STEPHEN
AND
MATILDA

STEPHEN AND MATILDA

COUSINS OF ANARCHY

MATTHEW LEWIS

First published in Great Britain in 2019 by
PEN AND SWORD HISTORY
An imprint of
Pen & Sword Books Ltd
Yorkshire – Philadelphia

ISBN 978 1 52671 833 4

A CIP record for this book is available from the British Library.

Printed and bound in the UK by TJ International
Typeset in Times New Roman 11.5/14 by
Aura Technology and Software Services, India

Pen & Sword Books Ltd incorporates the imprints of Pen & Sword
Archaeology, Atlas, Aviation, Battleground, Discovery, Family History, History,
Maritime, Military, Naval, Politics, Railways, Select, Social History, Transport,
True Crime, Claymore Press, Frontline Books, Leo Cooper, Praetorian Press,
Remember When, Seaforth Publishing and Wharncliffe.

For a complete list of Pen & Sword titles please contact
PEN & SWORD BOOKS LIMITED
47 Church Street, Barnsley, South Yorkshire, S70 2AS, England
E-mail: enquiries@pen-and-sword.co.uk
Website: www.pen-and-sword.co.uk

Or
PEN AND SWORD BOOKS
1950 Lawrence Rd, Havertown, PA 19083, USA
E-mail: Uspen-and-sword@casematepublishers.com
Website: www.penandswordbooks.com

Contents

Introduction

anarchy [an-ark-ee] *n* lawlessness and disorder;
lack of government in a state[1]

The Anarchy. It's a name to conjure with. It might be the perfect name for a civil war. The Wars of the Roses sounds a bit flowery and sporadic, and when the time came to give a name to the experiment with republicanism in Britain in the seventeenth century, The Civil War was the best that could be imagined. The Anarchy sounds like a *real* civil war, a country torn at the seams, with wolves snarling as they chew on the bones of a ruined nation. They knew how to throw an intestine – as the chroniclers were fond of calling it – dispute in the twelfth century: chaos, bloodshed, abduction, oppression and pillaging. That is a selection of what the contemporary writers in their monasteries recorded the reign of King Stephen as filled with.

Some of the most evocative and famous lines describing the strife in England come from *The Anglo-Saxon Chronicle*. 'They oppressed greatly the wretched men of the land with the making of castles; when the castles were made, they filled them with devils and evil men.'[2] If one quote springs to mind to recall The Anarchy, it will usually be that 'Wheresoever men tilled, the earth bare no corn, for the land was all ruined by such deeds; and they said openly that Christ and his saints were asleep. Such and more than we can say we endured nineteen winters for our sins.'[3] These are phrases and sentiments that have clung to the years 1135–54, the reign of King Stephen, but it is important to consider how accurate they really are, or at least whether the troubles they describe were as national and sustained as the writers explicitly claim.

The problems of getting to the root of what was really happening in England for those nineteen years when Christ and his saints slept are perfectly illustrated by the two main English chronicle accounts of the period. The *Gesta Stephani*, *The Deeds of Stephen* was possibly written by the Bishop of Bath, though the author's identity cannot be satisfactorily established. The first portion of this story favours King Stephen, portraying his cousin, Empress Matilda, as a divisive troublemaker whose personality made her unsuitable as a ruler. By the end of the account, almost certainly written after the accession of Henry II, the writer has grown careful to gently moderate his opinion to allow that the Angevin dynasty would ultimately succeed. It was no doubt wise to make such an adjustment in the years after 1154.

William of Malmesbury, a monk at Malmesbury Abbey, provides a parallel account that was written for Robert, Earl of Gloucester, the half-brother of Empress Matilda and military leader of her cause. He is at pains to make excuses for Robert at every turn, and so Stephen must be the oath-breaking usurper to allow Robert to fight for justice for his sister. Whenever a mistake is made by the empress's or the Angevin faction, it is Matilda's, usually made against Robert's advice or without his prior knowledge. The bias of both of these writers must be acknowledged and given consideration, but as contemporary accounts, both are invaluable.

Several common factors draw the two otherwise opposed accounts together. Both writers are religious men, as almost all commentators during this period were. They are careful to identify direct and tangible lines of causality between the sins of men and the punishment they receive from God. A typical example appears in William of Malmesbury's account of the death of Robert Fitz Hubert, 'a cruel and savage man' who 'used to boast gratuitously that he had been present when eighty monks were burnt together with their church'. William claims to have heard with his own ears that if any man taken by Robert secured his release and thanked God, Robert would reply, 'May God never be grateful to me!' Furthermore, Robert would 'smear prisoners with honey, and expose them naked in the open air in the full blaze of the sun, stirring up flies and similar insects to sting them'. When Robert died, it was 'God's judgment exercised upon a sacrilegious man', who fell not at the hands of his enemies, but those he considered friends. Almost every man's death could be directly linked to acts of religious barbarism that brought about God's wrath and vengeance.[4] That was how monks and priests saw the world and God at work within it. Whether these men really all sacked and burnt churches and dug up graveyards is open to dispute, but for men like William and the author of the *Gesta*, it was the reason they died, and no one escaped the judgment of the Lord.

Geography is also a critical factor in understanding the weight that should be given to these writers in particular. They are prone to paint a national picture formed around the view out of their local, cloistered worlds. Malmesbury Abbey in Wiltshire lay on the frontier of the dispute where the fighting and lawlessness would inevitably be at its height. Malmesbury Castle was a focal point of much action, and William extrapolated what he saw into a national catastrophe. Although not short of colleagues with whom he was in regular contact, William's view of the civil war was possibly the exaggerated perspective of a man on the front line. If the writer of the *Gesta Stephani* was not the Bishop of Bath, then he was almost certainly based in the south-west too, making his outlook similar to William's, though his notion of the causes and those ultimately at fault might differ.

A third prolific writer on this period is a monk named Orderic Vitalis. Born in Shropshire in 1075 to a French father and an English mother, Orderic ended up in holy orders at the Abbey of Saint-Evroul in Normandy. Much of what he writes of the civil war focuses on the Norman side of the struggle, understandably, but it is a signal of the ties that bound the duchy and the kingdom of England tightly together during the reign of the Norman kings. What was happening in England cannot be viewed as isolated or by any measure disconnected from events in the Duchy of Normandy. The preference on both sides of the Channel for a single master was a hard fact of Norman kingship, almost impossible to shatter. Powerful men held lands in Normandy and England, and serving two masters was never an easy task. Success or failure in Normandy could determine the security of England and vice versa.

After his death in 1135, Henry I quickly began to be viewed through rose-tinted spectacles that have proven hard to lift away. His personality and the state of affairs he left behind should be critically examined, but writers soon eulogized the dead king as a fountain of justice and peace. His brother Robert may have disagreed, and Henry scrapped for most of his life to keep what he had taken. His role in bequeathing to England and Normandy the nineteen years of trouble that followed his death was overlooked by those writing under subsequent rulers but should not be ignored and The Anarchy may have been a consequence or extension of the unresolved problems of his reign.

The Anarchy is a useful umbrella term for the civil war that dominated English politics in the middle of the twelfth century, but the question that must be asked is how accurate that term might really be. William of Malmesbury, the author of the *Gesta Stephani* and others were at pains to paint a picture of an entire nation tearing itself to shreds from coast to coast. Evidence of a total collapse of governmental authority across the country ought to be in plentiful supply if they are correct. I find myself wondering whether The Anarchy isn't much more of a nineteenth-century interpretation of Stephen's reign. To Victorian antiquaries and writers, in particular, the British Empire had been an inevitable consequence of the glorious, perfect and prolonged development of English and then British government. Those who had contributed to that inexorable flow were worthy forefathers of the nation, whilst those who added nothing to, or even sought to halt, the institutional progress deemed desirable were necessarily inconsequential blips.

Henry I was seen as a great stabilizer who brought the Exchequer into being and oversaw the birth of governmental machinery in England with his use of 'new men'. Henry II, his grandson, has been remembered as the father of the Common Law, a man who achieved a new pinnacle in empire unrivalled until centuries later. Whether Henry I's interest was more in money than establishing a platform for subsequent government was largely ignored. The Exchequer could not be a side effect of his greed because it was such a valuable, auspicious and venerable institution. Henry II's drive to standardize laws brought equity and certainty across disparate realms and regions. It was deemed universally positive and altruistic, with little thought given to whether it was meant merely to allow Henry to exercise his own rights and authority more firmly and more certainly across a wider area.

In Stephen, those looking back from the age of empire saw nothing positive or useful. He had not moved their notion of progress on at all, and may, in fact, have tried to take retrograde steps in devolving power that are only now becoming desirable and fashionable again. To earlier historians, King Stephen represented a brief spell of anarchy in the otherwise careful and unstoppable march toward the empire they took pride in. He made no grand contribution, and so warranted no praise and little attention. A consideration throughout this book will be the extent to which anarchy, as the total collapse or absence of government, can really be seen during Stephen's reign.

The names of those involved were drawn from an apparently narrow pool, usually of family appellations. This makes identifying individuals problematic. King Stephen is no problem, and King David in Scotland is the only significant man by that name. A few Baldwins and Fulks do little to confuse, and Waleran of Meulan has an invaluably unique name and title. After that, it becomes a bit trickier. Henry I is joined by his nephew, Bishop Henry of Winchester, the son of King David, Prince Henry of Scotland, and later by his grandson, the future Henry II, who is earlier identifiable as Henry of Anjou, Henry FitzEmpress, then Count Henry and finally Duke Henry. Matilda is a name that abounds too. Empress Matilda, Henry I's only legitimate daughter, is a focus of this story, but of no lesser consequence is Stephen's wife Queen Matilda, the daughter of the Count of Boulogne. Empress Matilda's mother was Matilda of Scotland, through whom her ancient English pedigree can be traced. I have tried to make the precise person under discussion as identifiable as possible. Where confusion is possible, and likely, I have endeavoured to fall back on a fuller title, which, though it may become tiresome to read over and over, will hopefully avoid muddling of personalities. Thus Henry I, Bishop Henry, Prince Henry and Count or Duke Henry might be easier to differentiate, and likewise Empress Matilda, Queen Matilda, Matilda of Scotland and so on. Wherever I fail to delineate these people accurately, I apologize both to you and to them.

Ultimately, this is the story of people. Two sides in a dispute that spilt into armed conflict. Stephen may be the leading man, but he has a supporting cast as worthy of attention as he is. His queen, Matilda – because why use different names when they can all share one? – provides not only staunch support but a telling contrast to the failings seen in his adversary. William of Ypres, a Flemish mercenary captain in Stephen's employ, was a vital support to his regime. The king's brother, Henry, Bishop of Winchester is an enigmatic figure who is difficult to detangle from some of his apparently contradictory decisions. The leading lady, Empress Matilda, had no less a dazzling supporting ensemble. Her half-brother Robert, Earl of Gloucester was a man almost universally respected and feared as a general and was one of the most powerful men in England and Normandy. Empress Matilda's husband, Geoffrey of Anjou, had his own agenda, and it was their son, Henry, who would pick up the mantle of his mother's persistent claim. All of this cast will be placed into difficult, sometimes impossible, positions and forced to make hard decisions. Two cousins waged war for the future of England. Only one could win. This is the story of Stephen and Matilda, and the civil war remembered as The Anarchy.

Prologue

The illustrious offspring of kings suffer shipwreck,
and sea-monsters devour those whom princes deplore.[1]

King Henry I had been in Normandy to subdue more trouble. On 25 November 1120, he took ship to return to England for Christmas, the duchy from which his father had conquered England secured, for a time at least. As the short evening sank into the long night, the king set off from Barfleur. Henry arrived back in England in good order, nothing appearing amiss. Orderic Vitalis noted, though, that 'a sad disaster happened which caused much lamentation and innumerable tears to flow.'[2] Just when the king believed he had won himself space in which to breathe, the worst catastrophe a monarch can suffer suddenly befell him.

Just before leaving Normandy, Henry had been visited by a man named Thomas who had explained to the king that his father, Stephen, had been in Henry's father's service all of his life. In fact, it had been Thomas's father who had transported the mighty William the Conqueror to England from Normandy when he made war on Harold for the crown. Seeking to follow in his father's footsteps, Thomas offered his services to Henry, telling the king that he had newly fitted out the *Blanche-Nef*, the *White Ship*, in a manner befitting the transport of a king. Henry accepted the offer, but not for himself. He already had his ship prepared and was not willing to change his plans. However, he would permit Thomas to take his sons William and Richard back to England with their party of young noblemen.

Henry I had more illegitimate children than any other monarch in English or British history, fathering at least twenty and perhaps twenty-four or more illegitimate sons and daughters. For a king, they were all well and good. Illegitimate children could be provided for and well loved, but inheriting, especially in England, was a different matter.

Henry's wife, Matilda of Scotland, had been carefully selected. She had the old blood of the House of Wessex running through her veins and gave English credibility to Henry as the third Norman king, following his father and older brother. Matilda was the great-granddaughter of King Edmund Ironside, and she had provided her husband with two legitimate children. They had a daughter, also named Matilda, born in 1102, and a son called William who was a year younger at seventeen. William had become known as William Adelin, a Norman variant of the Anglo-Saxon title Ætheling which had designated royal princes eligible to inherit the crown.

Overjoyed, Thomas prepared his ship for his prestigious passengers. As all the young lords piled on board, the mariners asked the prince for wine, and he ordered a considerable quantity to be brought on board. The crew and their passengers indulged quickly and heavily. As the ship slid out of the harbour, after the king and in the dark, almost everyone was drunk. Orderic Vitalis tried to work out how many were on board, and he believed there were 300 in total. He knew that several men, including two monks from Tyron, the king's nephew Stephen of Blois, William de Roumare and others had decided to disembark 'upon observing that it was overcrowded with riotous and headstrong youths'.[3] As soldiers shoved the fifty rowers off their benches, it may have begun to look like a wise decision. When they drunkenly laughed away the priests who had brought holy water to bless the voyage, Orderic could only see one end for them.

When the young men encouraged Thomas to try and overtake the king's ship, he allowed himself to be goaded into the attempt. As the rowers took back their positions and the inebriated pilot tried to navigate out of the harbour, the *White Ship* picked up speed, only for its starboard bow to grind into rocks just below the surface of the high tide. With the side split open, the ship quickly took on water and sank beneath the waves, the drunken panic on board saving none. Two men were reported to have been left clinging to the mast in the moonlit night; a butcher from Rouen named Berold and one of the young noblemen, Geoffrey, son of Gilbert de l'Aigle. At one point, the ship's master, Thomas, was said to have bobbed up and found the two men. 'What has become of the king's son?' he asked. When he was told that all but Berold and Geoffrey had been drowned, he despaired. 'Then it is misery for me to live longer.'[4] Allowing himself to slip beneath the surface again, he chose to surrender his life to the sea rather than have it taken by the fury of King Henry. Geoffrey lost his grip and his will in the freezing darkness and vanished. In the morning, only Berold, dressed in his meagre sheepskin overcoat, had survived the long, cold night. The poorest man in the company kept safe by his cheap but warm clothing.

In England, some from the king's fleet thought they had heard shrieks and screams in the night, but none knew the source of the strange noises. When word of the disaster reached that side of the Channel, none dared tell King Henry what had happened. Finally, after a day or two of those at court trying to hide their emotions, one of King Henry's nephews took control of the situation. Theobald, Count of Blois, whose younger brother Stephen was amongst those who had elected to disembark the *White Ship* before it left Barfleur, caused a young boy to throw himself, crying at the king's feet. When Henry asked the cause of his distress, the boy explained the fate of the *White Ship* and all aboard. Distraught, Henry fell to his knees and had to be picked up and escorted to his chamber by friends. There, he gave voice to his grief. 'Not Jacob was more woe-stricken for the loss of Joseph, nor did David give vent to more woeful lamentations for the murder of Ammon or Absalom.'[5]

Henry's grief was biblical in proportion and ferocity. So, too, was the problem he now faced. His wife had died two years earlier. He was fifty-two and suddenly without a male heir. He would remarry the year after the *White Ship* disaster, but he would father no more legitimate children. As personal loss devoured him, a constitutional crisis waited quietly, looming at the edge of his vision, silently demanding to be addressed. Who would succeed a king with no legitimate son?

1

The Death of Henry I

'Having now given a faithful account of the circumstances attending the death of this glorious father of his country, I shall proceed to describe briefly, in hexameter verses, the sufferings which turbulent Normandy, our wretched mother, underwent in the fangs of the viper brood, her own offspring: for, as soon as the death of her pious prince was known, in the first week of Advent, on one and the same day, the Normans rushed like raving wolves to the prey, and greedily entered on a course of the most infamous devastations.'[1]

King Henry I died at the hunting lodge of Lyon-la-Forêt, the Castle of Lions, near Rouen in Normandy. He was probably sixty-seven years old and had been King of England for just over thirty-five years. The Duchy of Normandy had also fallen to him in 1106 so that he had ruled there for twenty-nine years. Although Henry would almost immediately by lauded by writers such as Orderic Vitalis as the 'glorious father of his country', his rule had been far from smooth and the *White Ship* disaster fifteen years before his death had left a crisis that waited to explode.

As the youngest son of William the Conqueror, Henry had been born after his father's successful invasion of England, so was the only son born 'in the purple'. Nicknamed Beauclerc, most likely as a reference to his education and learning, he may have been intended for a career in the church. On the Conqueror's death, he had bequeathed the Duchy of Normandy to his oldest son Robert, known as Curthose, or 'short stockings'. The name was an insult derived from William's abuse of his heir. The two do not appear to have got on. The kingdom of England, a new prize, but a more prestigious one, since it offered a crown rather than a duchy, he left to his second son, William Rufus. Robert tried to stake a claim to the crown of England after his father's death but failed. In 1096, he joined the First Crusade, mortgaging Normandy to William Rufus to raise funds.

When William Rufus was killed in a hunting accident, which has been the centre of suspicion that he was in fact assassinated, on 2 August 1100, Robert was journeying back from the Holy Land. The youngest of the Conqueror's sons, Henry, who had been left money by his father with which to buy land, pounced into the vacuum and secured his own coronation as King of England on 5 August, just three days after his brother's death. Robert tried to unseat his brother in 1101, but failed and was forced to acknowledge Henry as king. In 1105, Henry invaded Normandy and the following year captured his brother at the Battle of Tinchebrai on 28 September. Robert was brought to England and remained Henry's prisoner until his death on 3 February 1134, aged around eighty-three and just a year before Henry would follow him to the grave.

After Henry's only legitimate son, William Adelin, had died in the *White Ship* disaster in 1120, Henry had been forced to try and resolve the issue of the succession. Few can have been more acutely aware than him of the perils of leaving a space that needed to be filled. Henry's heir presumptive, in the male line, was probably Robert's son William Clito. Henry's nephew's surname was similar to Adelin that Henry had used for his own son in that it was a Latinized word meant to mean something similar to 'prince'. Although Robert was still alive, he was a prisoner and Henry spent years opposing his active nephew until William died in 1128. As will be seen soon, Henry tried to provide for the continuation of his line through his only other legitimate child, Matilda, though he does not appear to have fully committed to her ruling England and Normandy. He caused his barons to swear loyalty to her on more than one occasion, but their relationship became tense after the king married her to Geoffrey, Count of Anjou.

Henry did not leave a kingdom quite as stable and secure as those quick to sing his praises suggested. If William Clito had not perished so conveniently for Henry, the king might have found his position even more fraught. In 1110, the county of Maine had left Norman control and given itself up to Anjou. At the Battle of Alencon in 1118, Henry had been defeated by an Angevin army. As late as 1127, the French were supporting William Clito as Henry's heir presumptive. When Charles the Good, Count of Flanders was murdered on 2 March 1127 at St Donation Church in Bruges, he left no heir. Louis VI of France promptly arrived with an army to impose William Clito on the county. Henry I responded by dispatching his favourite nephew, Stephen of Blois, to the region, leveraging the economic power of the English wool trade to encourage Clito's rejection and the installation of a neutral candidate in Thierry of Alsace. With Robert and William Clito both off the scene before Henry, it might have looked like a smooth succession should have been possible. As Henry's body was embalmed at Rouen and waited until 4 January 1136 to be buried at his own foundation, Reading Abbey, things were already unravelling.

Medieval government ceased on the death of a monarch. If there was no king, there was no king's peace to be kept. It was not until the end of King Henry III's reign in 1272 that a mechanism was implemented to allow the instant transfer of power, authority and government from one king on his death to his heir. Whatever their subsequent attitude to the argument that developed over the right to succeed Henry, most chroniclers agree that law and order broke down instantly. Orderic Vitalis complained that the Normans 'abandon themselves to robbery and pillage; they butcher one another, make prisoners, and bind them in fetters; burn houses and all that is in them, not even sparing monks, or respecting women'.[2] *The Anglo-Saxon Chronicle* laments that on the king's death there 'was treason in these lands; for every man that might robbed another'.[3] Chroniclers might exaggerate, but they painted a picture of a rapidly deteriorating situation. Scotland, under King David I, also saw an opportunity in Henry's demise. David quickly plunged an army across the border into England and took Carlisle, Wark, Alnwick, Norham and Newcastle. His advance was halted at Bamburgh, which he could not capture, and he moved on to besiege Durham. The Welsh were no slower to push back against Norman rule either. It was not a situation that could be permitted to persist.

Neither was the crown of England yet an hereditary possession. The Norman kings, with their background in a ducal capacity based much more closely on descent from father to son, wished to make it so. William the Conqueror had bequeathed the throne to his second son, not his oldest. Henry himself had further muddied the waters by snatching the kingdom from his oldest brother on the death of William Rufus. His subsequent efforts to firmly attach the succession to his own bloodline are, then, more than a little hypocritical and his fears that it would not work all the more understandable. Anglo-Saxon kings had been effectively appointed by a council, the Witenagemot, or Witan.

William the Conqueror had demolished that institution and its power, but the election of rulers was still a fact in, for example, the Holy Roman Empire and there may have been a preference for a return to this state of affairs in England too.

Before any move was made, there were probably four prime candidates to succeed Henry. His daughter, Empress Matilda, was perhaps the most obvious, but also in many ways the least attractive. Female rule was still something unheard of, at least in England, a nation that would have no queen regnant for another 400 years. The second possibility was Robert, Earl of Gloucester. Robert was an illegitimate son of Henry I, widely considered his favourite. He had extensive lands and power both in Normandy and England and was well respected. He was, however, illegitimate. That was less of a bar to power in Normandy: the Conqueror himself had been called William the Bastard. In England, it was unheard of. Legitimacy was still an absolute, marking the distinction between a duke and a king. Robert had everything required to follow his father except the right mother.

The two other contenders came from the House of Blois. They were Henry's nephews, the sons of his sister Adela and her husband Stephen, Count of Blois. Theobald, Count of Blois and Champagne was the senior male of the house, though his younger brother Stephen, Count of Mortain had been in England for years and was close to his uncle. They offered the prospect of legitimate, male successors as grandsons of William the Conqueror, albeit in a female line of descent. None of these solutions appeared perfect, and only one could win the throne. As it turned out, only two displayed an interest, and neither would give up during the nineteen years that followed.

2

Empress Matilda

'she should be nobly brought up and honourably served, and should learn the language and customs and laws of the country, and all that an empress ought to know, now, in the time of her youth.'[1]

Henry I's oldest legitimate child was born after he had taken the throne of England. Henry had been quick to marry Matilda of Scotland, the daughter of King Malcolm III. Her mother was Margaret of Scotland, daughter of Edward the Exile and her pedigree came from the House of Wessex, the famous Anglo-Saxon line of kings. She brought a good deal of perceived legitimacy and English authenticity to Henry's new rule. The date of the couple's first child's birth is poorly recorded but is often given as 7 February 1102. That date is based on the assertion that she was eight years and fifteen days old when she left England in 1110, but it remains speculation because dates of birth were simply not routinely recorded during this period.

In 1108, when Henry travelled to Normandy, he wrote to the recently reconciled Anselm, Archbishop of Canterbury, asking him to be the king's representative in England and also to care for his children. After claiming that he was not worthy of the role, Anselm agreed.[2] Matilda would later develop a deep and lasting affection for the monastery at Bec from which Anselm had been elevated to the archepiscopal see at Canterbury. Matilda's mother had been close to Anselm and had written to him frequently, so her daughter may have felt a similar affection for this venerable old man. The young girl was to be propelled onto the international stage in 1109 when ambassadors from the Holy Roman Empire visited Henry's court at Whitsun in June. Henry of Huntingdon wrote that the court was presented 'with extraordinary magnificence',[3] doubtless for the benefit of the prestigious envoys.

The embassy had come to request the hand in marriage of the eight-year-old Matilda for their master, Henry V, the Holy Roman Emperor. Although the emperor seems to have initiated the negotiations, it was a political coup for Henry I. Henry V was keen on English wealth and support to help secure his imperial coronation in Rome by the pope, a ceremony highly desired by any who held control of the Holy Roman Empire as a signal of their authority and prestige. Matilda's dowry was supposedly set at 10,000 marks of silver, which in order to raise Henry I set about taxing all of England, and preparations for her to leave her father's kingdom got underway. It can be no coincidence that Matilda's first appearance in official documentation came a year or so later. On 17 October 1109, Matilda witnessed a document to create the see of Ely during her father's council at Nottingham, identifying herself as '*sponsa regis Romanorum*' – betrothed wife of the king of the Romans.[4]

In February 1110, the emperor's envoys returned to collect his bride. Matilda was just eight years old and would not see England or Normandy again for sixteen years. Her husband was around twenty-five and had not been married before. She landed at Boulogne and travelled to Liège, where she met her betrothed for the first time. Very quickly, Matilda was involved in appealing for mercy for Godfrey, Duke of Lotharingia, who had fallen out of favour with Henry V, as an early introduction to the expectations of her position. She cannot have understood the complexities of her intended husband's relationships with his nobility yet, but he was acquiring a wife who could operate as a peacemaker and mediator across his sprawling territories. After travelling along the Rhine, through Cologne, Speyer and Worms, the entourage arrived at Mainz. Here, Matilda underwent a coronation ceremony on 25 July 1110, St James's Day. The archbishopric of Mainz was vacant at that moment, so the ceremony was undertaken by Frederick, Archbishop of Cologne, and Bruno, Archbishop of Trier. The young girl was then placed into the care of Archbishop Bruno to learn German and undergo her education to perform the role expected of her. The emperor instructed that 'she should be nobly brought up and honourably served, and should learn the language and customs and laws of the country, and all that an empress ought to know, now, in the time of her youth.'[5]

Between 1111 and 1113, Henry V visited Rome to secure his coronation by the pope as Holy Roman Emperor. The German church was locked in a dispute with the papacy about the right of the emperor to invest members of the church. Henry claimed it as an ancient privilege of his position, and the pope viewed it as an ecclesiastical matter in which the emperor's secular authority had no role. This kind of quarrel was typical both of the relationship between the empire and Rome, and the church's relationship with the secular world in general. Boundaries of authority were still fluid and matters cropped up with alarming regularity in which both princes and popes claimed rights. In this instance, Henry V refused to be cowed and took Pope Paschal hostage, forcing him to deliver the all-important coronation as Holy Roman Emperor. As soon as Henry left Rome, the pope denounced the ceremony, but it was too late. Henry had been invested, and his coronation was complete. He was fully entitled to be known as Holy Roman Emperor, consecrated by the pope. Significantly, he had left his bride-to-be at home throughout this episode. Although she would use the title Empress Matilda for the remainder of her life, she would never undergo the same coronation by the pope that made Henry V emperor.

In January 1114, just before her twelfth birthday, Matilda was married to Henry V at last, taking up her formal role as his consort. The splendour of the occasion was widely remarked upon. 'So numerous were the wedding gifts which various kings and primates sent to the emperor, and the gifts which the emperor from his own store gave to the innumerable throngs of jesters and jongleurs and people of all kinds, that not one of his chamberlains who received or distributed them could count them.'[6] Having completed her education, Matilda would now be expected to begin to fulfil the expectations of her office. German queens were involved both in ceremonial events and in government, so Matilda's education must have encompassed the workings of the empire's institutions. It was perhaps this exposure from a young age to structured preparation for involvement in rule that imbued Matilda with the conviction that she could do it and that her gender should not be a barrier.

At the end of 1115, Matilda was at Speyer with her husband and her former mentor Archbishop Bruno. Also joining them was the recently reconciled Archbishop of Mainz. Adalbert had been Henry V's closest advisor and had been promoted to the prestigious post to provide support to the emperor, only to immediately fall into dispute with his former master over the privileges of the church. Having seen how terribly wrong such a promotion could go, Matilda would live to see her son repeat the mistake in England with Thomas Becket. At Speyer, she witnessed a charter of privileges for the Cluniac monastery at Rüeggisberg and in early 1116, she journeyed to Augsburg with her husband as he prepared to travel into Italy. Matilda of Tuscany, Countess of Canossa, had left her property to Henry V, having previously promised to bequeath it to the papacy, so the emperor was keen to dart in and grab the lands before the pope could stake a claim.

By 11 March, Henry and Matilda had travelled through the Brenner Pass and reached the palace of the Doge of Venice. After a couple of days, they moved on via Padua, Mantua and Governolo Castle, finally arriving at Canossa Castle to a positive welcome. Henry's open-handed generosity had the desired effect of buying immediate support, and the region accepted him as their new feudal lord. Whilst in Italy again, the emperor also took the opportunity to try and build bridges with the pope. Henry had been excommunicated after abducting Paschal and was keen to remove the blot on his authority at home left by such a stigma. The household arrived in Rome before Easter 1117, and Henry made it known that he wished to wear his imperial crown and process through the city, as was traditional if an emperor was in Rome for any of the major feasts. Pope Paschal had fled the city south to Monte Cassino as Henry approached and the cardinals flatly refused to permit Henry to wear his crown formally in the circumstances. Maurice, Archbishop of Braga, who had been sent to the imperial court as a papal envoy, was convinced to help the emperor and Henry managed to gain entry to St Peter's Basilica, though they were forced to cross the River Tiber by boat when papal supporters refused to let them use the bridge.

During Pentecost, Maurice performed a coronation ceremony for both Henry and Matilda, theoretically bestowing on her the title of empress that she would scrupulously insist on using from then onwards. However, Maurice had been excommunicated by the pope between Easter and Pentecost for aiding Henry in spite of the pope's decision, so Matilda's imperial status was still unconfirmed. Her only real hope at that time of securing the prestige was to portray herself as Henry's betrothed at the time of his own coronation by Paschal, but it was a tenuous grip on the coveted prize at best. Henry and Matilda left Rome immediately after Pentecost without being reconciled with the pope. The remainder of the year was spent securing the Countess of Canossa's gift to the emperor, but Henry's absence was allowing dissent to foment in Germany. At some point in 1118, he took the decision to return to the empire but left his sixteen-year-old wife in Italy to govern his new territories for him. A large part of the army he had taken remained with Matilda too. She was now exercising independent authority at a young age, and nothing went awry under her gaze, though Henry's initial generosity had secured a positive opinion of them when they had first arrived.

By November 1119, Matilda was back with her husband witnessing a charter at Lotharingia. The next significant moment for her came in September 1122 at Worms, when three papal legates arrived to try and find a permanent resolution to the division between the emperor and the pope. Charters suggest that she was present, and two of those three legates would go on to become popes Honorius II and Innocent II, so she was in the presence of major players in the field of papal politics. Earlier that year, Matilda had tried to pay a visit to England but had been denied safe passage through the lands of Charles, Count of Flanders, who had perhaps sought to avoid offending Louis VI of France. Her brother William Adelin had died eighteen months earlier, and it is possible her father had recalled her to discuss the succession in England, perhaps to find out whether his daughter and son-in-law were likely to produce a male heir in the near future. Whatever the purpose of the attempted visit had been, it was abandoned.

After spending fifteen of her twenty-two years in the empire preparing for a long future alongside her husband, Matilda's world was turned upside down. On 23 May 1125, as he neared his fortieth birthday, Emperor Henry V died, possibly of cancer. The imperial couple had no children, and Henry left no heir. Henry bequeathed his royal insignia to his wife, as appears to have been the custom in Germany, for her to hand on to his successor. He asked his nephew, Frederick of Swabia, to take care of his widow after his death, though it was uncertain precisely what role she might have expected to fulfil in the future. Matilda handed over the imperial insignia to Archbishop Adalbert before a new emperor had been appointed and it is unclear whether she was deprived of it, coerced into handing it over to give Adabert more authority or willingly divested herself of the responsibilities. Unless she could find a new position in the world, which probably meant a second husband, she faced the prospect of heading into a convent at the age of twenty-two. It may be significant that her mother, Matilda of Scotland, had been sent as a child to a nunnery in Wilton under the care of her aunt Christina, the Abbess. She would later write of her experience that 'I went in fear of the rod of my aunt Christina, and she would often make me smart with a good slapping and the most horrible scolding'[7] and so her daughter might have sought to avoid a similar experience. Matilda of Scotland's time under her aunt Christina's care would have another part to play in her daughter's story over the coming years too.

The eventual election of one of Henry V's more rebellious subjects, Lothar of Supplinburg, as the new emperor must have confirmed that Matilda's long-term future did not lie within the empire, although she appears to have enjoyed her time there and felt secure. William of Malmesbury believed she was reluctant to leave Germany, 'because she had grown accustomed to the lands into which she was married, and had many possessions in them'.[8] In September 1126, sixteen months after her husband's death and aged twenty-four, Matilda crossed the Channel and returned to England, the kingdom of her father that she had left sixteen years earlier. Although she had received a solid, perhaps even exceptional, education and had been involved in government, Matilda had not faced any real crisis alone. On the death of her husband, her one piece of leverage that gave her a role in the future of the empire, the royal insignia, was swiftly abdicated to Adalbert for some reason. All of this may have given young Matilda a false sense of her own ability to perform the role of a ruler, by creating a notion that she had already done it before.

In January 1127, just as the Christmas court was due to break up, Henry gathered together all of the clergy and nobility. He was also joined by his brother-in-law King David of Scotland. David's sister Matilda had died in 1118, before the *White Ship* disaster, and although Henry had remarried in 1121 to Adeliza of Louvain, he had fathered no more legitimate children. As a result, the issue of the succession remained unsettled. Henry took the opportunity of the gathering to try and bring some form of resolution to the matter. *The Anglo-Saxon Chronicle* records that he 'he caused archbishops and bishops and abbots and earls and all the thegns, who were there, to swear [to place] England and Normandy, after his day, in the hands of his daughter'.[9] William of Malmesbury also noted the oaths sworn at this court that if Henry 'died without a male heir, they would immediately and without hesitation accept his daughter Matilda, formerly empress, as their lady'.[10]

William also stated that in 1131 Matilda received a confirmation of the oath from those who had sworn it before and took fresh pledges from anyone who had not been present in 1127.[11] It is worthy of note that, according to William of Malmesbury's wording at least, Henry did not cause them to recognize Matilda as his heir to the throne, or to promise to make her queen, but only to accept her as their lady. This may have had connotations of queenship, but it was sufficiently imprecise to leave room for interpretation of Henry's plans. That room would prove broad enough to cause serious problems.

Malmesbury recalled that William, Archbishop of Canterbury had been the first to take the oath in 1127, followed by the bishops and then the abbots. When it came to the turn of the secular lords, King David, as the senior amongst them and Matilda's uncle, went first. Her cousin Stephen was next to offer his pledge, followed by her half-brother Robert of Gloucester. The writer asserts that there was some dispute, or rather 'a noteworthy contest', as to who should have the honour of giving their pledge after King David. Stephen and Robert, 'as rivals in distinction', competed for the right to take the oath next, 'the one claiming the prerogative of a son, the other the rank of a nephew'.[12] If such a debate took place, it appears that Stephen was given precedence over Robert.

The marriage prospects of the widowed Matilda came almost immediately into sharp focus, not least because they were now to have a profound effect on the future of England and Normandy. Malmesbury points out that she was not short of suitors after her husband's death as 'some princes of the Lombards and Lotharingians came to England more than once in the following years to ask for her as their lady'.[13] It is interesting that the chronicler chooses to use the same word for those who wished Matilda to be the consort of their ruler as he uses to describe the role provided for her by the oath her father extracted. In terms of Henry I's foreign policy, there seemed to be a natural answer. His son, William Adelin, had been married to Matilda of Anjou, the daughter of Count Fulk V, a year before the *White Ship* disaster and an alliance with Anjou, on the south-western border of Normandy, must have remained desirable. Henry's nephew, William Clito, was still actively opposed to his uncle, but also probably viewed by many as a viable successor in England and Normandy.

On 23 March 1127, Louis VI had secured Clito's election as the new Count of Flanders. To further promote Henry's opponent, the French king had also given Clito Joanna of Montferrat as a bride. Joanna was the daughter of Rainer, Count of Montferrat and a maternal half-sister of Louis' wife Adelaide of Maurienne. It was a dangerous coalition, and Henry must have begun to fear that if Anjou were drawn into alliance with them, he would face overwhelming odds all along Normandy's borders. The county of Blois sat in a thin slither between territory directly under Louis' control and Anjou, and while Henry might be confident about the loyalty of his Blois nephews, the rest of his neighbours were a cause for increasing concern. Henry had secured an Angevin alliance before and must have felt compelled to ensure that it remained intact.

Against this background of mounting threat, Henry arranged a new union, this time between his daughter Matilda and Fulk's son Geoffrey. Geoffrey was born on 24 August 1113, making him eleven years younger than his proposed bride. Henry I knighted Geoffrey at Rouen on 10 June 1128, and on 17 June the couple were married at Le Mans, the union blessed by Guy, Bishop of Ploermel. Matilda was twenty-six and her husband just fourteen. Perhaps of even more concern to Matilda than the age difference was the diminution in her status that she underwent. The best demonstration of that outrage lies in her retention for the rest of her life of the title Empress Matilda; it is questionable whether she was entitled to use it. When Geoffrey succeeded his father, she became Countess of Anjou but continued to use the higher-ranking title.

Almost immediately after the wedding, Geoffrey's father left for Jerusalem, placing Anjou into the new groom's hands. Fulk was travelling to the Holy Land for his own marriage to Melisande, the only heir to King Baldwin II of Jerusalem. The plan was for the couple to rule jointly, though when they succeeded Baldwin in 1131 Fulk assumed full control of the kingdom and excluded his wife. This arrangement, made just before Fulk had returned from the Holy Land to Anjou to settle his affairs there, offers a hint at what Fulk and Geoffrey might have been envisaging from the match with Matilda. If Malmesbury is correct that Matilda was recognized as 'lady', Geoffrey might have believed, hoped or even been told that he would acquire Normandy and England as her husband. For Henry I, the final victory would, hopefully, be in a grandson following them onto the throne. Some of Geoffrey's later actions and claims offer some credence to this possibility, and the fact that none knew for certain what was supposed to happen is a testament to Henry I's failure to confirm the details, or to his decision to change them in the following years.

The situation altered radically within weeks of Matilda's marriage to Geoffrey. William Clito died on 28 July at the age of twenty-five. Having been pushed out of much of Flanders by Thierry of Alsace, who was supported by Henry, William had begun a counteroffensive. At the Battle of Axspoele just south of Bruges, William defeated Thierry and pushed north towards Ghent. Whilst laying siege to Aalst, William took a wound to his arm that became gangrenous and claimed his life. He was childless, and with his father still a prisoner in England, opposition to Henry was crushed and the prime purpose of the alliance he had made for his daughter evaporated. It is probably no coincidence that a year later, in July 1129, Matilda arrived back in Normandy, just after her father had sailed back to England. A year without the prospect of an heir may have concerned Geoffrey, especially since Matilda had not had any children throughout her previous marriage either. They may have found that their personalities ground against each other, exacerbated by her refusal to adopt the title of countess and her haughty insistence on remaining Empress Matilda. Events would soon suggest that the change in his own political landscape had caused Henry to rethink his policy and perhaps to deny Geoffrey what had been promised to him.

William of Malmesbury offers a sense of the complex and tangled problems that were to follow when the succession came into sharp focus. Roger, Bishop of Salisbury was the senior figure in Henry I's government and had been for many years. He had proven himself efficient in gathering money and managing the administration whenever Henry was required to leave England. In the near future, his role would become known as Justiciar, evolving later into Chancellor and a parallel in modern times would be the office of Prime Minister with a monarch still politically active. This made Roger rich and powerful, securing the bishopric of Lincoln for one nephew, Alexander, in 1123 and later the diocese of Ely for another nephew, Nigel, in 1133. Malmesbury Abbey had been brought, unjustly William felt, under Roger's authority, so William had contact with the bishop though perhaps disapproved of his worldly interests. He wrote of the previous oath to support Matilda that immediately after it had been given, 'all men began to assert, as though by some prophetic spirit, that after his death they would fail to keep their oath'. He was able to add, with some personal knowledge, the claim that

> I myself have often heard Roger, bishop of Salisbury, saying that he was released from the oath he had taken to the empress, because he had sworn only on condition that the king should not give his daughter in marriage to anyone outside the kingdom without consulting himself and the other chief men, and that no one had been involved in arranging that marriage, or had been aware that it would take place, except Robert, earl of Gloucester and Brian Fitz Count, and the bishop of Lisieux. In saying this I would not wish it to be thought that I accepted the word of a man who knew how to adapt himself to any occasion according as the wheel of fortune turned; I merely, like a faithful historian, add to my narrative what was thought by people in my part of the country.[14]

Although William is unwilling, or unable, to confirm what the bishop had said to him, it is clear that problems existed with the plans for the future. That men were looking for a way out of what they had promised, whether Roger's excuse had merit or not, was plain and did not bode well. It may be striking that Robert, Earl of Gloucester and Brian Fitz Count were to prove two of Matilda's staunchest allies, feeling themselves bound by their oaths, though William wrote for Robert and looked to promote the earl's image at every turn. If Henry planned to ensure Matilda succeeded him as the consort of her husband, it does not seem beyond the bounds of possibility that Henry agreed to give his nobles and prelates a voice in deciding who that husband might be. William's non-committal honesty leaves open the chance that Henry did not consult as promised, or that many disapproved of the Angevin match he made, but it also seems like clutching at very thin straws.

Roger's insistence that he and others were freed from their earlier pledges is made less convincing by the reiteration of their vow at a council in Northampton in 1131 when Matilda was still with her father after her breach with Geoffrey. Malmesbury insists that Matilda 'received an oath of fealty from those who had not given one before and a renewal of the oath from those who had'.[15] Henry of Huntingdon records only that this great council discussed Matilda's presence in England and that 'it was determined that the king's daughter should be restored to her husband, the Count of Anjou, as he demanded'.[16]

Shortly after, Matilda did indeed travel back to Geoffrey, and by the middle of the following year, she had fallen pregnant. Her first child, a boy named Henry, was born in March 1133 at Le Mans. A second son, Geoffrey, was born the very next year, but the birth, according to Robert of Torigny, nearly took Matilda's life. She organized the distribution of her lands and asked her father's permission to be buried at Bec-Hellouin. Although Henry initially insisted that she should be buried at Rouen Cathedral to reflect her status, he eventually agreed to her request. Robert of Torigny was impressed by Matilda's rejection of worldly glory in favour of a more holy place. 'She knew that it was more salutary for the souls of the departed if their bodies might lie in the place where prayers for them were offered most frequently and devoutly to God.'[17] This view of Matilda is perhaps at odds with later interpretations of her relentless pursuit of power, or at least of her worldly rights.

The extent to which the reforms and developments of institutions initiated by Henry were undertaken with an eye to female rule rather than his enduring political legacy may point to the extent of the problems he foresaw. A queen regnant would be a novelty, and it must have been uncertain to anyone who gave it thought precisely how it would function. The role of a king was to lead his men onto the field of battle and mete out justice. A woman could not have been expected to fulfil those roles so it may have fallen to her husband on her behalf. In Matilda's case, it would become abundantly clear over the years that followed that her husband had not the faintest interest in England. It seems possible that Henry envisaged a self-sustaining government, operating under Matilda in name but in practice able to continue its day-to-day working without the need to address the role of a woman in governing a kingdom in her own name.

In 1134, Geoffrey became impatient for the delivery of castles along the Norman border with Anjou that he claimed Henry had promised him as part of his dowry. The changing landscape after the marriage might have caused Henry to rethink the gifts, especially if his primary hope had been to bolster the border in case William Clito sought to make inroads with his French allies. Geoffrey began raiding across the border and, unlike a few years earlier, or perhaps because of her treatment in being sent back to her husband, Matilda chose to back Geoffrey against her father, who remained in Normandy. Henry of Huntingdon claimed of Henry that his 'daughter detained him on account of sundry disagreements, which had their origin in various causes, between the king and the Count of Anjou, and which were fomented by the arts of his daughter'.[18]

Henry I of England died in Normandy on 1 December 1135, his final year spent in dispute with his heir and her husband. Despite the almost instant perception of his reign as entirely peaceful and benevolent, it had not been; Henry had been successful, but only through seemingly unending adversity and repeated battling. If the primary aim of a king was to leave a male heir to succeed him, he had failed, and whilst he had done all that he could, what happened next was ultimately beyond his control. The king reportedly fell ill after eating lampreys, a favourite dish which his physician had warned him against indulging in. His body was taken to Rouen Cathedral, where it was disembowelled in preparation for the return to England. Henry had instructed that he should be buried within his own foundation at Reading Abbey. Henry of Huntingdon offers a final, less than pleasant comment on Henry's kingship in describing the fate of the man tasked with removing the dead king's head as his body was prepared for its final journey. 'Even the man who was hired by a large reward to sever the head with an axe and extract the brain, which was very offensive, died in consequence, although he wore a thick linen veil; so that his wages were dearly earned. He was the last of that great multitude King Henry slew.'[19]

William of Malmesbury recorded the confirmation of the succession on Henry's deathbed, a scene at which the writer was not present. 'When he was asked by them about his successor, he assigned all his lands on both sides of the sea to his daughter in lawful and lasting succession, being somewhat angry with her husband because he had vexed the king by not a few threats and insults.'[20] The *Gesta Stephani* insists that Robert of Gloucester was advised by some to claim the throne for himself as a powerful, popular nobleman who was also a natural son of King Henry. Robert was reportedly 'deterred by sounder advice' so that 'he by no means assented, saying it was fairer to yield it to his sister's son, to whom it more justly belonged, than presumptuously to arrogate it to himself'.[21] Henry of Huntingdon was clear that on her father's death, Matilda claimed England jointly with her husband, perhaps a recognition of the presumed form of the succession.

Matilda may have just become aware that she was pregnant again when her father died. Her third son, William, would be born at Argentan on 22 July 1136. Her presence there suggests that she had not moved to claim her inheritance. The pregnancy may have been difficult, as her second had been, but the delay was to prove disastrous. As soon as her father died, Matilda and Geoffrey began to occupy the disputed border castles that had been claimed as part of the marriage arrangements but went no further. Guigan Algason, Henry's castellan at Argentan, Exmes and Domfront immediately handed over control of the castles. Geoffrey also quickly gained control of other fortresses at Ambrières, Gorron and Châtillon-sur-Colmont. William Talvas accompanied Geoffrey and took Sées and Alençon, which he claimed to be his rightful inheritance, kept from him by Henry. A revolt in Anjou forced Geoffrey to abandon any further efforts to the north and return to his county, but Matilda remained at Argentan for the birth of the couple's third son.

In England, someone had moved much faster and the influence of events there was swiftly felt in Normandy.

3

King Stephen

> Stephen Count of Boulogne, a man distinguished by his illustrious descent, landed in England with a few companions. For this same man was by far the dearest of all his nephews to King Henry the peacemaker, not only because of the close family relationship but also because he was peculiarly eminent for many conspicuous virtues.[1]

Stephen of Blois's date of birth is not known but is usually placed around 1096. His parents, Stephen, Count of Blois and Chartres and Adela, daughter of William the Conqueror, married in about 1081 and Stephen was their third surviving son. Stephen's father left for the First Crusade in 1096, taking part in the successful siege of Nicaea on his arrival in May 1097. The count wrote an effusive letter home to his wife when the city fell, detailing his journey and the trouble-free crossing of the Bosphorus, which, despite its fearsome reputation, was 'safer than the Marne or the Seine'. He explained that the heavily defended Nicaea had fallen easily with very few casualties amongst the crusaders, ending his letter, 'I tell you, beloved, that from this Nicaea we will get to Jerusalem in five weeks, unless Antioch holds us up. Farewell!'[2]

Crusading zeal or overconfidence, and perhaps both, is plain from Count Stephen's excitement, but it was not to last. On 3 June 1097, the crusaders took the city of Antioch and laid siege to the castle only to find themselves almost immediately besieged, sandwiched between a large force and the citadel garrison. Towards the end of the long month, on 28 June, they made a daring sortie against the army of Karböghä which hemmed them in. It proved successful and has been credited with turning the course of the First Crusade. Count Stephen was not there. He had already fled, to his eternal disgrace. One story tells that Stephen and two companions threw ropes down from the sides of the city walls, climbed down and ran away.

Orderic Vitalis offers instead that 'Stephen, count of Chartres, had retired to Alexandretta for the recovery of his health, and was detained there for some time, as it is said, by sickness.' He adds that Stephen's return was desperately awaited 'as all the chiefs looked to him as their prime leader and counsellor; for he was a man of great eloquence and singular ability'. On hearing that the crusader army was pressed in hard at Antioch, he climbed the hills above Alexandretta and, seeing the vast covering of tents of the enemy's army, 'like the sand on the sea shore', he panicked. Returning to his base, he stripped it of everything portable and began to make his way back home. Orderic adds that Count Stephen met the advancing army of the Emperor of Constantinople as he retreated, warning him that all was lost and causing him to turn around so that 'the glory of victory and triumph over the Turks was reserved for others to whom it rightfully belonged'.[3]

By the time Stephen reached Chartres and his family, he was in disgrace. In 1101, he returned to the Holy Land to try and salvage his reputation. Having made a successful pilgrimage to Jerusalem, Count Stephen was killed during the Second Battle of Ramlah in May 1102, aged around fifty-seven. His career had been illustrious, and ultimately he had sought redemption in Jerusalem for what the rest of the world viewed as weakness at Antioch. Nevertheless, it was as a deserter and a coward that Count Stephen would be remembered, and it is important to consider the impact such a stain on the family honour may have had on his sons throughout their careers.

Adela, Countess of Blois and Chartres, and youngest daughter of William the Conqueror, maintained a far better reputation. Like her sister-in-law Matilda of Scotland, Adela seems to have developed a close friendship with Archbishop Anselm, who is credited with convincing her to become a nun after her husband's death. The countess gathered an impressive collection of tapestries, including ones depicting the stories of Noah, Soloman and the Fall of Rome. Around her bed hung a tapestry that told the story of her father's invasion and conquering of England, so that it was the last thing she saw at night and the first sight each morning. It was clearly an achievement she considered above anything else her family had attained. If her husband shared the bed with her, it is to be wondered what he made not only of someone else's achievements dominating his wife's thoughts, but also of his father-in-law looking down on him, spear in hand, in the marital bed.

Stephen and Adela had four sons. The oldest, William, probably named for his grandfather, was passed over entirely for the family's inheritance. There is some evidence that he began to be positioned as the next count in his early years but that his training was abandoned soon afterwards. Suggestions have lingered that he suffered from a mental illness, or physical disability, or even that he was so far in disgrace with the church that he lost everything, but none of these has ever been proven, and his exclusion remains unexplained. Instead, it was their second son Theobald, probably named for his paternal grandfather, who acquired the counties of Blois and Chartres, adding later in 1125 that of Champagne from his uncle Hugh.

In 1113, Adela sent her third son, Stephen, to England. The hope must have been that he would be able to make a future for himself across the sea at the court of her younger brother, King Henry I. The king did not disappoint either his sister or his nephew from Blois and seems to have taken a strong liking to Stephen. Almost as soon as he arrived, he was granted the title Count of Mortain on the western border of Normandy, near Brittany. The last count, William, had been captured by Henry at the Battle of Tinchebrai in 1106 when Henry had defeated and imprisoned his older brother Robert. Stephen also gained the Honour of Eye in Suffolk, confiscated from another of Robert Curthose's allies, Robert Malet. In 1118, Henry added to these with lands on the southern border of Normandy that had been taken from the rebellious William Talvas, who was to become an ally of Geoffrey and Matilda in 1135, seeking their return. The Honour of Lancaster was also granted to Stephen, and he founded Furness Abbey in 1126 using monks brought from the Abbey of Savigny in Mortain. Adela's choice had proven a good one and her third son was now amongst the wealthiest, most powerful and most popular men at Henry I's court.

Henry married his increasingly powerful nephew to another Matilda, the daughter and sole heiress of the Count of Boulogne. Eustace III owned vast quantities of land in England as well as a county across the Channel. Boulogne was a key port in northern France, and the port at Wissant gave the count significant control over the trade routes in the Channel. A large proportion of the English wool that found its way to Flanders passed through Wissant, providing not only an income but also strategic importance that Henry thought would be ideal for the loyal Stephen. His nephew was now a rival on both sides of the Channel to Robert, Earl of

Gloucester, though Henry may have seen their expanding authority as complementary rather than divisive.

Lavishing such favour on the capable son of his sister might also indicate that Henry's plans for what might happen after his own death were being re-evaluated, though he would never definitively change them. He could just as easily have believed Robert and Stephen would, together, be able to help Matilda hold the kingdom and the duchy of Normandy, but the succession, as previously discussed, was as yet unsettled. Of the previous four kings of England – Harold Godwinson, William the Conqueror, William Rufus and Henry I – none had been the oldest son of the preceding king. Neither was Henry I the oldest brother of his predecessor. It is feasible that Henry was giving thought to his nephew Stephen acting as a caretaker, to be succeeded by Henry's grandson and namesake in time. At this point in the story, that might feel like the application of a degree of hindsight that should ring alarm bells, but it may also help to explain the events in the immediate aftermath of Henry's death and the otherwise hard to comprehend settlement eighteen years later. It is perhaps a thought to keep on a backburner.

In the mid-1120s, and certainly by 1126, the youngest of the Blois brothers, Henry, had followed Stephen to England to try and find himself a future. In 1126, King Henry made his nephew, Abbot of Glastonbury, one of the wealthiest establishments in England, and in 1129 he became Bishop of Winchester, one of the richest sees in English history. Winchester was also still the location of the royal treasury, and it was by taking control of this city that Henry I had helped ensure his own successful accession in 1100. The king allowed his nephew, now Bishop Henry, to retain his office at Glastonbury too, indulging in pluralism to promote his family and bolster their status around him. Bishop Henry would prove a key figure during the civil war that followed, often dividing opinion on both sides, but his promotion during the decade that followed the death of William Adelin again begs the question as to what Henry I envisaged happening after his death. Was he building a wall to defend his daughter, or had the Angevin match with Geoffrey backfired, and been made unnecessary by William Clito's death shortly after it, so that he was actually seeking an alternative to leaving England and Normandy to Anjou? Henry made no provision to establish Geoffrey with land or titles in England or Normandy, nor did he ever make reference to him as an heir, jointly or in his wife's right, to either.

Neither did Henry provide anything similar for his oldest grandson, who had been born two years before the king's death. It is possible that he believed the oaths to Matilda that he had already extracted were enough, or at least as much as might be done, but as relations with his daughter and son-in-law disintegrated, it is equally plausible that Henry sought a different route to settling matters.

The only thing that is certain is that Matilda did not succeed her father. Stephen was in Boulogne when he heard of his uncle's death, and he immediately took a ship from Wissant to London. The *Gesta Stephani* suggests that law and order had begun to break down in England whilst Henry I had been absent in Normandy and that his death not only exacerbated the situation but also encouraged King David I to lead a Scottish incursion into the north of England, taking Carlisle, Wark, Alnwick, Norham and Newcastle in short order. Wales was also quick to buck against the yoke of Norman attempts to rule it. Stephen's arrival in London should not, therefore, be seen as the cause or spark of trouble in England, but his easy passage to the throne might suggest the authentic and pressing problems that precluded an absence of a government for any amount of time. If this was the case, then Geoffrey and Matilda's unhurried, almost nonchalant, move into Normandy was a grave mistake.

In London, the *Gesta* asserts that 'the elders and those most shrewd in counsel summoned an assembly, and taking prudent forethought for the state of the kingdom, on their own initiative, they agreed unanimously to choose a king.'[4] It is possible that the citizens of London saw a chance, both to undo what Norman rule had stamped in place regarding kingship, and to fall into line with other European systems. The Anglo-Saxon Witan had previously claimed the right to appoint a king, and in Germany, elections were the established norm. France was one of few crowns held predominantly by hereditary right, and it was that model that the Norman kings had tried to replicate in England. In 1135, London claimed 'it was their right and peculiar privilege that if their king died from any cause a successor should immediately be appointed by their own choice'.[5] The pressing nature of increasing unrest is felt in the *Gesta*'s insistence that 'they had no one at hand who could take the king's place and put an end to the great dangers threatening the kingdom except Stephen, who, they thought, had been brought among them by Providence; all regarded him as suited to the position on account both of his high birth and of his good character.'[6]

Stephen seems to have given or promised London something to win their backing, though it is nowhere made clear precisely what this was. He might have recognized their status as a commune, an important step in the city's political development. Harnessing the power (in wealth at least) of the merchants in the city, Stephen was able to offer preferential trade arrangements through his port at Wissant that would be instantly appealing. If the city, and other parts of the country, were uncertain or even fearful about female rule, or Angevin rule for that matter, then Stephen was a viable and preferable alternative. As unrest threatened, a king was needed to restore the king's peace, and Stephen was the man on the spot prepared to undertake the task, whilst Matilda and Geoffrey lingered in Norman border fortresses appearing to cause, rather than end, turbulence. Another alternative is that this had been what Henry I had envisaged towards the end of his life: the succession of his sister's son, either to ensure the continuance of the Norman dynasty or to act as a caretaker until his grandson came of age. Any one or a combination of a number of these possibilities might help to explain the ease and speed with which Stephen was accepted as the new king by the capital city. All that the *Gesta Stephani* is able to offer is that 'a mutual compact was previously made and an oath taken on both sides, as was commonly asserted, that as long as he lived the citizens would aid him with their resources and protect him with their power, while he would gird himself with all his might to pacify the kingdom for the benefit of them all.'[7]

Bishop Henry now moved to the forefront of matters. The coronation of a new king was a matter, traditionally, for the Archbishop of Canterbury. Henry I's had been performed by the Bishop of London whilst Archbishop Anselm had been in exile, but that see was vacant in 1135. As Bishop of Winchester, Henry was able to bring a degree of clerical backing to his brother's cause. When London had accepted Stephen, he quickly moved to Winchester, where his brother helped secure control of the royal treasury for him. Roger, Bishop of Salisbury, long-serving Chancellor to Henry I, supported Stephen, turning aside from his own pledge to Matilda, and aided in winning him control of the treasury. One final thing stood between Stephen and legitimate kingship, and it was the most important of all. He had swiftly secured the body of the kingdom, but now he had to win its soul.

The ceremony of coronation was never a simple confirmation of a man as a king. It was the act of undergoing a coronation that made a man into a king, transformed him from a mere mortal to one appointed and approved by God to rule over his people. It was this ritual that made him legitimate, unassailable and protected him from any challenge. With London, the former head of the government and his brother Bishop Henry behind him, Stephen asked William Corbeil, Archbishop of Canterbury, to consecrate him as the new King of England. It was here that Stephen hit his first hurdle. The archbishop, who was in his mid-sixties by this point, applied an abrupt break to proceedings. He insisted that the matter should not be undertaken lightly, but only after deliberation and thought. He perhaps resented the fact that he, as spiritual head of the nation, had been largely ignored up to this point until Stephen and his supporters tried to present him with a fait accompli:

> 'For,' he said, 'just as a king is chosen to rule all, and, once chosen, to lay the commands of his sovereign power on all, assuredly in like manner it is fitting that all should meet together to ratify his accession and all should consider in agreement what is to be enacted and what rejected.'[8]

The archbishop apparently joined the rest of the nation in believing that there existed a right to choose a king and that it should be reasserted now. This may also have been the first moment at which the issue that would dominate much of Stephen's kingship was raised. How, the archbishop asked, should men set aside the oaths that they had sworn during Henry I's lifetime to recognize his daughter? There is a vital point at work in what the *Gesta* tells us were the archbishop's objections. William Corbeil had already agreed that the selection of a king was preferable to the enforcement of lineal descent. To that extent, the relevant bodies had the power and authority to select, or elect, Stephen if they wished. He did not raise the matter of Matilda's position simply because she was the daughter of the former king. Instead, his concern was that whoever Matilda's father had been and whatever her perceived rights, all of the leading men of the country had sworn an oath to her. The succession might not fall to her because she was her father's daughter, but should it devolve on her because of the binding promise men had made that it would? The archbishop's concern was that 'it was presumptuous to wish to desire anything contrary to this arrangement, especially as the king's daughter was still alive and not deprived of the blessing of heirs.'[9]

The counter to this argument that was offered by Stephen's faction was that the oath had been extracted under duress. The *Gesta Stephani* recalled that King Henry had 'rather compelled than directed' those who had taken the oath 'with that loud and commanding utterance that nobody could resist'.[10] Given under duress, the oath was null and void. Whether this really satisfied the archbishop cannot be known but amid building pressure and the reality of disintegrating law and order, he agreed and on 22 December, three weeks after Henry I's death in Normandy and with his body still languishing there, his nephew was crowned King Stephen at Westminster Abbey. For the remainder of his rule, this moment above all others would remain significant and vital. Matilda could point to oaths that had been broken by men who should have been bound to her, but Stephen had been anointed as king. There was no known way to undo or break that sanctity while he lived, nor was any party particularly keen to breach such a fundamental tenet of kingship. To do so promised problems for all who relied on the security it offered.

Stephen's lightning manoeuvres in England helped to secure the other pillar of Norman rule across the Channel. The Norman barons were holding a council at Neubourg to discuss who should be their next ruler, clearly feeling no more bound or inclined to accept Matilda and her husband than England did. They were settling on the idea of offering the duchy to Theobald, Count of Blois, Stephen's older brother when envoys arrived from England to relay news of Stephen's smooth accession there. Instantly, the preference of men with lands on both sides of the Channel for a single ruler dominated the discussions. Although Orderic Vitalis understood that it was with Theobald's consent that the Norman barons immediately decided to make Stephen their new duke, he goes on to explain that Theobald, 'indignant at not being called to the throne, although he was the elder brother, departed in haste to transact important affairs which urged his attention in France'.[11] The chronicler is adamant that in abandoning Normandy and leaving it without an identifiable authority figure on the ground, Theobald doomed the duchy to lawlessness 'by his negligence'.[12]

Having swept to power in England and secured control of Normandy in so doing, Stephen had next to set about delivering his promises to restore order and peace. Despite the later belief that Henry I had been a great peacemaker who had bequeathed a settled realm, the new king was forced to address threats from almost every quarter. Scotland in the north, Wales in the west, internal strife within Normandy and the threat to the duchy's southern border from Matilda and Anjou. Only one of these was of Stephen's own making, and it seems likely that even Matilda would have faced the other problems had she been able to win control of England. David, King of Scots was her uncle and used his defence of her as the colour for his occupation of swathes of disputed land in the north, but he might well have tried to snatch them anyway. That we may never know, but the Welsh would almost certainly have risen in 1135 whatever had happened, and Normandy was only ever prevented from assaulting itself by an external threat, so in some degree, Stephen was helped here by Matilda's and Geoffrey's aggression.

4

Empress Matilda

> The Anjevins remained in Normandy thirteen days, securing by their irruption, not the dominion, but the eternal hatred of the Normans.[1]

Throughout the years that followed the death of Henry I and the succession of Stephen, Empress Matilda would press her rights to England and Normandy hard and without relenting. Her husband Geoffrey was never to appear remotely interested in England. He seems to have viewed Angevin control of Normandy as the main prize of his marriage to Henry I's daughter, and it was here that he would focus his attention with an uninterruptible dedication. It is hard to discern whether a crown held no appeal for Geoffrey, whether Normandy, from his position in Anjou, looked like the pinnacle of achievement or whether he saw danger in overreaching in a greedy effort to grab everything in one handful. If it was the latter, he was to be proven wise, but in making his choices, he left his wife to battle for what she wanted largely on her own.

The first Angevin drive into Normandy of Stephen's reign came in September 1136. After the border gains in the immediate aftermath of Henry I's death, this is often characterized as Geoffrey's second invasion of the duchy. It was unclear whether he came to press his wife's rights, their joint claim or that of his oldest son. He would surely have played to whichever was the most acceptable if any of them appeared to gain support, but his subsequent attitude suggests that he coveted Normandy for himself. Orderic Vitalis provides detail of this episode, but sets it against the backdrop of a duchy abandoned by Theobald, not yet reached by Stephen and lacking any firm government. He provides several colourful passages to describe the Norman tendency to fall to internal squabbling when they were not provided with either a strong leader or an external enemy.

> This province, however, though not disturbed by foreigners, by no means enjoyed security and peace, inasmuch as it was cruelly harassed by its own sons, like a woman in childbirth, was always suffering the pangs of labour.[2]

> But as discord make divisions among them, and fatally arms them against each other, while they are victorious in foreign lands they are conquered by themselves, and cut each other's throats without mercy, while their enemies in the neighbourhood look on and laugh, and their mother's eyes are often full of tears.[3]

> Such were the sort of outrages committed by the Norman, gnawing themselves with their own teeth like the beast allegorically represented in the Apocalypse.[4]

It was against the disunity of Normandy that Geoffrey erupted into the duchy, crossing the River Sarthe around 12 September with a large army.[5] With the Count of Anjou came William, Duke of Aquitaine (father of Eleanor of Aquitaine), Geoffrey de Vendôme, William, son of the Count of Nevers and William, Count of Ponthieu, who was the William Talvas who had joined Geoffrey in grabbing the border castles he claimed as his inheritance. It was no small-scale assault, but as much as Orderic lamented the internal squabbling of the Normans, he knew that this was precisely the kind of thing that would galvanize them.

Geoffrey's first target was the town and castle of Carrouges, just across the border into south-western Normandy. After only three days of siege, the fortress was taken, only to be snatched back by the castellan Walter as soon as the Angevin army moved on. At Montreuil-en-Auge, almost at the northern coast of Normandy, Geoffrey set another siege, but after three attempts to assault the castle, he was forced to abandon the effort. The place was too well defended and 'they gained nothing but wounds and retired, leaving many of their men dead'.[6] Moving east, Geoffrey next tried his luck at Moutiers-Hubert with more success. The castellan there, Paganel, was not, Orderic assures his reader, a popular man, having 'committed many outrages that same year', so that the monk is able to portray him as receiving his just desserts from God.[7]

Although King Stephen found himself waylaid in England, he had not entirely neglected Normandy. He had sent men led by Waleran, Count of Meulan to try and restore order to the duchy and repel the Angevins until he was able to visit Normandy himself. Waleran was to become a key figure in Stephen's reign, primarily for his long-held loyalty to the king. Waleran was the son of Robert de Beaumont, Count of Meulan and Earl of Leicester. Waleran was also a twin to Robert, and the Beaumont twins were heavily relied on by Stephen for many years, offering him sterling service until a breach eventually divided them from the king. When Geoffrey moved from Moutiers-Hubert to nearby Lisieux, Waleran sent Alan de Dinan to defend the castle there.

As the Angevin army approached Lisieux, it became clear to Alan that they were too numerous and too powerful to be held at bay. His response was to gather all of the residents within the castle walls and burn the city to the ground. It was a demonstration of defiance designed to warn the enemy of what Lisieux was capable, but it also denied them the plunder they would have won in sacking the houses and businesses. Orderic reflected that the Angevins 'learned the resolute character of the Normans, and admired the bitterness of their implacable hatred, which led them to prefer losing all their wealth in the conflagration, than to save it while they bent their necks to foreign power'.[8] Finding themselves unable to get close to the fortress in the singeing heat of the blazing buildings, the Angevin army gave up and turned instead toward Sap, hoping for an easier time there.

At Sap, Geoffrey found the inhabitants arrayed ready for battle, waiting for them. Perhaps keen to vent some of his army's unspent adrenalin, the count ordered an advance, and there was a skirmish during which buildings were again set on fire. Orderic is clear that in this case, both sides were torching the town, 'the inhabitants and the foreigners.'[9] Sap eventually fell to Geoffrey, though at some point during the fighting the count was wounded in the foot. Empress Matilda had arrived to reinforce him with several thousand men, demonstrating her ability to offer support to her husband in a manner recognizable, and acceptable, to her contemporaries. She was too late, though, and despite some success amongst the setbacks, the campaign had to draw to a close.

Orderic blames the sudden failure on 'their profanation of sacred things',[10] and men getting what they deserved for violating churches would become a theme of The Anarchy that offered chroniclers a way to rationalize and explain what was happening. Doubtless, the moral warning also served to protect church property and the clergy by demonstrating the consequences of such sacrilege. The Angevins were afflicted by what was probably dysentery, Orderic claiming that they had 'gorged themselves with crude eatables'. He provides a typically graphic depiction of their retreat from Normandy. Geoffrey and his army 'were, by God's just judgment, attacked with bowel complaints, and suffered so severely from diarrhoea that, leaving foul tokens of their passage along the roads, numbers of them could scarcely crawl home'.[11] Gross, but fitting punishment for daring to try and invade Normandy.

Having blazed into Normandy intending to subdue it, Geoffrey was carried away in a litter, pale and suffering from the wound he had sustained. He had lost many men and gained nothing substantial or permanent. Orderic heard that on his way back through the woods at Maleffre, south of Alençon in his own county, Geoffrey's chamberlain was assassinated and all of the count's clothes and treasures were stolen so that 'he lost more by his own people than by the enemy'.[12] The rivalry between Normandy and Anjou is assumed to have been a long-standing feud. Certainly, Henry I had lost Maine to them as well as a battle, but he had also made marriage alliances for both his son and his daughter with children of Count Fulk. If Orderic is to be believed, the real meat of the hatred was born of Geoffrey's attempts to take control of the duchy after Henry I's death.

For Matilda, it was a poor signal of her prospects. She might have done better had she marched into Normandy alone and insisted on the recognition of the oaths men had taken to her. Instead, the threat Geoffrey had loudly made reverberated not only around the duchy but across the narrow sea to England too. In a fortnight, Geoffrey had succeeded in galvanizing Normandy and England against Matilda.

5

King Stephen

I, Stephen, by the grace of God with the assent of the clergy and people elected king of the English, consecrated by William archbishop of Canterbury and legate of the Holy Roman church, and confirmed by Innocent, pontiff of the holy Roman see, out of respect and love of God do grant freedom to the holy church and confirm the reverence due to her.

King Stephen's Charter of Liberties, 1136[1]

Stephen had taken a coronation oath in 1135 not dissimilar to that his uncle Henry I had sworn in 1100. The next year, he reiterated and expanded upon it at Oxford. It seems likely that the wide-ranging freedoms of the church that he promised to uphold had formed a part of the price to be paid for his brother's easy and crucial support of his accession. They may also have smoothed the Archbishop of Canterbury's agreement to Stephen's coronation. The fact that Stephen was willing to return to the church any forests taken from it by Henry I is a possible signal of the weakness of his position and his desire to shore up clerical support, though he reserved any previous exactions intact. Secular matters barely received a passing mention, though the king confirmed that 'I wholly abolish all exactions, injustices and miskennings wrongfully imposed either by the sheriffs or by anyone else.' He added only, 'I shall observe good laws and ancient and lawful customs relating to murder fines, pleas and other suits, and I command and ordain that they be observed.'[2] This was a statement of policy, and as much as the church may have campaigned for the rights it felt it was owed by the king it had supported, it was not really novel and formed part of the continuing negotiation of the relationship between church and state.

The great council that met at Oxford to hear this pledge was the first the king had been able to call. Given the widespread unrest in England on his succession and his promise in London to restore peace as soon as possible, he had much to do. The incursion by King David of Scotland was high on the list of Stephen's priorities. David held the Honour of Huntingdon in England and much of the north, around what had been the Kingdom of Northumbria, was hotly contested territory as the border between England and Scotland remained fluid, ebbing and flowing with the fortunes of each nation. David would portray his invasion on the death of Henry I as an entirely altruistic move to help protect the inheritance of his niece, Empress Matilda, the daughter of his sister. Such a motive is not impossible, but neither is an opportunistic move to regain lands that David asserted belonged to Scotland. Stephen's accession only served to make David's motives look all the more unselfish and reasonable.

David surely felt confident that in the troubles of the commencement of a new reign, particularly if Matilda and Geoffrey were likely to stake their claims from the south, Stephen would be ill-equipped to respond to his land grab. He was quickly proven wrong. With a speed and unexpectedness that were to become a powerful trademark, Stephen arrived at Durham with a huge mercenary army, funded from the overflowing treasury Henry I had left at Winchester. Henry of Huntingdon described the force as 'one of the greatest armies levied in England within the memory of man'.[3] David was caught unawares and forced to come to terms with the new King of England. Stephen was able to buy David's compliance so easily that shock and panic are the only real explanations. Part of the key to Stephen's swift success, which would become another trademark many would argue served him less well, was his reluctance to seek punitive terms for peace. It made conciliation quick and bearable for his opponents, but would also leave them strong enough to continue to threaten him. Richard of Hexham noted that King David refused to do homage for his lands in England to Stephen, but transferred them to his son and heir, Prince Henry, who did swear fealty to Stephen. David was also left in control of Carlisle and Doncaster, and a rumour quickly sprang up that Stephen had promised not to give the earldom of Northumberland to anyone until Prince Henry's claim to it had been adequately examined in court. In return for these concessions, David returned Wark, Alnwick, Norham and Newcastle-upon-Tyne to Stephen without the need for a siege or confrontation.[4]

On the surface, the arrangements do not seem like an outright victory for Stephen, and they were far from it. David was left with a claim on Carlisle and Doncaster, but in the circumstances, it ought to be considered a positive result for Stephen. David had relied on his inability to stop him at all but had been forced to return four of the five castles he had taken. Beyond that, Prince Henry had done homage to Stephen for his lands in England and left the north in the company of the King of England, ensuring a degree of friendship between the two nations. David was Empress Matilda's uncle, but he was also the uncle of Stephen's wife, Queen Matilda. Her mother was Mary of Scotland, the youngest child of David's father Malcolm III and Margaret of Scotland. As much familial leverage as Empress Matilda could exert, Queen Matilda could rely on too, the only differentiation being David's continued reference to the oath he had given to the empress years earlier.

Had David's real motivation been the protection of the empress's inheritance, his incursion into England would have been a miscalculation. Stephen had been given a clear passage to the throne precisely to restore order and bring peace, so an invasion from Scotland was only likely to galvanize a panicked nation behind the new king. It was not all plain sailing for Stephen, though. The mighty Earl of Chester, Ranulf de Gernon, had interests and ambitions in Northumberland, and particularly Carlisle, that were thwarted by the terms Stephen granted David. When Prince Henry arrived at Stephen's court, Ranulf stormed out, and when the prince was later permitted to sit at Stephen's right hand, the Archbishop of Canterbury left, enraged because the position should have been his.[5] It was an early lesson for Stephen that there were no easy answers in the tangled mess he was having to try and weave order from. The scales would need to be carefully balanced and the degrees to which some men could be upset without jeopardizing the unity of the realm had to be weighed with thought.

When Stephen held his Easter court on 22 March 1136, most of the barons arrived to recognize him as king. The way in which he had dealt with David apparently inspired confidence in the majority of the nobility. The perception of Stephen as the accepted and legitimate king was spreading, and it was against this background that the court moved to Oxford, where Stephen gave his charter of liberties. He was not in a particularly weak position. Instead, the church, according to the author of the *Gesta Stephani*, had been unreasonably and intolerably abused by Henry I. The clergy complained they had been 'a prostrate and downtrodden handmaid and had suffered most disgraceful wrongs'.

If anyone had dared to challenge Henry's exploitations of the church, 'at once he was intimidated by the king, assailed by injustice, vehemently persecuted by him and his agents, and could get no hearing for any request or complaint until he had oiled the king's palm and publicly confessed himself guilty of presumption'. For further dramatic effect, the situation was called 'this second oppression of Pharaoh'.[6] In promising to restore the church's rights and holdings to the situation before Henry had become king, it was this perceived injustice that Stephen was promising to reverse, re-establishing rights rather than granting away fresh ones. Although undoubtedly Stephen wanted clerical support for his position on the throne, that was not necessarily his only or overriding concern.

Wales was proving less easily quelled, but it is doubtful many saw that as a failing of Stephen's rule. A new reign traditionally brought fresh unrest and border skirmishing in Wales and the early part of 1136 had seen fighting in Gower and a Welsh raid over the border that had led to the death of Richard Fitz Gilbert. In October, English forces were ploughing into Cardigan in revenge, but it is likely that no one viewed this unrest as particularly unusual or concerning.

By the end of April, Stephen had secured perhaps his greatest propaganda coup to date. Robert, Earl of Gloucester had been in Normandy since the death of his father Henry I, but now, with fortune appearing to favour Stephen's cause, he came to England and submitted to the new king. As Henry's illegitimate son, Empress Matilda's half-brother and one of the most significant landowners on both sides of the Channel, it represented a major step in Stephen's building of support. If it was genuine. Robert would become the mainstay of Empress Matilda's efforts in England, and it remains unclear whether he intended from the outset to deceive Stephen. William of Malmesbury, always keen to excuse any apparent failing on Robert's part, clung firmly to the belief that his submission was never intended to take precedence over the vow he had made to Matilda. The earl, he claimed, meant only to gain access to the other nobles of England in order to promote his half-sister's cause. 'The most prudent earl was indeed anxious to convince them of their fault and bring them to a sounder opinion by personal conversation.' As proof, William offered that Robert 'did homage to the king conditionally, namely for as long as the king maintained his rank unimpaired and kept the agreement'.[7] Bishop Henry was keen to make the most of the gathering in of potentially one of

Stephen's most powerful foes. Writing to Glastonbury Abbey, where he remained Abbot, he told the monks, 'King Henry my uncle having gone the way of all flesh, and my brother Stephen having succeeded in the kingdom, the aforesaid Robert did homage and swore an oath of fealty as was the custom, together with the other magnates of the land.'[8]

To all outward appearances, Stephen was in the ascendant, and he was fulfilling the promises he had made to secure peace in the kingdom. Virtually all of the barons were behind him, the church was supportive, peace with Scotland had been achieved, and the mighty Robert, Earl of Gloucester had sworn fealty. Even William of Malmesbury conceded that the new king was appealing to many. 'Stephen besides, when he was a count, by his good nature and the way he would jest, sit and eat in the company even of the humblest, had earned great affection, so great that it can hardly be imagined.'[9] If the spring had been challenging but rewarding, it was not a situation Stephen was able to enjoy for very long.

6

Empress Matilda

But the king took what had happened good-humouredly and showed no annoyance over it, saying that he would eventually have a day of real rejoicing if divine providence brought it about that all the enemies of his peace were shut up in one small spot.[1]

Matilda remained largely quiet after her husband's enforced retreat from Normandy. It is mainly for this reason that the next instalment of her story did not involve her personally, but rather gave hope and life to her cause in England. As Geoffrey licked his wounds, both metaphorical and literal, events were evolving in England that would cause the empress to believe that all was not lost. Whether or not Robert had gone ahead to lay the groundwork for staking her claim, and whether or not she knew he had some subterfuge in mind, his oath to Stephen, though it might be excused if the king's legitimacy were to be challenged or the earlier promise to Matilda upheld, at least appeared a blow.

Although it does not seem to have been for any particular affection toward the empress or her status, Baldwin de Redvers in the south-west of England had refused to accept Stephen. He was conspicuous by his absence from the Easter court and never swore fealty to the new king, so neither was he confirmed in his lands like other barons were. Those possessions in Devon and on the Isle of Wight were not insignificant, but Stephen seems to have decided to make an example of Baldwin. When Robert, Earl of Gloucester submitted to the new king, Baldwin was willing to make his peace too, offering to do homage if Stephen would confirm him in his lands. The king refused. It was risky since it might drive Baldwin and others into more open opposition, but Stephen was within his rights to refuse to confirm Baldwin's titles and must have felt that it was just too little too late.

The disgruntled Baldwin decided to seize Exeter, where he had been castellan for Henry I, but the residents, unimpressed, sent word to Stephen asking him for help because Baldwin 'was loudly threatening fire and sword against all who did not yield to his presumption'.[2] When the king arrived, faster than anyone had imagined, it was with another mercenary force, but this time it was bolstered by a deliberate display of baronial support. Robert, Earl of Gloucester was amongst those attending on the king, and it may have been an unwise choice to take him towards rebellion so close to his own heartland. On the other hand, as one of the most powerful magnates in the region, Stephen may have sought to rely on Robert's influence to end the matter swiftly. With the city against him, Baldwin took his men into the security of the castle and locked the gates against the besieging royal force. The garrison at nearby Plympton Castle, Baldwin's men, quickly submitted to the king's horde, which must have been an unnerving sight.

The *Gesta* explains that a man named Alfred, whose father Joel was an ally of Baldwin, also abandoned his own castle because it could not possibly be defended against Stephen. Instead of surrendering, he took his men to Exeter and slipped in amongst the besieging army; 'for among so many clad in mail it is impossible easily to distinguish one from another'.[3] Alfred managed to get one of his men into the castle amidst the priests and prisoners who were occasionally allowed to move between the two armies. When they let Baldwin know that they were there to support him, a plan was hatched. Baldwin's men launched a sharp assault out of the castle against the king's force, only to quickly retreat. Their aim had not been to cause any real damage, but rather to allow Alfred's men to rush to their side and enter the castle with them. The gates were tightly shut up once again with more men inside. Perhaps the besieged should have considered that more men only meant more mouths to feed.

The king laughed off the apparent setback and refused to be disheartened. He told his barons that 'he would eventually have a day of real rejoicing if divine providence brought it about that all the enemies of his peace were shut up in one small spot.'[4] It was perhaps a moment that foreshadowed more serious events later on, but for now, Stephen appeared pleased to allow his enemies to gather together, packed within the walls of Exeter Castle to be dealt with in one action. In what chroniclers would unflinchingly paint as the will of God, the wells within the castle began to dry up. As water ran low, the defenders were forced to use the copious amounts of wine stored within the castle instead. As it became critical, the garrison was reduced to making bread with wine and to boiling their food in it too. Understanding the growing crisis, Stephen ordered that lighted torches should be launched over the walls, setting the castle's wooden service buildings on fire. Those within were now forced to extinguish the blazes with what remained of their wine.[5]

Several months after the siege had begun, the garrison finally sent word that they wished to negotiate with the king. When the delegation arrived, they asked for permission to leave the castle, but Stephen's brother, Bishop Henry, counselled him to refuse their request and maintain the siege. He pointed to their wasted bodies, their lips drawn tautly over their teeth and their pale, sallow complections. They could not, the bishop suggested, hold out much longer and then the castle would be surrendered on the king's terms, not theirs. It may have sounded like good politics, but it was hardly counsel based on Christian charity. When their embassy returned with the bad news, Baldwin's wife emerged, barefoot, her hair down and tears rolling down her cheek. She now pleaded for mercy and terms, and although the king was minded to refuse her requests too, his barons intervened. Some, including Robert, advised him to now show mercy. Relenting, Stephen allowed those within the castle to leave, permitting them to take all of their possessions with them and to become the followers of any lord they chose.[6]

Moments like this are often used to demonstrate either Stephen's weakness in dealing decisively with his enemies or the fact that he was dominated by his barons. Certainly, he seemed to lack a killer edge that his predecessor had been willing to display. If he allowed his brother to advise him to be more cruel and then capitulated to the baronial insistence that he should show mercy, it is hard to see which might have been the better option. Either way, he would have been open to accusation that he was being controlled. It seems likely that the emergence of Baldwin's wife in a pitiful state, dishevelled and crying, was a perfectly stage-managed moment for both sides. Chivalry and honour would have demanded that a man protect such a lady, even his enemy's wife. By allowing his barons to plead the lady's cause with success, Stephen displayed his own magnanimity, capacity for mercy and maintained his honour in recognizing the suffering of a woman. The king was allowing his nobles to perform the role his own wife may have fulfilled had she been present, interceding to ask for his mercy on behalf of those who may not have deserved it or otherwise been able to obtain it.

Baldwin himself fled Exeter to Carisbrooke Castle on the Isle of Wight. Stephen moved to Southampton and hurriedly prepared a fleet so that 'Baldwin, utterly astonished at his sudden and unexpected arrival, appeared before him, at the persuasion of friends, as a downcast suppliant'.[7] Too far gone in his disobedience, Baldwin was spared but forced into exile. His immediate response was to seek out Geoffrey, Count of Anjou. In doing so, he must have given Empress Matilda some hope that her cause, or at least opposition to Stephen's rule that might be harnessed, was alive. The novel situation faced by Stephen, and Matilda, and those surrounding them, was the potential of a viable alternative. Nobles rebelled – that was nothing new – but they would generally find themselves reconciled, executed or exiled. Thrown out of England, they might find a hearth amongst their king's enemies, in France, for example, but they could do little to destabilize things from there.

The exceptional situation in 1136 was that Baldwin was able to seek out a person who could challenge Stephen's position, his legitimacy as king, and offer his allegiance and support to that cause. Matilda could still claim that the oaths made to her entitled her to Stephen's crown. She was not just an enemy, but a rival for the throne. Henry I had suffered problems with William Clito, his nephew, but Clito had only ever been seen as Henry's potential heir, not a figure who could depose Henry and replace him as king, unless it was by conquest. In his cousin Matilda, Stephen faced a claim to legitimacy that could be considered as good, if not better, than his. From this moment on, anyone who fell out with Stephen could seek out Empress Matilda and promote her cause. There was no imperative to seek a reconciliation with Stephen and exile was not the end of the matter either. It left the king in an almost impossible position. How could he enforce order amongst his barons when they could simply transfer their support to Empress Matilda at any moment? Many of the traditional levers available to a king to maintain law and unity were removed from Stephen by the existence of this rival claimant to his throne.

It was precisely this situation that Empress Matilda and her husband needed to seek to exploit if their desire to gain control of England and Normandy was to come to anything. It seems likely that, as raids into Normandy failed to produce meaningful results, other than to galvanize the Normans against the Angevins, and therefore Matilda too, Baldwin's arrival lit a taper in the gathering darkness. Questions remained to be answered, though. Would Matilda seek regnal authority in England and Normandy? Did she want just England, satisfied to leave Normandy for Geoffrey? Was she planning to try and maintain the claim of her oldest son, Henry of Anjou, as his grandfather's heir? Few seemed confident of what Henry I had really planned, or how much it had changed by the time of his death. A year later, the same lack of clarity might affect Matilda's efforts to gain that which she claimed was rightfully hers. If Baldwin was the spark that lit a fuse, it was to prove a slow-burning business that would struggle to reach anything explosive for several years. Nevertheless, the resistance had begun in earnest.

7

King Stephen

> The news of his coming filled with joy the hearts of the poor people, who for a whole year had been left to oppression and desolation.[1]

In the spring of 1137, King Stephen finally felt able to leave the shores of England and deal with the problems that kept his duchy of Normandy lawless and under threat from the Angevins. Stephen had been accepted as Duke of Normandy in the immediate aftermath of his accession in England, benefiting from the unwillingness of most to serve two masters. He did not need to fight for recognition, but rather to establish law and order and unite the feuding Norman polity against the threat from Geoffrey of Anjou. Having invaded in 1134, 1135 and 1136, it must have seemed inevitable that the count would soon try his luck again on Stephen's borders.

In March, the king sailed from England to La Hougue. His younger brother Bishop Henry had spent the winter in Normandy, seeing first hand the suffering of those whose houses had been burnt to ashes. He was perhaps sent, or at least was able, to report back to Stephen on the state of the duchy. Orderic saw a sinister motive in the bishop's journey too. William Corbeil, Archbishop of Canterbury died in November 1136, and there seems to have been a widespread expectation that Bishop Henry would be given the most senior role in the English church. Orderic believed Bishop Henry had crossed the sea to begin lobbying Pope Innocent II to approve of the promotion,[2] while the matter would not be settled quickly, each brother's motive remaining a source of contention.

Another setback was the extensive drought, the like of which 'no one in our times has witnessed before'.[3] It was during this same year that *The Anglo-Saxon Chronicle* offered the famous lament that 'Wheresoever men tilled, the earth bare no corn, for the land was all ruined by such deeds; and they said openly that Christ and his saints were asleep. Such and more than we can say we endured nineteen winters for our sins.'[4] The only satisfactory explanation men could divine for such extreme weather conditions causing crop failures was the disapproval of God. Although the chronicler must be referring to the entire reign of Stephen and the period of civil war that lasted nineteen years, the overt signal of God's displeasure is not the devastation of war, but of drought. The crops do not fail because of battles and torchings, but rather because of the weather.

On 25 March, Stephen arrived at Evreux where he met with his brother Count Theobald. Any lingering grumbles from the Count of Blois about missing out on England and Normandy were ended by a promise of a pension of 2,000 marks a year. In May, the king went on to meet Louis VI at the border between Normandy and France, receiving his approval of Stephen as Duke of Normandy as a fief of the French crown. Stephen's oldest son Eustace did homage to Louis for the duchy, and the two kings agreed a peace between themselves that ensured Louis would not help the Angevins and left Stephen able to focus more fully on Geoffrey. If Stephen had expected the count to try again on the Norman border this year, he was not disappointed. In early May, Geoffrey crossed into Normandy and assaulted Exmes. He took the castle quickly and moved north-west to Argences, where he joined up with the rebellious Rabal de Tancarville, the chamberlain of Normandy, in search of allies. In the Hiémois region, Geoffrey's men reportedly torched Bazoches-au-Houlme, burning sixteen people alive inside the church in the kind of sacrilegious action that would, if the chroniclers are to be believed, proliferate the emerging civil war.

Geoffrey's intentions this time are perhaps not hard to discern. He reached Mézidon with Rabal, a town just ten miles from Caen, the Norman seat of Robert, Earl of Gloucester. If William of Malmesbury had been correct that Robert had made his peace with Stephen only as a mask for his real loyalty to his half-sister, then his moment had arrived to join Geoffrey and strike against the king while he was on Norman soil. Orderic understood that Robert, and others, were under suspicion of sympathizing with Empress Matilda and Geoffrey. When it came to the acid test, Stephen might have been a little perplexed. Caen held firm against the Angevin assault and refused to surrender.[5] Was this with Robert's blessing, or against his wishes? Had Robert decided that the time to play his hand had not yet arrived? Was Geoffrey making for that region in search of intelligence from Robert as much as gains of land? It is also possible that at this point Robert had absolutely no intention of betraying Stephen. William of Malmesbury was keen to make excuses for the earl's willingness to submit to the king, assuming he had an ulterior motive and a plan in motion, but in the evolving situation, Robert and his city of Caen remained loyal to Stephen and resisted Geoffrey's assault.

Stephen began a muster at Lisieux in June, intending to put as large an army in the field as possible and force Geoffrey to give battle. The king believed that to be the clearest and quickest route to victory, but his barons were less convinced. The twelfth century was still a time when pitched battles were an uncertainty to be avoided at any cost. Even larger numbers were no guarantee of success. Prestigious noblemen could expect to be taken prisoner and ransomed rather than run through, but that could leave them financially crippled. Besides, there was no way to mitigate the possibility of being killed in a general melee. Castle warfare was the standard method of asserting authority, though sieges were slow, expensive for those outside and, as supplies ran out, harsh for the inhabitants, as Exeter had demonstrated. Still, it was preferable to battle: more predictable, with established rules for negotiating a surrender that guaranteed the survival of all but the most belligerent garrisons.

Orderic Vitalis believed Stephen was 'very desirous to bring him [Geoffrey] to a general engagement' and that the plan was to besiege Argentan and other castles the Angevins had taken so they would be drawn into a pitched battle. As Stephen's nobles tried to suggest that his plan was flawed, a brawl erupted between the Norman men-at-arms and a group of Flemish mercenaries in the king's pay. The Normans apparently resented their presence and men on both sides were killed in the ensuing fight. Quick to take the opportunity of backing out of a plan they disapproved of, most of the nobles took their retinues and left without seeking Stephen's permission to do so. Stephen found himself embarrassingly chasing his own men as they ran away from him.[6]

Giving up on the idea of confronting Geoffrey, not least because he couldn't be sure his own army would come to him, Stephen changed tactic. He sought to end the incessant incursions into Normandy and Geoffrey agreed to a two-year truce between them. Orderic was pleased to see 'peace and tranquillity' re-established in the duchy, though Geoffrey was not the only source of trouble and the quiet was short-lived.

Roger le Bègue stirred up trouble and Stephen managed to gather an army together, taking Roger's castle at Grosoeuvre in Evreux. In Avranchin, Richard Silvanus was brought to terms, and the castle at Guitry in the Vexin was torn down.

Given Stephen's reputation as an ineffectual ruler, his first (and only) visit to Normandy during his reign was an almost complete success. He had made accords with Theobald and Louis VI, received confirmation of his possession of Normandy from the French king, put out the small fires of rebellions across the duchy and bought time to deal with the Angevin threat. Outbreaks of unrest are not necessarily a comment on Stephen. His contemporaries suffered similar problems so that Geoffrey only had to leave Anjou to enter Normandy and trouble erupted behind him. It is true that he managed little more than to postpone a resolution to the issue with the Angevins, but a two-year peace bought vital time. A strong presence and decisive action were foiled, in the end, by a lack of unity amongst his army. Precisely who was to blame for that cannot be untangled with any certainty, but as their commander, Stephen must shoulder both the blame and the consequences. A swift and crushing victory on the battlefield against the Angevin invaders would have gone a long way to securing the king's dominance of his duchy, ensuring too the respect and affection of the Norman lords. Although Stephen didn't lose, the fact that he was forced to forgo a confrontation, seek peace and leave the problem unresolved left room for doubt.

Reports of trouble in England caused the king to begin to arrange a swift return. This in itself was, to some extent, instructive. Normandy was the traditional patrimony of the Conqueror and his descendants, but as a kingdom, offering a crown and consecration, England was the bigger prize in terms of prestige. It always seems to have been viewed as a land overflowing with money too. The Holy Roman Emperor's primary motive in seeking a match with Henry I's daughter was believed to be his need for cash. When the papacy took a controlling interest in England during the thirteenth century, they were convinced that the land flowed with gold and silver to fill up the coffers of the Roman Church. Quite how accurate the perception was at any given point can be hard to determine, but it existed nevertheless.

Stephen had not finished his work in Normandy, at least not entirely. He arrived in March 1137 and left in November, spending just eight months of his nineteen-year rule in the duchy. Orderic Vitalis was unimpressed by the king's decision to go. 'Thus was unhappy Normandy torn by such storms as these, mangled by blows mutually given by the swords of her own sons, and plunged into grief by the slaughter perpetrated on all sides. She suffered the most cruel calamities, and had daily to apprehend still worse evils, because she saw, to her sorrow, the country left without a governor.'[7] Even before he mentions Stephen's departure, the monk considers Normandy an ungoverned land, ripping itself apart. With law and order not yet fully restored and the Angevin threat still hanging over the border regions, the duchy's ruler left. Stephen left William de Roumare and Roger the Viscount with a handful of others, 'commanding them to accomplish what he had been unable to effect in person, to do justice to the inhabitants, and procure peace for the defenceless people.'[8] Orderic was profoundly uninspired by the turn of events that left Normandy prone to the hungry wolves not only prowling her borders but at her own hearth too.

There was one more incident ascribed to Stephen's visit to Normandy that would gravely affect the remainder of his reign, whether it really happened or not. Robert, Earl of Gloucester was under suspicion of planning to betray Stephen but had conspicuously failed to do so when presented with the opportunity at Caen. Stephen and Robert had been rivals, perhaps friendly ones, at Henry I's court and precisely what their personal relationship had evolved into by 1137, with Stephen as king and Robert as his vassal, cannot be determined with certainty. Stephen appears to have been suspicious, but was he right to be? Robert seems loyal in his actions, but what were his true intentions? A legendary moment took place in Normandy which Robert and his sympathizers would point to as the cause of later problems between the two men, though it is far from certain that the event genuinely took place.

Stephen relied heavily on Flemish mercenaries, the dislike of whom was given as the cause of the Norman lords abandoning him at Lisieux. The leader of the Flemish forces was William of Ypres, a man frequently credited with being one of the first professional mercenary captains in medieval Europe. Born around 1090, William is believed to have been an illegitimate son of Flemish nobility, a grandson of Robert the Frisian, Count of Flanders. He therefore had some potential claim to that county and launched two failed bids to be accepted before Flanders selected Charles the Good as their new count in 1119. At that point, William turned his attention to building up a mercenary force to earn his money and make a name for himself. His association with Stephen was to prove long and largely fruitful for both of them, though he and his men seem to have been disapproved of by the Norman, and frequently the English, nobility. In the early years of mercenary work, it was easy to see such men as lacking in chivalry, honour and a moral code if they chose to fight only for money. They could also acquire significant wealth and influence without a landed patrimony or noble lineage to demonstrate that they had 'earned' such a place.

It may be significant that the incident that occurred before Stephen left Normandy is widely blamed on William of Ypres. If it is untrue, it served an end, and the mercenary captain was a natural and easy target for accusations of behaving dishonourably. It is asserted that William of Ypres, with Stephen's approval, set an ambush to try and kill Robert, Earl of Gloucester. William of Malmesbury reports the incident with the certainty of a man keen to accept the reasons given for his patron's subsequent behaviour. He insists that 'the king, instigated by a certain William of Ypres, tried to catch him in an ambush' but that Robert 'was forewarned about it by someone in the secret and avoided the trap prepared for him.'[9] Following the incident, Robert kept away from Stephen's court, ignoring frequent invitations to attend.

If Stephen did initiate, or even just allow, the ambush, then it was a reckless and foolish move. Robert had demonstrated his continuing loyalty, at least in public, at Caen. If Stephen remained suspicious of his true intentions, then attacking him would not solve the issue. If anything, it would drive Robert into opposition even if that had never been his intention. William of Malmesbury probably garnered much of his information from Robert himself. Dislike of the influence wielded by William of Ypres, to the detriment of his own, and the need to find a reason for his later breach with Stephen may have led to the creation of a story of an ambush. Malmesbury could now assert that Stephen 'never showed the earl unqualified friendship, always regarding his power with suspicion'.[10] To ensure that the point was driven home, Malmesbury added that 'Robert, as one placed on a watch-tower, was looking to see how things would end, and considering carefully how he could avoid being branded before God and man as a traitor to the oath he had taken to his sister.'[11]

Suddenly, Robert was hit with the pangs of guilt at his failure to uphold his oath to Empress Matilda. It seems clear that Robert blamed

Stephen, through William of Ypres, for causing him to have to reassess his allegiance to the king. When Robert had done homage to Stephen, it was carefully made clear that it had been conditional on Stephen maintaining his own faith with Robert. An attempted ambush might constitute a sufficient breach of that agreement to activate the conditional clauses in Robert's oath. Freed from fealty to the king, he could safely, in good conscience, return to the otherwise contradictory pledge he had made to Empress Matilda to uphold her rights on their father's death. The neatness of this does not preclude some attempt to be rid of Robert on Stephen's part, as foolish as that might have been. Neither is it implausible that the ambush was a literary device meant to represent a longer-running sense of mistrust between the two men that led to a break-down in their relationship and bring it into sharper, more immediate focus. It is also possible that Robert invented the ambush as his justification for a change of allegiance, blaming Stephen for breaking the accord between them and thereby avoiding a charge of dishonouring the homage he had given.

Stephen's visit to Normandy had begun to set things right, and he made good early progress. Peace was secured with his brother Theobald and with France. He was recognized as the legitimate Duke of Normandy. Internal rebellions were efficiently quashed, and peace with the Angevins negotiated. It cannot be known for certain what might have happened had Stephen remained in Normandy any longer, not least because the effect of his absence in England cannot be measured. It seems likely, though, that Normandy wanted and expected him to say longer, to finish the job properly and give them complete peace and security. That he chose to leave a few men behind and take the majority of the great Norman barons, including the Beaumont twins, back to England with him must have felt like a betrayal. When Henry I had taken the crown of England, he had fought long, hard and tirelessly to keep Normandy within his possession too. The duchy may have grown concerned that despite its preference for a single lord shared with England, it was fast becoming the poor relation to the more prestigious crown of its neighbour across the water. For a proud people, that must have been hard for the Normans to face up to. It appeared that Stephen was not willing to fight to be their lord in the same way as Henry I had. He had done the bare minimum and scurried back to England at the first sign of a problem there, leaving the duchy's issues unresolved.

Perhaps that would be a harsh interpretation of Stephen's visit in 1137, but it may also have been what was felt on the ground, and the fact that he would never set foot there again can only have served to reinforce the idea as time passed by. Normandy had been the premier possession, and its people could be proud that their ruler had conquered a kingdom. Now, as it looked more and more as though the balance was shifting in England's favour, it might have been reasonable for Norman lords to question their commitment to a shared ruler, and to Stephen. They did not reject him, ever, but it is hard to establish how much of the resistance maintained against Geoffrey was a result of the perception of an invasion by a foreign power rather than affection for Stephen, and whether any headway made by the empress in England directly affected her husband's prospects in Normandy.

8

Empress Matilda

Then Geoffrey of Anjou entered Normandy at the head of
four hundred men-at-arms; and, taking service on his
wife's behalf, carried on an active campaign.[1]

If Henry I had created uncertainty about what precisely he had meant to happen on his death, his son-in-law Geoffrey, Count of Anjou did little to clarify the matter for those keen to understand. Orderic Vitalis was under the impression that when Geoffrey entered Normandy he did so 'on his wife's behalf', but also that the Angevin was viewed as an invader rather than a liberator. Throughout Geoffrey's annual assaults on the Norman border since 1134, his wife had remained conspicuously absent, detached and kept in the background. Empress Matilda was perhaps Geoffrey's greatest weapon in the fight for Normandy, but he kept her firmly in reserve. It is a decision that makes the likelihood that Geoffrey saw Normandy as his own prize, not one he wanted to hold on behalf of his wife, seem more compelling.

Stephen's arrival in Normandy in 1137 had gone some way toward galvanizing Norman resistance to the Angevin cause but had also exposed the size of the job required to restore internal order to the duchy, never mind protect it from external threats. The disunity that had torn Stephen's army apart can only have been food for Matilda's table. The arrival of campaigning season in 1138 presented another opportunity to test the waters. The trouble was begun by Reginald de Dunstanville, another of Henry I's plethora of illegitimate children. Reginald set about unsettling the area around the Cotentin in northern Normandy in the name of his half-sister, Empress Matilda. Reginald was supported by Baldwin de Redvers, the exile from Stephen's court, and other opponents of the king, including Stephen de Mandeville.[2]

The rebels were opposed to great effect by Roger the Viscount, one of the men left behind in Normandy by Stephen to keep order. Unable to defeat him in the open, the rebels resorted to ambushing Roger, hiding in the woods, laying in wait, until they 'burst from their lurking-place like hungry lions, and fell on the others unawares, butchering Roger without mercy'.[3] Despite Roger loudly pleading for mercy and promising a ransom for his release, the attackers, having no interest in allowing him to return to the front line, ensured that he was dead. In typically dramatic style, Orderic bemoaned the chaos that resulted from this incident. 'The governor being slain, the whole country was reduced to a state of desolation, and the savage fury of the freebooters exercised on the peasants is to this day unbridled.'[4]

The two-year truce that Geoffrey had agreed was broken. The dishonour in breaching his promise in ruthless pursuit of his aim is often overlooked; his word should have kept the peace for another year. It is likely that the swelling opportunities were just too much of a lure for Geoffrey to resist. Ralph d'Esson, castellan of several fortresses, was abducted by those loyal to Empress Matilda and taken to her. According to Orderic, she had him placed in a dungeon for a long time until he agreed to hand over control of his castles to her.[5] In May 1138, Waleran of Meulan and William of Ypres sailed back to Normandy to try and settle the situation. They focused first on Roger de Conches, a troublesome baron, finding him emboldened by recent events and the possibility of a rival cause to that of Stephen. As the situation mounted, Geoffrey re-entered Normandy in June.

Almost as soon as the count launched his assault, Robert, Earl of Gloucester submitted Caen and Bayeux to the control of his half-sister. It cannot be known beyond doubt whether Robert had merely been waiting for the right moment to move against Stephen, or whether the suspicion he was under, possibly the attempt to ambush him and his lack of prospects at his cousin's court, caused him to re-evaluate his loyalties. Whatever the truth may have been, this was the moment that real civil war was ignited. If Geoffrey was an outsider, an invader against whom Normandy should be defended, then Robert was the opposite: an insider, an influential and respected landowner who had allied himself with the Angevin cause. Waleran and William of Ypres swiftly put an army into the field to counter Geoffrey's new invasion, and their response caused the count to fall back. Robert himself remained within the walls of Caen and did not physically hand the city over to his brother-in-law. Frustrated, Waleran and William took their army to Robert's town and tried to lure him out by ravaging the lands around, but he would not be drawn. Eventually, they too were forced to withdraw.

By 1 October, Geoffrey had regrouped and laid siege to Falaise, almost thirty miles south of Caen. Robert, Earl of Gloucester was with the count for the assault, his decision now firmly and openly made. The Angevin army cannot have appeared too impressive, or at least the garrison at Falaise felt confident in their own supremacy. The captain, Richard de Lucy, took to opening the gates every morning and daring the Angevin army to come inside, closing them each night when they refused to accept the challenge. Orderic noted that Geoffrey and Robert 'toiled before it in vain for eighteen days' before being forced to abandon the siege of Falaise, defeated by the valiant Richard de Lucy.[6] The Angevins left in such a rush that they left supplies, including tents, weapons, wine and food behind. A rumour or false report of another approaching army under Waleran and William of Ypres may have spooked them. When it proved unfounded, they slunk back some ten days later to recover as much of their property as they could.

In search of a victory for his men that might avoid another embarrassing, empty-handed return to Anjou, Geoffrey moved on to Touques in November. Forty miles north-east of Falaise, it lay beyond Robert's city at Caen and on the Norman coast. Robert himself must have been equally keen to gain something tangible from his decision to switch sides. In the succession of unsuccessful assaults launched by Geoffrey, he may well have begun to question his choice. Gaining a foothold on the coast would be an essential step forward, not least if part of Robert's concern was to look across the Channel to his half-sister's prospects in England. Around the same time, Walchelin Maminot was taking control of Dover Castle to try and secure a port in England for Empress Matilda's cause, but he was thwarted by Stephen's wife, Queen Matilda, who was able to call upon a fleet from Boulogne. The earl may have helped to identify Touques as a soft target. The Angevins, sure enough, easily gained control of the town as the people fled in panic. So comfortable were they that Geoffrey and his army took lodgings in the abandoned houses and put their feet up at the hearths of families they had driven out. They relaxed, but they did so far too soon.

Many of the townsfolk had made for the nearby castle of Bonneville-sur-Touques, the most likely next target for Geoffrey's army if they were to tighten their grip on the town. William Trussebot, the castellan receiving the fleeing refugees, had no intention of waiting for a siege to come, nor of letting the Angevins enjoy a restful night at Touques. William and the townspeople laid a daring and bold plan to take the fight to the Angevins. Perhaps stirred by the effect of the burning of Lisieux two years earlier, William gathered a group of young boys and women who knew the town well and sent them to infiltrate the four quarters of Touques. When all were in place fires were set in forty-six different spots throughout the town at the same time, throwing the relaxing attackers into disarray. Awoken by the sound of their sentries' cries and the crackling of blazing wood, the Angevin soldiers stumbled out into the street and were driven to panic. Abandoning horses, armour and anything else they were not already wearing or carrying, they tried to leave the smoke-clogged, unfamiliar streets. As they did, William Trussebot and his garrison waited for them.

The plan was almost perfect. It was foiled only by the inability of William and his men to see the enemy through the thick blanket of smoke that obscured the light cast into the darkness by the flames. With neither side able to work out where the other was, the terror of the night increased. Count Geoffrey was eventually forced to try and find shelter with as many of his men as remained close to him in a graveyard within the town, seeing out the night there. As the smoke cleared and the morning light broke over the scene, the Angevins saw once more the Norman willingness to burn their own houses and property rather than see it fall into the hands of an invader. Orderic took some delight in yet another Angevin retreat from the duchy. 'As soon as the dawn appeared, he fled with the utmost speed, and having had some experience of Norman daring, never held bridle till he arrived, not without disgrace, at Argentan.'[7]

Robert, Earl of Gloucester had now cast the die. He issued a *diffidatio* to King Stephen, an oddly medieval piece of chivalric convention that has no modern parallel. A *diffidatio*, or a 'defiance', was a formal statement renouncing the allegiance and homage done to a lord. It was usually provided alongside detailed justification for the breach. In Robert's case, he was relying on the charge that Stephen had broken his own oath to recognize and protect Empress Matilda's inheritance by seizing the throne for himself. A *diffidatio* is subtly but crucially different from rebelling. Revolting against a lord brought with it charges of breaking fealty, breaching the accompanying oath, and treason; it was a path to infamy that risked execution, exile and possibly excommunication too, depending on the king's relationship with the church. By absolving himself of his allegiance to Stephen, Robert ensured that he was not rebelling. He placed himself in much the same position as Geoffrey, and that may have been no accident. Without a lord, Robert was unable to call on some of the protections he might expect from Stephen, but he was no longer looking to rely on them. The statement was designed to demonstrate the permanence of Robert's new position. In his relations with Geoffrey, it also prevented him from being one of Stephen's vassals appearing to defect to serve Geoffrey. Instead, he was a man with no lord, free to make his own decisions and decide his own direction.

William of Malmesbury recorded the issuing of the defiance by stating that Robert 'sent representatives and abandoned friendship and faith with the king in the traditional way, also renouncing homage, giving as the reason that his action was just, because the king had both unlawfully claimed the throne and disregarded, not to say betrayed, all the faith he had sworn to him.'[8] Whatever Robert's long-term plan had been before his formal breach with Stephen, it must be wondered whether it was this moment rather than anything Matilda or Geoffrey was able to effect, that really led to civil war in England. Empress Matilda had no foothold or landed interest in England. There was no group there showing her any special affection or attention. Baldwin de Redvers, sent into exile, had found a willing sponsor in the empress, but still, her cause, or that of her husband, was making little or no headway in Normandy, never mind appearing to near an attempt on England. Geoffrey was being beaten back at every turn in his assaults on the duchy. Even if Stephen were not held in particularly special regard by the Norman barons or the populace, they would not willingly accept invasion and conquering by the Count of Anjou. It is significant that only after Robert's decision to formally renounce his fealty to King Stephen did the Angevin cause appear to build a real head of steam that would propel it across the Channel and into England.

Robert, Earl of Gloucester remains a central figure in the struggle that now began to gather momentum, yet he is also a problematic figure to give real, corporeal form to. Having been one of Henry I's favourite illegitimate children, if not his favourite one, Robert utterly spurned any opportunity of promotion to rule on his own account. None of Henry's other children had been built up on both sides of the Channel to the same extent as Robert was. Stephen seems to have been the only rival to Robert in terms of Henry's affection, his generosity, and the wealth and authority this generated. There was, the author of the *Gesta Stephani* insists, an element amongst the polity who saw Robert as his father's most likely and most acceptable successor: keeping to Henry's blood but bypassing the inherent issues of female rule or Angevin domination. The earl refused to countenance such an idea.[9] Reginald de Dunstanville had begun to take an active part on Matilda's account before Robert, at least openly, but would never attain the position reserved for Robert at the empress's side.

There can be little doubt that Robert enjoyed an enviable reputation as a military leader, a nobleman of high standing and a man who wished to be seen as a paragon of chivalry. William of Malmesbury's constant need to justify the earl's actions and excuse any errors are plain to see, but behind them lies a motive that probably came from Robert himself. He was trapped in an awkward position by his oath to Empress Matilda and the contradictory homage he had paid to Stephen. The two were mutually exclusive, but he risked losing face, and honour, by breaking one or both of them. Many excused their breach of the loyalty promised to Matilda by claiming it relied on consultation about her marriage, but that they had been excluded from any discussion of the match with Geoffrey of Anjou. If it is true that Robert and Brian Fitz Count were the only men in England consulted by Henry I, then they could not plead the same extenuating circumstances. Bound by conflicting oaths, Robert had to break one and concentrate on the fulfilment of the other. His *diffidatio* was the only answer available, marking the homage he had given to Stephen as an error and reversing it. There remains some question as to the legal status of a defiance in England, but that is perhaps moot. Everyone knew what it meant. It meant war.

9

King Stephen

> There was no man of any dignity or substance in England who was not building or strengthening fortifications in England.[1]

Hot on the heels of Robert, Earl of Gloucester's *diffidatio* just after Whitsun 1138 came revolts in England at Bedford and then in the west, led there by Geoffrey Talbot. King Stephen cannot have helped but see a link, even if there was not one. Robert remained in Normandy but sent word to his men, based at his seat of power in Bristol, that they were no longer subject to Stephen's authority and that they were to cause whatever havoc they might and defend his lands until he arrived. Naturally, the king's response was to raise an army and take it to the walls of Bristol to try and break Robert's power before he came in person to lead the cause.

All of this unrest and rebellion seemed to do little to upset the energetic Stephen. Malmesbury wrote that 'he was not broken in spirit by any man's rebellion but appeared suddenly now here, now there, and always settled the business with more loss to himself than to his opponent.'[2] The king seemed to have been able to mobilize large forces at very short notice and cover unexpected distances, not unlike King Harold was able to do in 1066, but Stephen would sustain this effort for much longer. The problem pointed to by Malmesbury was that in attempting to meet all of these outbreaks and move on to the next, Stephen often reached terms that were not in his own best interest. There is a perception of Stephen as a weak man who could not keep a tight grip on what he had, but it must also be considered that given the wars he faced on several fronts – in Normandy, from Scotland, now in the west under Robert and localized trouble in England, often in the east – his options were severely restricted. Many kings faced one of these threats in isolation and struggled. Stephen was confronted by them all at the same time.

When the royal army arrived at Bristol, they found an almost impenetrable fortress prepared to hold out against them. As it became clear that there would be no swift victory, contradictory advice began to reach Stephen's ear that caused concern in some quarters. A portion of those with the king thought that they should lay a siege and pursue it to the end, no matter how long it took to ensure that Robert's power was shattered. These men promoted a plan to block the River Avon, preventing supplies from reaching the town and possibly flooding it. Others began to suggest that Bristol was too well protected and prepared so that a long siege might never succeed. There was suspicion in some quarters that these were men sympathetic to Robert and perhaps to the empress too, and that their advice came from a desire either to promote their cause or at least not to be seen to be standing in its way. The *Gesta Stephani* recorded in exasperation that

> others, and especially those who only pretended to serve the king but really favoured the earl, confuted the sound and acceptable advice of these men, and urged that it would be a waste of time and a profitless labour to try and block up the unfathomable sea with masses of timber and stone, since it was very clear that anything rolled in would either sink and be swallowed up from the mere depth of the water, or else would be entirely washed away and brought to nothing by strong flooding tides.[3]

Whether their advice was genuine or not, there was already emerging concern that some were preparing, or were prepared, to leave Stephen, and the risk of that must have figured in the king's thinking from that moment forward. It is impossible to establish at this distance whether Bristol might have fallen or would have stood firm indefinitely, sapping Stephen's cash and resources so that all the other fires at his borders and within his lands would necessarily be left to burn out of control. The veracity of the counsel provided to the king is therefore hard to establish, but if the *Gesta* is to be believed, suspicion was rife, and loyalties were in doubt. Part of Stephen's failings may well lie in his inability to recognize that enforcing his dominance and asserting his will would never have been 'a waste of time and a profitless labour'.

Although it is easy to spot with the benefit of hindsight, allowing Bristol to defy him and remain unassaulted was to cause long-term problems. Deeming it too strong to take made it a focus for all his enemies seeking protection and if he ever had a chance to break the castle, it was before Robert arrived to take command in person. Standing before the city's walls in 1138, balancing all of the other pulls on his time and attention, Stephen decided that those telling him to abandon the siege were probably correct. It was to prove a fateful calculation, but Stephen cannot have known that as he ordered his men to pack up and prepare to move on. They ravaged the land around Bristol, destroying or carrying off supplies and any goods that could be moved to deprive those within the city of access to food wherever possible.

The king elected to try and make some quick gains, doubtless hoping that these would serve to diminish the resistance of Bristol and Robert's adherents. He was able to quickly take Castle Cary from Ralph Lovel and Harptree Castle from William Fitz John. These satellites might well have fallen in the shockwave of a successful siege at Bristol, but as they were taken into royal hands, Stephen was able to point to firm victories, simultaneously denigrating Robert for his failure to come and protect the men resisting Stephen in the earl's name. If that was the intention, then it did not have the desired effect. Stephen's continuing and mounting problems were aptly described by the author of the *Gesta Stephani*:

> Having finally been victorious over Castle Cary, as has already been said, the king hastened, always armed, always accompanied by a host, to deal with various anxieties and tasks of many kinds which continually dragged him hither and thither all over England. It was like what we read of the fabled hydra of Hercules; when one head was cut off two more grew in its place. That is precisely what we must feel about King Stephen's labours, because when one was finished others, more burdensome, kept on taking its place without end and like another Hercules he always girded himself bravely and unconquerably to endure each.[4]

Throughout the summer of 1138, Stephen continued his vigorous efforts against those encouraged and emboldened in their opposition to him by

Robert and by the opportunity such trouble between great men might present. The king quickly took castles at Overton, Whittington, Bryn and Ellesmere in Shropshire along the Welsh border from William Peverel. When Shrewsbury, one of the primary towns along the Welsh border, rebelled, Stephen made a direct line for it. William Fitz Alan, married to a niece of Robert, Earl of Gloucester,was stirring up the trouble and in August the king arrived to assault Shrewsbury. William took his wife and children and fled from the city, leaving the effort to resist the king to his uncle, Arnulf of Hesdin. Arnulf refused to agree terms for the surrender of Shrewsbury to the king, and so the siege was pursued to its bitter end.

When Shrewsbury Castle finally fell, Arnulf and the garrison of ninety-three men were hanged. Stephen was well within his rights to behave in this apparently cruel manner in dealing with his vanquished enemies. Castle warfare was regulated by a set of well-established and accepted rules of conduct. Those within were, when their cause became hopeless, usually entitled to appeal to their master to send relief or to permit them to agree on terms for surrender. If no help came, that would be taken as permission to find conditions under which they could give up the castle. In that circumstance, the besiegers were generally expected to offer those within the opportunity to leave, perhaps with their possessions and wealth, but certainly with their families and their own lives protected by the leader of the besieging force. If, having made their appeal and found it unanswered, those within continued in their defiance, they could no longer expect to be entitled to mercy. Their lives were forfeit if the struggle was lost.

Arnulf and his garrison paid the traditional price, the one they would have expected to be extracted when the castle was lost. For Stephen, it was an opportunity to send out a firm message to those others considering joining Robert and resisting royal authority. There would be no mercy for their defiance. It would help to encourage others to hand over the keys to castles they controlled more easily if they understood that Stephen would pursue the rules of castle warfare to their ultimate, justified conclusion. Generally seen as a man whose unnecessary and boundless mercy hampered his cause when more ruthless action might have won the day, this is an instructive episode. Stephen was not cruel and vicious, but neither was he a pushover. If he offered mercy, he must have seen some advantage to it in minimizing the disruption that might otherwise be exacerbated by rushing to executions. Although he might not have been keen on reprisals that meant death for his enemies, he was both willing to and capable of exercising his rights to extract the ultimate toll when required. It should not be forgotten either that a degree of mercy and certainly adhesion to the rules of war were expected of any good king and served to restrict the kind of behaviour that was acceptable.

While Stephen was kept busy in the south, King David of Scotland took another opportunity to cross what might loosely be called the border and stake his claim to chunks of northern England. Just as Geoffrey's incursions into Normandy were becoming an annual affair to the king's south, so King David ensured that Stephen was not free from threats at the northern edges of his territories. Able to plead that he sought only to defend the rights of his niece, Empress Matilda, David's motives, as demonstrated by his swift move to peace with Stephen in 1136, were not quite so clear-cut or honourable. In July, King David crossed the River Tees with a Scottish army that included a large contingent of Picts. Two Scots barons were sent to lay siege to Wark as David marched south. Eustace Fitz John, who had been deprived of control of Bamburgh Castle by King Stephen, saw the benefit of being presented with an option for his own allegiance and made contact with David. Eustace still retained control of Alnwick Castle and another fortress at Malton, and when he added his forces to those of David, the Scots army decided to march past Bamburgh to demonstrate their presence and power. The garrison, believing themselves unassailable, taunted the Scots from the safety of their barricades. Enraged, the invading army attacked, quickly broke down the walls and slaughtered those within the castle.[5]

Henry of Huntingdon ascribed traditional atrocities to the attackers. 'They ripped open pregnant women, tossed children on the points of their spears, butchered priests at the altars, and, cutting off the heads from the images on crucifixes, placed them on the bodies of the slain, while in exchange, they fixed on the crucifixes the heads of their victims.'[6] Stephen was unable to travel to the north himself, committing to try and deal with Robert's defiance, but he contributed to the effort against the Scots and must have sent instructions too. Bernard de Baliol, 'a man well skilled in military tactics', hurried north with soldiers sent by King Stephen.[7] Bernard and another baron, Robert de Bruce, went to see King David and offer what must have been Stephen's terms for peace. If the Scots army would leave England immediately, David's son,

Prince Henry, would be given the earldom of Northumberland. David declined the offer, upon which Bernard and Robert denounced their previous homage for lands they held from him and returned to the English army.

The organization of the effort to resist David was given to Thurstan, Archbishop of York. Nearing seventy by this time, Thurstan had been archbishop since 1115, though a dispute with Ralph d'Escures, Archbishop of Canterbury had led to a delay of four years in his consecration. Ralph had refused to approve of Thurstan's appointment unless he submitted to Canterbury as the senior archdiocese. York continued to assert its independence and, as his predecessors had done, Thurstan refused Ralph's demands. He was eventually consecrated by the pope and had become a fast ally of Stephen on the new king's accession in 1135. Placing Thurstan in military control was an interesting decision. It prevented any baronial squabbling over supremacy, but with the considerable Pictish element in David's army, it allowed the campaign to take on the air of a crusade under the archbishop's guidance. It was a powerful motivator, and Thurstan set about securing God's favour for their undertaking with three days of fasting, almsgiving and absolutions.[8]

Thurstan marched the English army to Northallerton in Yorkshire, about thirty miles north-north-west of the city of York. On a piece of land belonging to St Cuthbert's, increasing the religious significance of the moment, Thurstan arrayed his force to face down the Scots on 22 August 1138. The archbishop had a ship's mast brought up and secured to a cart at the top of a hill where he had placed the army. On the mast were hung the banners of St Peter, of St John of Beverley and of St Wilfrid of Ripon. Above the apostle and two northern English saints' emblems was placed the 'Body of the Lord, to be their standard-bearer and the leader of their battle'.[9] Thurstan sent his bishops and priests amongst the men to pray with them and take their confessions. Although he and the other religious men then withdrew from the field, the preparation for a crusading battle to save the north was complete. The fight was in the hands of knights, soldiers and God. Henry of Huntingdon places a rousing speech into the mouth of Ralph, Bishop of Durham, reminding the men who they were and the reputation they fought to uphold:

> Brave nobles of England, Normans by birth; for it is well that on the eve of battle you should call to mind who you

> are, and from whom you are sprung: no one ever withstood you with success. Gallant France fell beneath your arms; fertile England you subdued; rich Apulia flourished again under your auspices; Jerusalem, renowned in story, and the noble Antioch, both submitted to you.[10]

As the English army, drinking in the bishop's stirring exaltation, bellowed 'Amen! Amen!' in response, the Scots issued their own battle cry of 'Alban! Alban!'. The vanguard of the Scottish army advanced, all cries and bravery, but without armour, sufficient weaponry or much hope. The men of Lothian had reportedly demanded the privilege of joining battle first, and David had reluctantly agreed. 'Naked, and almost unarmed, these men advanced against battalions clad in mail, and thereby rendered invulnerable.'[11] The lightly armoured Scots crashed against the rocky shore of the English army that stood, resolute, beneath their standard. English archers picked off the Scots and knights hacked them down. 'For the Almighty was offended at them, and their strength was rent like a cobweb.'[12]

The rest of the Scots army, which had begun to engage in various spots around the field, saw the plight of the men of Lothian and understood the hopelessness of the task facing them. They began to flee, first piecemeal, but soon in larger and larger groups. King David had selected the flower of Scottish knighthood from amongst the many clans he had united to act as his personal guard. Though they wore armour, they too began to fall away as the army of York proved immovable. The final handful with King David urged him to call for his horse and retreat before he was captured and killed, and he was forced to see the wisdom of their counsel. His son, Prince Henry, 'heedless of what his countrymen were doing, and inspired only by his ardour for the fight and for glory', led a cavalry charge to try and make a breakthrough, but it too failed; 'a brilliant but unsuccessful attack'.[13]

After three hours of fighting, with a reported 11,000 Scots killed on the field and only a small handful of English casualties, the army of York stood victorious. Some called the field Bagmoor for a time, a jibe at the amount of baggage left behind by the fleeing Scots. As they wandered the countryside lost, many more were killed by locals who found them in woods and cornfields. The English did not pursue, seeing no need.[14] The day had been an unmitigated success, a victory won by God's own hand, under whose banner the men had fought what they viewed as a crusade. The encounter became known as the Battle of the Standard and proved a vital success for Stephen despite his absence. Henry of Huntingdon explains that when news of the victory reached the king, 'he and all who were with him offered solemn thanks to Almighty God'.[15]

Stephen was not ignorant of the more temporal rewards the events required. Amongst the leaders of the force in the field was Walter de Gant,[16] Earl of Lincoln and William le Gros, Earl of Albermarle,[17] and others received rewards for their contributions. William le Gros was made Earl of York to add to his Norman title, and Robert de Ferrers became Earl of Derby.[18] Stephen would soon implement a policy of creating regional magnates, and it is possible that the aftermath of the Battle of the Standard demonstrated the possibilities of offering coveted rewards to loyal men whilst simultaneously strengthening royal authority in the regions through them, allowing them to also take some of the workload of keeping an increasingly fragile peace.

The year 1138 had proven very successful for Stephen as autumn began to fall and the Scots limped back across the border. Robert, Earl of Gloucester had issued his *diffidatio* but had also remained across the Channel in Normandy. Bristol had not fallen, but Stephen had elected not to try and bring about its capture. Instead, he had harried the surrounding lands, won swift victories at Castle Cary and Harptree before working up the Welsh border region to enforce his authority. The king is perhaps denied credit for the crushing victory at the Battle of the Standard because he was not present in person, but it seems unreasonable not to allow him a part in the result. Stephen had sent men, presumably with instructions about what he expected to happen. Placing the preparations into the hands of the Archbishop of York demonstrated an understanding both of the power of a crusading message and of the art of effective delegation. It is worth considering not that Stephen was not present to win the glory of the victory, but rather that his army was victorious despite his inability to be there himself.

Aside from trusting his subordinates with such a vital task as defending against a Scots invasion and creating an opportunity in which they were able to win convincingly, Stephen's attractions as a leader must be noted. King David was a charismatic and well-respected figure. Although increasingly viewed as an enemy across the border, Scotland maintained claims to swathes of hotly disputed territory in the regions where the two kingdoms abutted each other. If King Stephen was an entirely unappealing, forlorn and broken monarch, then his northern subjects had the opportunity in August 1138 to welcome rather than repel King David. Instead, Thurstan was easily able to coordinate a unified resistance with an army that remained disciplined even when victory appeared assured. If there was an emerging sense of Empress Matilda's rights being championed by King David and Robert, Earl of Gloucester then the whole kingdom was being offered an alternative. It was one, in 1138, that all but Robert's lands conspicuously turned away from to defend Stephen.

A further demonstration of the king's willingness and ability to successfully delegate responsibilities was taking place on the south coast too. With Stephen still in the west and Thurstan organizing the fight against the Scots in the north, it was left to Queen Matilda to take back control of Dover Castle for her husband. It seems likely that Robert hoped to use it as a foothold in England at which he could arrive, and Orderic Vitalis is clear that the fall of this fortress was entirely the work of the queen. It was she who laid the siege on the land side, and it was her family and contacts in Boulogne who sent ships to blockade the sea route. With war threatened on so many fronts, Stephen could not possibly tackle them all personally, but he was able to rely on key people to represent him successfully. That is a testament both to his ability to delegate and to the desire in many quarters to preserve him on the throne.

Stephen's wife, Queen Matilda, is a figure whose role in the events of her husband's reign would prove critical in keeping his cause alive and functioning, but she also offers a stark contrast to her own cousin, Empress Matilda. Stephen was first cousin to the empress through their joint descent from their grandfather, William the Conqueror, but Queen Matilda shared maternal grandparents with the empress. Queen Matilda's mother was Mary of Scotland, a daughter of Margaret of Scotland and therefore a sister to Matilda of Scotland, the empress's mother. King David consequently found himself trapped between the causes of two nieces rather than merely championing a single relative. Victory for one niece meant the destruction of the other. It also offered him a pleasing fallback if he ever wished to maintain a position floating between the two.

Queen Matilda would frequently show just how effective a woman could be in medieval England if she carefully operated the levers of her influence. Never accused of the pomposity and manliness that would afflict the empress's personal reputation, Queen Matilda nevertheless played a prominent role in government and raised men to fight. Perhaps the critical difference, not least for those being commanded by her, was the understanding that she did all these things in her husband's name. Empress Matilda sought to rule in her own right. Although subtle, the distinction is key to understanding the success of one and the setbacks faced by the other. Nevertheless, the empress and her husband never harnessed the demonstrable power of a wife acting to promote her husband's cause. Had they united in this manner, their campaigns might have been more successful more quickly, and Empress Matilda might not have been left to languish in the distaste of the memories of men she tried to rule. It is a stigma she has been unable to shake off for almost a millennium.

The year must have felt like a successful one against mounting odds for the king. Before it was out, there was one more incident that has cast a shadow over the years that followed. On 24 December 1138, Theobald of Bec was elected as the new Archbishop of Canterbury. The previous incumbent, William de Corbeil, had died on 21 November 1136 and the office had been vacant for two years when Theobald, the abbot of the Benedictine Abbey of Our Lady of Bec was selected. There may seem little in this. Stephen appears to have approved of Theobald, who was probably nearing fifty. The election had been overseen by Alberic of Ostia, a papal legate, and Alberic would consecrate Theobald in his new office on 8 January 1139, so there was no potential for a dispute between the king and Rome. It is possible that the Beaumont twins, Waleran and Robert, were involved in Theobald's selection too, as Waleran was a lay patron of the Abbey of Bec. If so, their motive might have been an attempt to block the promotion of Henry, Bishop of Winchester, the king's brother with whom they appear not to have been on good terms. There has long been a lingering sense that Bishop Henry had coveted the archbishopric for himself.

There is no extant record of Bishop Henry's desire for the position, though he was at St Paul's officiating at the ordination of deacons when the election took place and reportedly stormed out when the news reached him, leaving the ceremony incomplete. Even if Bishop Henry had hoped to grasp the office, he would not have been an appealing candidate to the monks of Canterbury. Henry was a pluralist, holding onto the post of Abbot of Glastonbury when he became Bishop of Winchester. The monks had last faced the same sort of problem with Stigand before and after the Conquest, and there had been calls for his deposition for his unsuitability which ultimately led to papal intervention to unseat him. Although Canterbury might have carried more prestige, it would have meant giving up two of the wealthiest offices in England. Henry was a political animal too, something that would have made him more unappealing to the monks of Canterbury. For Stephen, there was some benefit in having his brother wealthy and influential enough to offer political support, but also slightly detached. Empress Matilda had seen the problems of trying to move a partisan into a senior church office in Germany and Theobald would be a patron of his own successor, Thomas Becket, who would also demonstrate the dangers of mixing politics and religion too closely. Perhaps Stephen saw the risks more clearly than others. It is possible too that his brother's desire for the office has been overstated or even assumed. Bishop Henry would soon receive ample compensation if he did feel that he had missed out in the election to Canterbury.

10

Empress Matilda

Robert found that in England the nobles were either hostile or gave no help, apart from a very few who had not forgotten the faith they once swore.[1]

In an effort to resolve the issues created by the papal schism after the death of Anacletus II, Innocent II summoned almost a thousand prelates to attend the Second Lateran Council in April 1139. The session would confirm the prohibition on marriage for the clergy, order bishops and archbishops to stop wearing ostentatious clothes and forbid tournaments and jousts that endangered life. Empress Matilda took the opportunity of the gathered Church to launch a formal, ecclesiastical challenge to Stephen's kingship.

Ulger, Bishop of Angers attended the Second Lateran Council at the instruction of Geoffrey, Count of Anjou to plead the case for Empress Matilda's right to Normandy and England. The case was based on the assertion that Stephen had defrauded Matilda of her inheritance and that the oaths made to her invalidated the fealty given to Stephen later. Ulger also took the chance to make the false claim that Matilda had been consecrated as empress in Rome when married to Henry V, an event that had never taken place and can hardly have furthered their case. The appearance is that Matilda and Geoffrey were making a bid for control of Normandy and England in her right. Geoffrey may have realized that his own incursions into the duchy had made no lasting headway because he was seen as an invader rather than a liberator or rightful ruler. His wife was able to stake her own claim as the legitimate ruler so the appeal may have been an attempt to significantly change the emphasis of their efforts. Alternatively, it is possible that the empress took the opportunity to voice her grievances in front of the gathered Roman Church to ensure that the matter was not yet forgotten, would not be overlooked and could be kept alive for her sons if she was unable to enforce her rights.

After the death of her first husband Henry V, Matilda could reflect on the career of his nephew Conrad of Hohenstaufen. Foiled in his efforts to succeed Henry as Holy Roman Emperor, Conrad opposed the election of Lothair III, who was carried to power by the support of the bishops. Marching into Italy, Conrad had himself crowned King of Italy, and although he was forced to recognize Lothair in 1135, when the emperor died in 1137, Conrad had succeeded him as King of Germany. There was perhaps some instruction for Matilda in the story: that a claim kept alive and in the face of the world could succeed eventually, even if the short term appeared gloomy. If she sought more encouragement, Roger of Sicily had been excommunicated for usurping a throne, just as Matilda was alleging Stephen had done. Roger had managed to alter papal policy by force of arms so that Innocent had acknowledged him, so the pope's mind could be changed. Although Stephen had received papal recognition, both sides of Roger's story offered Matilda some hope.

Arnulf, Archdeacon of Sées, who would later become Bishop of Lisieux, led Stephen's representatives to answer Matilda's and Geoffrey's case. Arnulf's rebuttal relied almost entirely on a scandalous accusation that Matilda herself was illegitimate and therefore incapable of succeeding her father. He did not seek to depend on a notion that female rule was impractical or illegal. Nor did he claim that the oaths extracted by Henry I had been given under duress, or invalidated by the old king's failure to consult on the question of his daughter's marriage. Arnulf went right to the core of all of Matilda's arguments and sought to tear them down in one go by questioning her status as a legitimate member of the royal family. This was a compelling argument, one that seems to have precluded the otherwise eminently suitable Robert, Earl of Gloucester from following his father. Perhaps not in Normandy, but certainly in England, illegitimacy was an absolute bar to rule, accentuating the difference between a duchy and a kingdom, in which a ruler is appointed by God and consecrated by the church.

The allegation against the empress was not entirely new. It related to the period that Matilda of Scotland had spent in the care of her aunt Christina at Wilton Abbey, during which she had complained about living in fear of the beatings she received. Arnulf resurrected the allegation that Empress Matilda's mother had been a confirmed nun during that time and that Henry I had abducted her from the nunnery in order to marry her. Given that Henry could not legally marry a nun, that would invalidate the marriage and make any offspring from the union, including, and now limited to, Matilda, illegitimate and incapable of inheriting. In 1144, Gilbert Foliot, then Abbot of Gloucester, would write to Brian Fitz Count, giving a full account of this episode in his letter. Gilbert had been present at the council in the company of the Abbot of Cluny, in whose house he was then serving. Gilbert recognized the charges that had been made but insisted that in his belief, the fact that Anselm, Archbishop of Canterbury at the time, had blessed the wedding meant there could be no impropriety.[2] On the continent, Herimann of Tournai claimed that the accusation was correct and that Anselm himself had prophesied trouble from the unholy union. The death of William Adelin in the *White Ship* disaster and Matilda's barren first marriage were, Herimann believed, the fulfilment of that forecast.[3]

Pope Innocent II threw the case out. Significantly, he did not offer a pronouncement on the merits of either case, leaving both able to maintain that they still held a valid position. The pope sent written confirmation of Stephen's legitimacy as King of England and Duke of Normandy, appearing to rule in the king's favour, but he had not examined the case thoroughly and never denied Matilda's claims. It was a setback, perhaps one that triggered the empress's next move, her boldest so far, but her case in Rome was not done with. By refusing to rule on the matter, Innocent had sidestepped a sticky decision. If he found in Empress Matilda's favour, he would have been forced to renounce a predecessor's decision and would risk condemning England and Normandy, neither of which were openly rejecting Stephen as their ruler, to civil war. At a time when crusading was on the minds of many, a civil war in northern Europe was in no one's interest and hardly held with the church's responsibility to maintain and promote peace amongst Christian men. Had Empress Matilda's claim been formally rejected, it risked alienating Geoffrey, whose father was currently King of Jerusalem. Furthermore, if the Angevin assault on Normandy, then potentially England, were to succeed, Innocent would be faced with having to recognize a claim he had previously deemed baseless from a woman he had ruled to be illegitimate. The easiest answer was to throw his papers in the air and everyone out of the room. He could then avoid giving a definitive answer. It left both sides unsatisfied, but neither bereft nor hostile.

In August 1139, Empress Matilda had apparently decided on a radical adjustment in her efforts, though her husband seems to have kept at arms' length from her new and risky activities. Matilda did not lack an adventurous spirit and demonstrated a willingness to take the fight right to the enemy's door in an act of daring that would almost certainly have been loudly applauded in a man. It was not a distinction or restriction she was ever to fully acknowledge, at least not for many years. Baldwin de Redvers was sent to secure Wareham Castle in Dorset on the south coast to provide a secure landing spot in England for the empress. Baldwin failed and was forced back to Corfe Castle slightly further inland. His connections in the south-west were letting him down.

Changing her focus, on 30 September 1139, Empress Matilda landed at Arundel Castle near Worthing, further east than Wareham. The castle belonged to William d'Aubigny, who had been created Earl of Sussex (though often referred to as Earl of Arundel) in 1138. William had married Queen Adeliza, the young widow of Henry I who was Empress Matilda's stepmother. Adeliza was a year younger than her stepdaughter, and it is possible the two had a reasonably good relationship, though they are unlikely to have been close. William was a devoted supporter of King Stephen, so his reception of two of Henry's children seems odd unless it was at his wife's instigation. She may have believed she was simply receiving a visit from her stepchildren, or have thought her responsibility still lay in finding a reconciliation between the arguing factions that were emerging. That had been her role as a queen, and she might have believed she could help now, with her husband's closeness to the king and her own relationship with Henry I's children.

The *Gesta Stephani* stated that Robert 'landed at the castle of Arundel, as though he were merely to be a guest there, and was admitted with a strong body of troops.' William of Malmesbury says Robert brought with him 'no more than 140 knights'.[4] It seems that Robert's early reports did not bode well for them. His intelligence suggested that the overwhelming majority were not seeking to abandon their allegiance to Stephen and that only a small handful could be relied on to uphold the oath they had sworn to Empress Matilda.[5] Almost as soon as they had arrived at Arundel Castle and the empress had been safely installed there, Robert left with a dozen knights to ride west towards his power base at Bristol. He was met along the way by Brian Fitz Count, who rode out of his castle at Wallingford to meet the earl. Brian is the man

William of Malmesbury believed had been consulted alongside Robert about Matilda's marriage to Geoffrey, and he may have been a softer target because of that. He could have been reminded that whatever release others believed they had secured from their oaths, Robert and Brian could not claim the same breach and so remained honour-bound to help the empress.

Robert's departure from Arundel was timely, perhaps deliberately so. Stephen, with his characteristic speed and vigour, arrived outside the walls with an army threatening to lay siege to the fortress. Robert may have expected, and planned for, precisely this. The ease with which the king was able to raise men and travel unhindered through the kingdom was in itself a setback for the empress's cause that showed a realm united behind their leader rather than one ripe for rebellion. Had Robert been at Arundel, Stephen would have been justified in immediately launching into hostilities. His *diffidatio* meant that he was not one of Stephen's subjects and was not entitled to any protection that came with that status. Having been deprived of all of his lands and offices, Robert's arrival could have been viewed by Stephen as nothing less than a hostile invasion. In hindsight, that was what it undoubtedly was.The *Gesta Stephani* offers further weight to the notion that it was Robert's arrival, not Empress Matilda's, that was causing the greatest consternation. 'England at once was shaken and quivered with intense fear, affected in different ways, because all who secretly or openly favoured the earl were keener than usual and more eager to trouble the king, while those who obeyed the king were brought low as though cowering beneath a dreadful thunderclap.'[6] The impression the chronicler gained was that Robert was the man inspiring those who considered opposing Stephen and worried those who would remain loyal to the king. Arriving at Arundel to find Queen Adeliza and Empress Matilda changed the complexion of the confrontation completely for Stephen.

What followed has long been a source of criticism for King Stephen, as it seems to have been at the time. As with many such moments, it was not a simple matter. As Stephen settled down for a siege and it became clear that Robert had left, the king was faced with the prospect of assaulting not only a former queen but also his cousin. Adeliza insisted that she had not let her stepchildren into Arundel to use it as a base for hostilities against the king. Robert, who might legitimately be viewed as an enemy, had left. Empress Matilda had not yet declared any intention to lead a revolt against Stephen. Her submission at the Second Lateran Council must have alerted the king that she had not forgotten the rights she claimed, but her failure to secure papal backing made her current position unclear. Was she there to stir up revolt, or to attempt a reconciliation that might relieve Stephen of problems both in Normandy with Geoffrey and in England now with Robert? Uncertain what her intentions were, if Stephen laid siege to Arundel Castle he risked a perception that he was attacking a woman, who was his own cousin, a daughter of the previous king, and a non-combatant who had not openly threatened him. Aside from the dishonour such a move might bring, it would risk creating a well of outrage and sympathy from which the empress's cause might drink deeply. An attack might drive support to Matilda.

The solution Stephen arrived at, possibly at the suggestion of his brother Bishop Henry, was to allow the empress to leave Arundel under a safe conduct and travel to Gloucester, to her half-brother Robert. It sounded like madness, particularly with the benefit of hindsight, but Empress Matilda held all the cards within the walls of Arundel Castle, and Stephen was left dangerously short of options. Bishop Henry and Waleran, Count of Meulan were provided as escorts to take the empress most of the way to the west. William of Malmesbury explains the king's apparent generosity as no more than meeting the chivalric requirements of his situation. 'Then the king gave the empress the escort of Henry, bishop of Winchester, and Waleran, count of Meulan, escort which it is not the custom of honourable knights to refuse to anyone, even their bitterest enemy.'[7] It was a weight of expectation that Matilda and Adeliza might have been able to play up to their own benefit, but Stephen really had little choice other than to act as he did. Robert came to meet her at an arranged handover spot, somehow already marking the extent of the earl's unchallengeable influence, and Stephen's duty was discharged.

For the king, it was not a result without benefit. When attacking Baldwin de Redvers he was credited with saying that he preferred all of his enemies to be gathered together in one spot so that they were easier to tackle. It must have quickly become evident that the empress was not there to mend their fractured relationship, let alone offer him homage or an end to her husband's assaults on Normandy. That meant she could only be there to cause trouble, but until she did so openly, the king's hands were tied. If he left Matilda where she was, even if she was not getting active support from Adeliza or William d'Aubigny, he risked opening up yet another front in the war to retain control of his territories. Scotland was still a potential threat in the north, Anjou a more certain one in the south, now Robert was in his well-protected, if technically forfeited, lands in the west and if Empress Matilda could raise any support from Arundel or allow men to arrive there from across the Channel, he would face a threat in the east too. Surrounded, it would take little to encourage King David to a fresh assault, Geoffrey could march into Normandy and Stephen would be squeezed in England from west and east. There was some sense in moving Empress Matilda to join another, existing threat. In fact, it may not have suited her plans at all. If that was the case, then Stephen had outwitted her.

That Matilda might not have been entirely happy with the outcome is suggested from the very brief time that she remained at Bristol with Earl Robert. The empress moved quickly to Gloucester, the seat of her half-brother's earldom but not his own base. There she was warmly received by Miles of Gloucester, the castellan for Earl Robert who had been a loyal servant of Henry I and, from this moment forward, would never waver from his daughter's cause. The writer of the *Gesta Stephani* claimed that 'he was so unquestioning in his loyalty to King Henry's children as not only to have helped them, but likewise to have received the Countess of Anjou herself with her men and always behaved to her like a father in deed and counsel.'[8] Miles was viewed as a mentor of sorts to the empress and she appeared to value his support and advice for the remainder of his life. Matilda's motives in seeking to base herself at Gloucester may have lain in the fact that, unlike Bristol, Gloucester was a royal castle and her pretensions were to the crown that Stephen wore. She would not hide behind Robert's stout walls at Bristol but rather was keen to show herself in conspicuous possession of royal property in her own right.

Nearby Hereford was quickly taken for the empress. The garrison tried to hold out within the castle but to no avail. Stephen arrived to attempt to relieve them but was unable to get close. Forced to withdraw, he took his cavalry south and harried the area around Bristol again, burning villages around Dunster and trying to deny his enemies any supplies or food.[9] The initiation of a bid to reclaim that which Empress Matilda believed herself deprived of had been difficult, but not without promise. Perhaps the most substantial step forward was that she was now in England as a figurehead for her own cause. If she had expected more support when she arrived at Arundel, then the empress must have been disappointed to find herself marched almost the width of England and deposited with her half-brother. Queen Adeliza's role in the affair remains uncertain: she may have sought to help her stepdaughter but been foiled, or her aim may only ever have been to try and help find peace. No significant baron or noble other than Robert had declared for her, though Brian Fitz Count and Miles of Gloucester were to prove invaluable and unshakeable. A few of those dispossessed by Stephen and dissatisfied enough to seek the empress out found their way to Gloucester 'where all those attacked by the king had assembled as though it were a receptacle of filth',[10] but these men necessarily brought no land, power or influence to Matilda's table, only disgruntled hopes of vengeance.

Nevertheless, they had held Bristol, Gloucester and Hereford against King Stephen's best efforts to drive them out. Robert had a firm grip on his power base and had been able to demonstrate that he could not be assaulted at Bristol. The empress had struck out for Gloucester to make her own, independent bid for authority and is not often given the credit she deserves for doing so. It was a daring move. The easy option was to remain safely at Bristol and rely on Robert to make military gains in her name. The spanner that Empress Matilda frequently threw into the workings of medieval politics was her refusal to recognize or accept that kind of traditional female role for herself. Sometimes it was to the detriment of her cause, but even then it is admirable. If the men of her age were unable to comprehend what it might mean for them and how it should work, that is their failing, not hers, even when she may have been better served in the long term by acquiescing just a bit. If a prince had landed in England and swiftly gained control of large chunks of the West Country and Welsh Marches, fending off attacks from the king, it would surely have been seen as the beginnings of an epic adventure. It was when the empress's son tried it. Matilda's sex was not her fault, but perhaps her inflexibility in making allowances for the intransigence of the men she looked to rule hampered her cause. Then again, as she would probably reflect more than once in the coming years, how could she rule like a king without behaving like one?

11

King Stephen

> It may be remarked that this permission given by the king was a sign of great simplicity or carelessness, and prudent men regret that he was regardless of his own welfare and the kingdom's security. It was in his power at this time to have easily stifled a flame which threatened great mischief, if, with a policy becoming the wise, he had at once driven away the wolf from the entrance of the fold, and, for the safety of the flock, crushed the deadly efforts of those whose enterprise threatened the country with pillage, slaughter, and depopulation, by smiting them with the sword of justice.[1]

Orderic Vitalis was not sympathetic to King Stephen's decision to allow Empress Matilda to leave Arundel Castle to join Robert, Earl of Gloucester. It is interesting to think what he, and other chroniclers, might have made of any other decision. Should Stephen have assaulted the castle, taken his cousin prisoner and thrown her into a dungeon indefinitely? Indeed, he might be applauded had he managed to do that at Bristol against Robert, but to a woman who had not declared against him openly? What if she had been killed? Would he then be a vicious, tyrannical murderer of women? Had he left her at Arundel, and another front in the war against him had been opened up, surely commentators would blame his inaction for exacerbating his problems. In reality, what Stephen did was probably the best, or the least terrible, option available to him, certainly without the loss of honour and reputation that he would have found unpalatable.

If 1138 had been a generally successful year for Stephen, if not quite decisively so, then 1139 was to prove filled with problems, of which Empress Matilda's arrival might not have even seemed the most serious or pressing. On 9 April 1139, Stephen concluded a peace treaty with King David of Scotland that had primarily been negotiated by his wife,

Queen Matilda, another of David's nieces. The contents of the agreement were kept secret until the following year, a sure signal that the terms were not as favourable as Stephen might have hoped. David's son, Prince Henry, was given all of the lands he had held in 1138, apart from the towns and castles of Newcastle and Bamburgh. For the withholding of these, he was given two towns of equal financial value in the south. Prince Henry was also created Earl of Northumbria, a vast province that encompassed Northumberland, Durham, Cumberland, Westmoreland and parts of Lancashire north of the River Ribble. He was also confirmed as Earl of Huntingdon. Although it was agreed that the English laws of Henry I would remain in force in those regions, barons within the earldom were permitted to do homage to Prince Henry, saving only their allegiance to Stephen. In return, King David and Prince Henry promised permanent peace and provided four hostages. The prince was also to be married to Ada de Warenne, a half-sister of the Beaumont twins.

The appeal of this to the English king is plain. As trouble mounted in Normandy and Empress Matilda made her case in Rome to be recognized in his place, Stephen had too many problems mounting up before him. Having crushed David's invasion at the Battle of the Standard, he had the opportunity to force a settlement that would relieve him of one of the fronts continually being opened up against him. The effect was that much of England north of the River Tees fell under Scottish control, but it appeared to resolve the issues there. Prince Henry joined Stephen's court, and the two seem to have enjoyed a reasonably good relationship, as will soon become apparent. Any punitive settlement Stephen might have felt able to force on David in the aftermath of the Battle of the Standard would not bring the permanent end to troubles that the English king needed. David would be left itching for an excuse to break the treaty. By giving him tangible benefits, even if it meant ceding control of a large chunk of land, Stephen bought himself time to focus on other problems.

If Stephen missed a trick during the negotiation of the Second Treaty of Durham, it was in his failure to recognize precisely what had happened the year before. David had attacked, and in the king's absence, the barons and clergy of the north had united to put an army in the field to defend their lands. By extension, whether they meant to or not, they had also defended Stephen and his legitimacy as King of England. That was a coup for a man generally viewed ever since as an unpopular disaster. The willingness to give Scotland what it had been unable to take in 1138 undid all of that northern unity, pride and vicarious support. Although it might have meant leaving war bubbling just beneath the surface, Stephen might have chosen to bolster those who had defended him the previous year instead of the enemy they had defeated. If the nobles, barons and leading clergy of the region had been empowered to resist David, Stephen would have been free from concern about his northern territories. The added benefit would have been that his northern lords and the populace would have been kept busy and left no time to contemplate the merits of Empress Matilda's cause or to join anyone else seeking to inspire trouble against Stephen. In hindsight, it is possible to view this as a better option, but as other matters grew increasingly pressing, Stephen was forced to try and find the fastest route to a lasting settlement. For now, that would be giving ground to David, but it was probably not meant to be a permanent arrangement. The north may have grown tired and disaffected by a protracted war effort, particularly if a view developed that Stephen had abandoned them. David might begin to appear a preferable option, even if his military efforts could be kept at bay indefinitely. If war was coming in the south and in the west, Stephen may have considered that tying up all of the men and barons of the north in something that could be avoided would be an unwelcome drain on his stretching resources.

Hugh Bigod is an intriguing figure during King Stephen's reign, and indeed after it. It was Hugh who had borne witness to a deathbed change of heart by Henry I, insisting that the old king had set aside his daughter in favour of Stephen. Although Hugh was accused of not having been anywhere near Henry I's deathbed, he swore oaths that helped Stephen become accepted as king. A rumour of Stephen's death following an illness in 1136 seems to have caused Hugh to seize Norwich Castle, probably for his own ends. When it became clear the king was not dead, he refused to give up the fortress and Stephen was forced to lay a siege to recover it. Hugh would sometimes appear a loyal friend to Stephen and then abandon him, raising trouble in East Anglia that was an unwanted distraction for the king. It is striking that Hugh never seems to have particularly favoured Empress Matilda or the Angevin cause, which was becoming the obvious home for disaffection. Perhaps his part in denying Matilda her inheritance placed him beyond hope of a position in her camp, but it is likely that his efforts were exclusively on his own behalf in response to problems he found with Stephen. It was another front on which Stephen was required to fight and keep watch. Hugh will come to the forefront as civil war escalates, but he demonstrates the breadth of the problems the king was attempting to deal with all at once.

Part of the reason that Stephen's reign is frequently viewed as backward and worthy of scorn is his failure to push forward the centralizing institutionalization of government driven by his predecessor and successor. Apart from the earls of York and Derby created in the wake of the victory against King David in 1138, Stephen had also promoted the faction centred on his close favourites, the Beaumont twins. Robert Beaumont was already Earl of Leicester, a title inherited from his father. Waleran had acquired the county of Meulan but in 1138 was also made Earl of Worcester, placing him directly against the border with Robert, Earl of Gloucester's lands and into the centre of the trouble that would follow Empress Matilda's arrival. The twins' younger brother Hugh, known as the Pauper, received the earldom of Bedford around the same time.[2] The king must have seen some immediate and tangible benefit to delegating responsibility for local law and order to a local level. The earls seem to have had primarily a responsibility to keep the peace in their locality. After his success at the Battle of the Standard, it is not unreasonable that Stephen sought to face dispersed challenges by entrusting a few men with representing him in the regions.

The Beaumont's brother-in-law, Gilbert de Clare, was created Earl of Pembroke in Wales, while their family and associates were accruing power in Normandy too. Their father's former confessor had been made Abbot of St Evroult in 1137, and in 1139 their cousin Rotrou became Bishop of Evreux. The Beaumont faction was being relied on heavily by Stephen and was reaping the rewards of their service, but it was rare that such preferment failed to cause either resentment in one quarter or the desire for more power in another, all too often leading to both, and trouble. The Beaumont twins had been working hard for Stephen in Normandy, and now he needed their help in England. In early 1136, Stephen had betrothed his two-year-old daughter Matilda to Waleran in an effort to tie them more closely to his cause, and though the child would pass away in 1137, it serves to show the regard Stephen had for the family and the reliance he was placing on them. They might well have seemed to some to be gaining a stranglehold on the king's favour on both sides of the Channel. That might not have been an issue if there wasn't already a dominant faction in England that was being squeezed aside to make way for the king's favourites.

Roger, Bishop of Salisbury had been a towering figure in Henry I's England and had continued in office under Stephen. As a priest in Caen, he had impressed a young Henry before he came to the throne and was taken into his service. On his accession, Henry made Roger his Lord Chancellor but removed him from that office the following year to make him Bishop of Salisbury. Throughout Henry's reign, Roger continued to impress and win favour. He would become the most senior figure in the administration, performing the role of a Justiciar without ever being officially appointed to that role. Roger had been left in control of England on numerous occasions when Henry travelled to Normandy and is widely credited with having created the Exchequer system of finance for which Henry I is usually applauded.

With the king's trust came rewards in terms of influence and wealth. Roger nominated William Corbeil as Archbishop of Canterbury and saw him successfully elected. One of Roger's nephews, Alexander, gained the bishopric of Lincoln and acted as his uncle's assistant. Another nephew, Nigel, became Bishop of Ely and was Treasurer. Roger le Poer – the Poor, so called because he lacked a bishopric – became Stephen's Lord Chancellor. His relationship to Bishop Roger is clouded in – perhaps deliberate – mystery; he may have been another nephew, but is also referred to as Bishop Roger's son. Henry I had left the government of England almost entirely in the hands of Bishop Roger and his family. Roger became wealthy after all of his years of service too. He held castles at Old Sarum, Devizes and Malmesbury and was understood to have a horde of treasure stashed away.[3]

Roger had initially welcomed Stephen's assumption of the throne. He is the man William of Malmesbury quoted as claiming release from his oath to Empress Matilda because of her father's failure to consult on her marriage as he had promised. In 1135, Roger had been easily convinced to hand over the royal treasury at Winchester to Stephen. After a few years of Stephen's reign, during which they had retained their positions and influence, the Beaumont family were beginning to encroach on their authority, driving their fingers into the stranglehold the bishop had on the English administration. It is into this mix that suspicion was poured. Whether it had a basis, was invented by one side to undo the other or sprung from the harassed mind of the king cannot be known, but Roger and his family were about to undergo a spectacular fall from grace that would leave Stephen's kingship tarnished forever.

William of Malmesbury, who knew the bishop, wrote that Roger had been nervous at the thought of setting out for the king's court in June 1139. 'I heard him speaking to this effect: "By my blessed lady Mary, somehow I am disinclined to this journey, I know not why! This I do now, that I shall be as useful at court as a colt in battle." Thus did his mind forebode the evil to come.'[4] It is worth considering whether William saw, or insinuated, some admission of guilt in Bishop Roger's words. There may have been a building sense of suspicion around the bishop that he was aware of as the Beaumont family rose to match his own and Bishop Henry held his brother's ear as Roger had done under Henry I, or he may have feared that his plots, had he any, had been uncovered. The root of the issue may have lain in his possessions around Wiltshire. Old Sarum, Devizes and Malmesbury all stood between Earl Robert's lands and the king. If Stephen was aware that the empress and her half-brother were planning to come to England, it is not unreasonable to think that they would contact Roger, their father's loyal man who might be able to ease their passage and provide them with valuable support at key castles. If he was being pushed aside, he might have been ripe for the plucking. If he had not intended to betray Stephen, then the fear of the possibility made it a certainty.

The *Gesta Stephani* gives credence to the idea that Bishop Roger was planning in secret to back the empress's cause as soon as he could:

> He promised, but in secret, to avoid offending the king, that he would most loyally keep faith with them and grant them zealous aid, and his castles, which he had built elaborately, he was filling on a very lavish scale with weapons and supplies of food, shrewdly combining service to the king with waiting till the time should duly come when those others arrived in England and he could help them with the utmost vigour and speed. And because he hoped that their arrival in England would be soon, according to frequent messages they had sent from Normandy, everywhere he went, and especially to the king's court, he was encircled by a large and numerous bodyguard of troops.[5]

The writer, at least at this juncture, is favourable to Stephen, and may have been the Bishop of Bath; certainly he was an ecclesiastic of some level. That such a figure would allow for a bishop of Roger's standing to have been plotting against the king, and that he might approve to some extent of what followed, is telling when it might reasonably be expected that applying secular justice to a man protected by benefit of clergy would raise more concern than sympathy in the author.

Whatever the truth, the spark for the resolution of the issue was a brawl at Oxford. As the *Gesta* notes, Bishop Roger travelled with an armed entourage, and with his nephews 'assembled at court with the utmost ostentation'.[6] A fight broke out between Bishop Roger's knights and those of Alan, Count of Brittany, apparently over lodgings in the city. Alan's men fled, the count's nephew barely escaping with his life, and though victorious in the brawl, Bishop Roger's men were left bloodied, and one of his knights lay dead on the inn floor.[7] This created the opportunity for Stephen to act since the men of the count and the bishop had broken the peace of his court. It also opened several interesting legal questions as it progressed, but some were certain that Waleran of Meulan had connived the incident to give the king a reason to move against Bishop Roger. The *Gesta Stephani* notes that the fighting 'arose between the bishops' knights and the king's knights at the instigation of the crafty Count of Meulan and some others.'[8]

Stephen used the incident to arrest Roger, Bishop of Salisbury and his nephew Alexander, Bishop of Lincoln. Nigel, Bishop of Ely had not yet arrived in Oxford and immediately fled to his uncle's castle at Devizes. Several issues were instantly created for the king irrespective of the merits of any case against Roger that he was plotting with Empress Matilda. The uncertainty and the wide open space for debate is symptomatic of a period in which the relationships between princes and popes was still fluid, shifting and uncertain. Both sides sought to retain the authority they had and to snatch some from the other wherever possible in the grey areas. William of Malmesbury summed up the issue by recalling that 'This action of the king opened the mouths of many to express different opinions. Some were saying that they thought the bishops had rightly been deprived of castles they had built in defiance of the canon law.'[9] Henry, Bishop of Winchester was simultaneously arguing that 'If the bishops had in anything stepped aside from the path of justice, then it was not for the king to judge them, but for canon law.'[10]

The first question to be answered, but which seemed to defy resolution, was whether Roger and Alexander had been arrested as bishops or as laymen holding castles. Stephen was keen to portray it as a political matter, brought about by their secular interests. His brother contended that even then, benefit of clergy prevented Stephen from arresting and judging them. Rendering castles to a feudal lord in times of crisis was an accepted custom in Normandy, but it had never been formally introduced into England. That appears to be what Stephen was trying to do in 1139. It is hard to deny that the times warranted such a measure. Robert, Earl of Gloucester, just to Bishop Roger's west, had issued his defiance and within weeks he would be in England with Empress Matilda, something Stephen might reasonably have suspected. Even if Bishop Roger was not suspected of sympathizing with them, his castles were on the frontier of Robert's territories, and so Stephen might have felt control of them was necessary to handle the looming emergency. Bishop Roger's refusal to hand them over, whatever his reasons and whatever rights he sought to defend, can only have made Stephen more uncertain of the powerful bishop's intentions.

Nigel, Bishop of Ely shut himself up in Bishop Roger's stout castle at Devizes. That can hardly have allayed Stephen's fears. The king gathered an army and marched to the town, demanding the surrender of the castle. He threatened to hang Roger le Poer from the walls if the castle held out. Bishop Roger starved himself, willingly according to some and as a punishment from the king by other accounts, until Nigel agreed to a parlay. Bishop Roger criticized his nephew for running to Devizes rather than his own diocese, thereby bringing trouble to Bishop Roger's doorstep. The castle quickly surrendered, the three bishops were stripped of all their secular offices and properties and then set free to return to their sees. Bishop Roger and his family had risen sharply, and grown rich, from service to Henry I, reaping the rewards of his willingness to rely on men outside the central circle of senior nobility to get his work better done. Henry's government was remarkable in that aspect, and Stephen's removal of the bishops from the administration represented a return to an older way of running the government.

The arrest of the bishops in 1139 has been seen as a turning point in Stephen's reign. He might have been justified in requiring the rendering of the castles in Wiltshire, he may have been suspicious, with or without justification, of Bishop Roger's plans and certainly once he refused to hand over control of the tactically significant locations, Stephen was backed into a corner. He could not permit such open defiance when an enemy might land at any moment. He would appear weak if he could not enforce his will, but he also placed the church in England on immediate alert by arresting men of the cloth when they refused to obey a secular command in a secular matter. The prickly question of jurisdiction was raised and hotly contested. Seen as the moment barons as well as churchmen became wary of Stephen, who should not have arrested anyone whilst they enjoyed the peace and security of his court, the incident set everyone on edge. The king's options were limited. Whether by some scheme or not, Bishop Roger had broken the peace of the king's court and Stephen cannot have been expected to ignore the breach. When he refused to hand over castles held as part of his secular role in government, Stephen could hardly have shrugged his shoulders and dropped the matter, hoping for the best. As with so many of Stephen's decisions, it was one without a right answer, only a balancing of unsatisfactory choices.

Philip d'Harcourt was appointed chancellor in place of Roger le Poer. Philip was dean of Waleran Beaumont's College of Beaumont-le-Roger, strengthening that faction's grip on power. A new seal was ordered to be made to draw a line in the sand, demonstrating that Stephen saw this moment as a turning point in his government of England. The new seal showed him on horseback, lance in hand and banner unfurled. This was how Stephen had been required to appear for the majority of his rule to date, and it must have been a recognition that more military action was expected and that Stephen was ready for it. It was also perhaps a direct challenge to the position of Empress Matilda. The conspicuous inability of a woman in the twelfth century, at least in England, and at least in an acceptable way, to put on armour and lead an army into battle was a significant problem with her claim to the throne. By showing himself fulfilling that role, which his cousin could not, Stephen was making a clear distinction between them, appealing to the misogyny considered entirely right and proper at the time to try and prevent the loss of any support to the empress's cause.

The return to an earlier style of government is supported by the creation and regional empowerment of earls during these years. By 1140, Stephen would have almost twenty shires under the direct control of locally based earls. These men were not administrators transplanted into areas to be directly controlled by the king. They were exclusively military men, given the freedom to maintain law and order and Stephen's authority as they saw fit. It opened the door to localized corruption and abuse of that power, but these men remained ultimately answerable to the king, and Stephen had shown himself a capable and effective delegator. Faced with so many problems on so many fronts, it seems a reasonable response to try and tackle all of the issues using trusted men rather than flying from flashpoint to flashpoint and solving nothing. As soon as Stephen was forced to leave an area to solve another problem, trouble could simply erupt in the dust cloud of his horse's hooves, and he had no way to personally deal with so many crises. William le Gros, Earl of York would defend against the Scots. Gilbert de Clare, Earl of Pembroke was responsible for keeping Wales under control, in as much as that was possible. Alan of Brittany, the man who had been involved in fighting with Bishop Roger's men yet escaped any punishment, became Earl of Cornwall to counter Baldwin de Redvers' threat and offer some challenge to Robert, Earl of Gloucester to his west. Hervey Brito, an ally of Stephen who had been no friend to Henry I, was made Earl of Wiltshire and Waleran Beaumont Earl of Worcester to hem Robert in at Bristol and Gloucester. It seems like a sensible response, but the devolution of previously centralized power is part of what has led, perhaps unfairly, to a poor general opinion of Stephen amongst later historians.

Another delicate moment arrived at the end of August 1139, delivered by Stephen's brother, Bishop Henry. A Church Council was summoned to Winchester on 29 August by Bishop Henry. He unveiled a papal commision to act as Legate, making this a Legatine Council and giving him precedence over the Archbishop of Canterbury. If Bishop Henry had been disappointed with failing to obtain the archbishopric, he now had his compensation. William of Malmesbury believed that Henry had held the document appointing him Legate since 1 March, but had kept it until it was needed to bring Stephen to account.[11] If that was the case, then it suggests Bishop Henry was not quite as desperate for authority as might be believed if his ruthless pursuit of the see of Canterbury is accepted. The council does not seem to have been aimed at denigrating Stephen, and there is little sense of the adversarial fraternal relationship usually ascribed to the king and the bishop. It appears more likely that a genuine question about the extent of the authority of the king and church had been exposed and there were efforts to find a satisfactory answer that protected both parties. Though it is likely Bishop Henry favoured the church's interests over secular ones, the council was convened because two authorities had come into conflict in a way that was not good for the kingdom. Henry could, had he wished, have simply condemned his brother's actions, but he instead offered a platform for their justification and a long-term settlement of an unanswerable question.

King Stephen initially sent some of his barons to uncover more detail about the summons. He would not have been keen to be seen to be at the beck and call of the church in his own kingdom, but he also did not refuse to attend. The barons returned to inform Stephen that they felt he had a case to answer. The bishop's forceful reply was that

> one who remembered he owed obedience to the faith of Christ should not complain if he had been summoned by Christ's ministers to give satisfaction when he knew himself guilty of an offence such as our times had nowhere seen; for it belonged to pagan times to imprison bishops and deprive them of their property.[12]

Stephen now acquiesced and agreed to answer the charges that were being laid before him. Aubrey de Vere gave the king's response at Winchester, which boiled down to an insistence that the bishops had not been arrested as men of the church, but as servants of the king. Aubrey claimed that 'Bishop Roger had inflicted many wrongs on King Stephen. He had very seldom come to court without his men raising a brawl, presuming on his power.' He added that 'The bishop of Salisbury secretly favoured the king's enemies, though for the time being he dissembled, until circumstances should change.'[13] Bishop Roger vehemently denied the claims made against him and insisted that he remained loyal to Stephen, but de Vere went on that 'Everyone was saying that as soon as the empress came he would take her side together with his nephews and his castles. Roger then had been arrested not as a bishop but as a servant of the king, who both managed his affairs and received his pay.'[14]

As the debate raged on, Stephen requested an adjournment until the next day. Then he asked for another until the Archbishop of Rouen had arrived. Hugh of Amiens was a staunch supporter of King Stephen, and his intervention proved decisive. William of Malmesbury recalled that all those gathered waited in expectation of what he would contribute to the proceedings. His pronouncement was simple, and devastating to the church's case. Hugh told the council 'he would allow the bishops to have their castles if they could prove by canon law that they were entitled to have them; but, as they could not, it was a mark of extreme wickedness to wish to strive against the canon law.'[15] In conclusion, William places these words into the archbishop's mouth:

> 'So the bishops' whole case will fall to the ground. For either it is unjust, according to canon law, for them to have castles, or, if this is permitted by the king as an act of grace, they ought to yield to the emergencies of the time by delivering the keys.'

The Council broke up on 1 September with the matter settled in the king's favour. Hugh of Amiens was a Cluniac monk, as Bishop Henry was, so their beliefs cannot have been too far apart. Later commentators often see Bishop Henry as being incensed by the outcome, but he had brought about the platform from which the decision had been made. He must have known Archbishop Hugh would be sympathetic to Stephen and that Cluniac reform ideals involved a degree of humanism and a willingness to work with secular authorities. It is to be wondered whether Henry wasn't party to Hugh's summoning, since it would remove any hint of him favouring his own brother over the church. Bishop Henry is often seen as working against his brother when he may well have been offering support. After all, the outcome of a Legatine Council summoned and overseen by Bishop Henry had been the complete exoneration of Stephen's actions. Clerical reform frequently disapproved of bishops becoming too entangled in secular politics since it prevented them from properly performing their pastoral role. This may have been an opportunity to condemn bishops such as Roger and his nephews who allowed themselves to become embroiled in politics and to accumulate wealth at the expense of their real duties. If that was the case, Henry had helped his brother whilst appearing to uphold the church's rights.

The Council at Winchester was disbanded just four weeks before Empress Matilda and Robert, Earl of Gloucester arrived at Arundel Castle. It was against this backdrop that Stephen faced the choice of a siege or of allowing Empress Matilda safe passage west. If Bishop

Henry offered advice that Stephen should let Matilda go, it had a sound strategic basis and fulfilled the bishop's responsibility to try and keep the peace between Christians. It need not have been a trick of any kind, or a sign that Bishop Henry was working against his brother. The king was in campaigning mode once more in the west as he travelled up and down the Welsh border trying to prevent the empress's cause from getting a secure foothold in his kingdom. Miles of Gloucester took a force around the king to relieve Wallingford, perhaps taking a leaf out of the Welsh campaign manual that generally involved keeping away from the enemy and harassing their lands where possible. Miles sacked Worcester to distract Stephen's attention from Bristol, and it worked. The king arrived with Waleran, the new Earl of Worcester, just as Miles withdrew to safety. The king took back Sudeley Castle in Gloucestershire but heard there of the death of Bishop Roger on 11 December. He immediately made for Salisbury to secure the see and the bishop's treasure.

Another front was opened up almost immediately when Bishop Roger's nephew Nigel, Bishop of Ely took control of the Isle of Ely and set about causing trouble in the surrounding areas. He was not, at least openly, attached to Empress Matilda's cause but more likely lashing out at the loss of his family's position and authority, and now the death of their patriarch. Bishop Nigel 'put on the man of blood', 'entirely abandoning the weapons of the Gospel and the discipline of the church', hiring mercenary knights who were 'prepared for any crime'.[16] The king led an assault on the island, arriving with his usual speed and determination. After taking advice on the best way to reach the impenetrable island, he arranged for a collection of boats to be tethered together at a narrow point to make a bridge. Taking those on the island by surprise, a small castle was quickly won and several of the bishop's knights captured. Nigel was unable to fend off the royal forces, and the revolt was quickly crushed. The *Gesta Stephani* noted triumphantly that 'by gaining this wonderful and famous victory over his opponents he struck very great dread into his enemies all over England', and it is at this point that Nigel slunk away to Gloucester, 'where all those attacked by the king had assembled as though it were a receptacle of filth'.[17]

The civil war proper was about to begin. Stephen had so far put out the small fires but had been unable to extinguish Geoffrey's burning desire for Normandy or Empress Matilda's blazing conviction that England was rightfully hers. It remained to be seen whether the smouldering Scottish peace would burst into flames again. Henry of Huntingdon recorded a lament for the state of the kingdom at this moment.

Oh! for a fount of tears to flow,
And weep my country's bitter woe.
Clouds shroud her in the darkest gloom.
And thicken round her day of doom;
Fated intestine wars to see,
Fire, fury, blood, and cruelty.
Rapine stalks boldly through the land,
Ruthlessly baring the strong hand;
A castle's walls are no defence
Against the sons of violence;
All truth is fled; unblushing fraud
And flaunting treason walk abroad:
Churches, in vain, and holy ground
Which erst religion fenced round.
Open their gates to shelter those
Who refuge seek from bloody foes.
The monks and nuns, a helpless train,
Are plunder'd, tortur'd, ravish'd, slain.
Gaunt famine, following, wastes away
Whom murder spares, with slow decay.
Who for the dead shall find a grave?
Who England's hapless children save?
The cup of mingled woe she drains,
All hell's broke loose, and chaos reigns.[18]

12

Empress Matilda

Meanwhile the earl behaved with restraint, and avoided nothing more carefully than even a slight loss of men to gain a battle.[1]

Empress Matilda's entry into England must have been far less glorious than she had hoped. There had been no wholesale rejection of Stephen on her return. If she had expected the support of Queen Adeliza and Stephen's man William d'Aubigny to kickstart her cause, she was sorely disappointed. The granting of free passage from Arundel to Robert's custody in Bristol can only have served to drive home the depth of her predicament. She was accepting Stephen's mercy and being delivered, like a possession rather than a queen-in-waiting, into her half-brother's care. Miles of Gloucester appeared willing to recognize the empress in her own right, but precious few others did. Disaffection with Stephen rather than any devotion to her seemed to pave the roads of those who did come to her at Gloucester.

Matters did not seem to improve for Empress Matilda. Robert Fitz Hubert, a Flemish mercenary in the pay of Robert, Earl of Gloucester, managed a significant coup when he took Devizes Castle, the key fortification Stephen had been so keen to take control of from Bishop Roger. When Robert Fitz Hubert captured the castle on 26 March 1140, it might have been a bright moment for the empress and her cause, except that the mercenary immediately refused to hand it over to Earl Robert and decided to keep his prize for himself. William of Malmesbury would have no truck with this mercenary soldier, whom he described as 'a cruel and savage man, well suited to the stratagems of war'. William considered him 'the cruellest of all men within the recollection of our age, and also a blasphemer against God'. This Robert was known to brag that he had set fire to a church once with eighty monks locked inside, burning them all to death. The matter was made personal to William by the threats Robert issued that he would do the same at Wilton and at William's own Malmesbury Abbey in vengeance for their perceived support of Stephen, a charge William vehemently refuted.

Robert Fitz Hubert must have been well known in the area. William of Malmesbury was able to relate that he had heard 'with my own ears' that if ever a prisoner was released by Robert, a rare thing in itself, and thanked him in God's name, Robert would retort, 'May God never be grateful to me!' One of Robert's favourite forms of torture was to smear his captives in honey, tie them up naked outside in the sun and stir up flies and other insects to sting and bite them.[2] This kind of behaviour was intolerable to William's sensibilities, and he was certain a fitting punishment from God was coming Robert's way. Having taken control of Devizes, from where he believed 'he would gain possession of the whole district from Winchester to London', Robert began to send to Flanders for knights to act as his personal bodyguard, clearly intending to establish himself as a serious magnate in England. If nothing else, the understanding of Devizes's strategic importance makes Stephen's move against Bishop Roger seem a little more reasonable.

Marlborough Castle was the next target Robert Fitz Hubert set for himself. The castellan there was John Fitz Gilbert, known as John the Marshal, an office he held under Henry I and Stephen. One of his sons, William Marshal, would go on to play a defining role in English politics into the next century but in 1140, John's loyalties seemed subject to some doubt. When Robert set his gaze on John's castle, the Marshal did not wait for the attack to come. Instead, he managed to capture Robert and display the truth of his loyalties by ransoming the mercenary to Robert, Earl of Gloucester rather than King Stephen. Earl Robert took his prisoner to the walls of Devizes and threatened to hang him if his men failed to hand over the castle, just as Stephen had done there with Roger le Poer. This time the garrison refused and their commander was duly hanged.

William of Malmesbury was able to see the delivery of God's sentence on the wicked Robert Fitz Hubert. 'Wondrously was God's judgment exercised upon a sacrilegious man, in that he earned so shameful an end not from the king, to whom he was an enemy, but from those whom he seemed to favour.'[3] The writer of the *Gesta Stephani* had no more sympathy. He concluded that 'by a wonderful judgement of God his wickedness returned upon himself, since according to the maxim inspired by God "Wherewith a man sins, thereby shall he likewise be tormented."'[4] Eventually, the castle surrendered, but to King Stephen's new Earl of Wiltshire, Hervey Brito, in return for a substantial payment.

By Whitsun, Stephen was staying at the Tower of London, most of the bishops, except 'him of Sées',[5] refusing to attend on him either for fear or disdain. William of Malmesbury found the world in a piteous state in 1140. 'That whole year,' he lamented, 'was troubled by the brutalities of war. There were many castles all over England, each defending its own district or, to be more truthful, plundering it.' He was in no doubt where the blame lay. 'Under King Henry many foreigners, displaced by troubles in their native land, sailed to England and lived in undisturbed peace under his wings. Under Stephen many from Flanders and Brittany, who were wont to live by plunder, flew to England in the hope of great booty.'[6] These complaints echo those of other chroniclers, but are perhaps an exaggeration of the real picture, at least at a national level. William, in his cloister at Malmesbury, was in the eye of the storm but did not find it calm. His home lay on the frontier between King Stephen and Earl Robert, not to mention the tribulations of having a man like Robert Fitz Hubert threatening to tear down his abbey. There were undoubtedly local revolts across the country, but they were most likely in response to increasing uncertainty, and the opportunity that afforded for some, and would have been of little consequence under normal circumstances. William is relentlessly unwilling to criticize Earl Robert, so heaps all of the blame at Stephen's feet.

Nevertheless, the situation in England was far from ideal. Normandy had, at least for the moment, fallen quiet and Stephen might have been able to reflect on success there and against Scotland, but in England, he had more than enough problems to replace those solved. Around Whitsun, Bishop Henry intervened to try and find peace. It is possible to infer into this some ulterior motive on the part of the king's younger brother, perhaps that he secretly favoured the empress's cause because he felt undervalued by Stephen. It is, however, as likely that as Papal Legate to England, Bishop Henry felt the weight of the church's expectation that he would contribute to the finding of a diplomatic solution to the throbbing issue of civil war. It did not serve his brother to face so many challenges, nor was England able to enjoy peace and prosperity. If Normandy and Scotland had at least been quelled for a time, resolving the struggle with Empress Matilda and Earl Robert was the last piece of a jigsaw. If Scotland and Anjou attacked again while the west of England was in open and organized revolt, Stephen's position would quickly become very precarious. Bishop Henry was perhaps not the agent of mischief he is frequently considered to have been.

Against this backdrop of a potential final resolution to opposition to Stephen, Bishop Henry spent Whitsun arranging for the two sides to meet and thrash out a deal. When representatives of the two factions gathered near Bath, it must have seemed promising. Earl Robert and others attended for the empress, and Stephen's delegates included his wife Queen Matilda, his brother Bishop Henry and Theobald, Archbishop of Canterbury. The nature and content of the discussions are not known, but the talks eventually broke down without resolution. William of Malmesbury complained that 'vainly, vainly, I say, they wasted both words and time and parted without making peace,' though he ascribed predictably different reasons to each party. The empress, 'more inclined to good', had sent word that she would be prepared to place the matter before the church for a final ruling. It is odd that she would propose this course of action when the pope had only recently thrown her case out of his court at the Second Lateran Council. Perhaps we are meant to understand that the English church would be more sympathetic to her claims and that she had received assurances to that effect. Alternatively, knowing full well that the English prelates could not easily go against the papal decision to confirm Stephen as king, the empress was trying to place Stephen in an impossible predicament. He would be forced to refuse the step, not for fear of the outcome, but because it would put his right to the crown and position as king into the hands of the church. When princes and popes vehemently argued over authority and jurisdiction, the king would never grant the church in England the power to assess and rule on the validity of an anointed king's rule.

Unfortunately, the *Gesta Stephani* is silent on this meeting, perhaps due to a section that remains undiscovered,[7] so a more royalist account of the negotiations does not survive. William of Malmesbury offers only that Stephen 'was most concerned to guard against this' imposition of the church. The assertion is clearly that the king feared what his bishops might conclude, but given the lead provided by the pope himself, it seems unlikely that the outcome was what he hoped to avoid, but rather the submission of his own authority to that of the church. William believed that Stephen was unduly influenced by the advice of those around him 'who desired nothing less than peace, while they were able to manipulate him to their own advantage'.[8] It is a constant feature of the commentaries on Stephen's reign and the decisions that he made that he is either seen as belligerently ignoring good advice or weakly acquiescing to wicked counsel. At one moment he will listen to no one, in the next, he is led by the nose by his barons. Both are unlikely to be true. The perception that all of the lords and nobility of England invested themselves in disrupting peace and prolonging turmoil for their own selfish ends is oft repeated but hard to justify. It must be wondered what barons gained from lawlessness. Effective management of their lands and the maximizing of their revenues relied on peace and the ability of administrators to perform their roles unhindered. Disruption across the countryside necessarily disrupted their affairs and their incomes. As trouble intensified, it is worthy of note that many of the lords in England would seek out ways to establish and maintain peace with their neighbours independently of a weakening and uncertain royal writ. They looked for ways to mitigate the problems, not magnify them.

King Stephen attempted to assert his authority in the south-west once more. He planted Alan of Brittany, already Earl of Richmond, into the region as Earl of Cornwall, but they found it impossible to improve royal influence in the area. To counteract the measure, Robert, Earl of Gloucester appointed his half-brother Reginald de Dunstanville, the illegitimate son of Henry I who had been quick to rise in Empress Matilda's name in Normandy, as a rival Earl of Cornwall. It is striking that Earl Robert was assuming the authority to make such a gift of high office. William of Malmesbury is keen to insist that it was his patron Earl Robert who took the decision, 'in view of the great difficulties of the time, he made his brother Reginald Earl of Cornwall'.[9] Unless there was some unreported breakdown between the empress and her leading general, Robert must have given Reginald the post at her command, or with her permission at the very least. It may be that William was keen to overplay the earl's position, but it is also possible that he was taking an increasing amount of responsibility in his half-sister's faltering efforts to establish herself.

In August 1140, Earl Robert led an attack on Bath to try and take the town but failed to make any headway. The following month, he switched his attention to a more obscure and unexpected target. Along with Ralph Paynel of Dudley, Earl Robert took a band of knights to Nottingham.

It may have been their intention to distract Stephen from his own efforts in the south-west, but given what would follow in early 1141, there might have been some sense that the East Midlands was an area ripe for the plucking in the empress's name too. Despite William of Malmesbury's insistence on Earl Robert's probity, the attack on Nottingham was little more than a raid which involved the burning of as many buildings as possible, including a church with people trapped inside. The lack of a desire to take control of the city and castle demonstrates the weakness, narrow appeal and short reach of the empress's cause at this moment. Robert may have been probing soft targets to try and expand their influence, but if he was, the results were less than encouraging.

September also saw a renewed effort from Bishop Henry to bring about peace as the unrest began to intensify. The Bishop of Winchester took himself across the Channel and arranged to meet his oldest brother Theobald, Count of Blois as well as the new King of France, Louis VII. Louis le Jeune – the younger – had succeeded his father in 1137 and was married to Eleanor of Aquitaine, a fabulously wealthy heiress who brought the large Duchy of Aquitaine into the possession of the crown of France, extending its reach south to the Pyrenees. At twenty, he was a young man, but Bishop Henry saw the authority he now wielded as key to helping end the troubles in England. Normandy was, for the moment, quiet as the precarious truce held but Louis would have a pivotal role to play in keeping his vassal, Geoffrey of Anjou, under control and it was Geoffrey's wife who was fomenting the trouble in England. Bishop Henry must also have felt that Theobald had a role to play as the senior figure of the Blois family, not least in helping to maintain Stephen's possessions in Normandy. It is possible Count Theobald still harboured some resentment that he had missed out on the duchy and a crown in England, and perhaps Bishop Henry appealed to him to set those feelings aside in the interests of securing the family's future.

William of Malmesbury believed that Bishop Henry had also met with a number of senior churchmen in his quest to secure peace. It is possible to see something underhand in the bishop's activities, and there have been lingering accusations that he secretly favoured Empress Matilda and worked against his brother, but there is little to substantiate that belief. It is more likely that Bishop Henry took his position as Papal Legate intensely seriously and understood that the responsibility to bring peace between the Christians under his care lay firmly with him.

Having been given the role, particularly if he felt he had been overlooked for the See of Canterbury, he had to make a good impression and deliver the main concern of the church: peace. Amongst Christians, at least. There was still sporadic war in the Holy Land, and England and Normandy would be in no position to provide valuable men and money for that effort if they were consumed by civil war.

Bishop Henry also remained uniquely well placed to negotiate a settlement. He was Bishop of Winchester, a rich see, but he was also the king's brother, the empress's first cousin, Earl Robert's first cousin, the brother of the Count of Blois, Chartres and Champagne, not to mention Papal Legate and a man able to access the King of France. It might have been the easy option for Bishop Henry to throw his considerable political, financial and religious weight directly behind his brother, but he may not have viewed that as the best way to reach a final resolution. It would mean war in England and was likely to lead to the same in Normandy when Geoffrey was free to try and assault the duchy again. Rather than working against his brother, it is possible, and maybe more likely, that Henry was looking for the best way to resolve his brother's problems whilst also fulfilling his responsibilities as Legate.

The suspicion that Bishop Henry was not entirely on his brother's side is added to by William of Malmesbury's assessment of the results of the bishop's efforts. Henry returned from the continent in late November with a set of proposals for peace that he had arrived at with the aid of Theobald, King Louis and the church. Empress Matilda and Earl Robert immediately agreed to the terms, but Stephen delayed giving his opinion 'and finally made the whole plan to no avail'.[10] Sadly, no record of what Bishop Henry proposed has survived to assess the reasons for the empress's swift agreement and Stephen's vacillation. The insinuation from William of Malmesbury is that the terms favoured the empress's cause and were therefore rejected by Stephen, thus portraying Bishop Henry as sympathetic to his cousin, but Malmesbury is always keen and quick to paint his patron as the font of all reasonableness. Here, he wished it to appear that Empress Matilda and Earl Robert wanted only peace and a resolution to the troubles, but Stephen was bent on war.

Given that the empress would soon make it clear that she would settle for nothing less than the crown atop her head, it seems unlikely that she would have agreed to a compromise that left her bereft of the power that Stephen currently held. By the same token, Stephen appeared to be in an entirely dominant position in 1140. He was facing problems, but he was doing so with success. The empress was cornered in the south-west and failing in every attempt to expand from that region. Why would the king agree to terms that must have sought to offer the empress something tangible at this point? Without hindsight, it is hard to see why he would have felt the need to acquiesce to his brother's settlement in 1140. The terms of the proposals cannot be assessed to try and determine who was being unreasonable, but it might have been evident, even in late November 1140, that no one would benefit from their rejection. Bishop Henry had failed to deliver peace as Papal Legate. Empress Matilda remained confined to a narrow region, lacking in support and failing in attempts to widen her sphere of influence. Stephen passed up the chance to be free of an internal threat, perhaps believing it would be easily crushed soon enough, but such confidence had little basis. He had been unable to shake the empress and Earl Robert from their strongholds so far. If there was any concern as Christmas approached in 1140 that a golden opportunity had been missed, such prescience was to be proven spectacularly accurate very soon.

13

King Stephen

In the year of our Lord 1141, the fourth indiction, there were grievous troubles in England, and great changes occurred, to the serious loss of many persons.[1]

Ranulf aux Gernon, Earl of Chester was a proud and powerful magnate in King Stephen's England. His nickname, *aux Gernon*, means 'the moustaches' and referred to his impressive facial hair. The earl's father, Ranulf le Meschin, *the younger*, had been 3rd Earl of Chester, boasting an impeccable Norman pedigree, and both his father's and mother's families were closely tied to King Henry I. Ranulf le Meschin had acquired the earldom of Chester from his cousin Richard d'Avranches after the latter's death in the the *White Ship* disaster that had claimed King Henry's son William Adelin and ultimately led to the divisive problems now clutching at England. As part of the deal to allow Ranulf le Meschin to inherit the earldom, King Henry had insisted on the handover of Carlisle and Cumberland. The present earl coveted them as part of his patrimony; they had not, after all, been taken away for any treason. Had Stephen chosen to return them to Ranulf aux Gernon, he might have caused the earl to defend them, and by necessity the north-west of England, from the Scots. As it was, they had both been given to Prince Henry of Scotland as part of the deal to secure peace with his father, King David, much to Ranulf's chagrin.

After Michaelmas 1140, Ranulf planned to attack Prince Henry as he returned to Scotland, but when Queen Matilda got wind of the plan, she convinced her husband to accompany the Scottish heir personally, thus thwarting Ranulf. Frustrated, the earl snapped and, according to the most exciting version of the story, hatched a plan with his maternal half-brother, William de Roumare. Waiting until the garrison was out enjoying some hunting, the two men's wives strolled into Lincoln

Castle to visit the lady there. After a short time of merriment with the castellan's wife, Earl Ranulf appeared at the castle gates, wearing no armour and accompanied by only three attendants, to collect his wife and sister-in-law. With no reason to suspect foul play, he was freely granted entry and escorted into the heart of the castle. With blinding speed, he and his few men overpowered the handful of men-at-arms left to guard the castle. They quickly found weapons, drove the men outside and barred the gates. Having secured the fortress, William de Roumare arrived with a small army and was let into the castle to help take control of it and the city of Lincoln.[2] It was a bold move, but one they can hardly have expected to go unnoticed.

Stephen had barely returned to London from his impromptu, enforced trip to the Scottish border when an appeal arrived from Lincoln. The citizens implored the king to come with all haste to relieve them from the cruelty of Ranulf and William, who had taken the castle and city and were oppressing the people in their triumph. The message advised the king that if he came quickly, the men might be caught unawares and overpowered. Quick and easy was just what Stephen liked and the plan appealed to him, offering swift vengeance against a new source of rebellion. The fact that the people of Lincoln looked to King Stephen as their saviour is perhaps more telling than is usually allowed. If he was an unpopular and ineffective king, why would his subjects turn to him so quickly for aid? Ranulf and William were obviously not seen as preferable alternatives, and neither did those suffering under their yoke reach out to Empress Matilda or Earl Robert for succour. The decision to call for Stephen suggests that he was not only still viewed as the rightful king, responsible for the defence of his subjects, but that he was also regarded as someone capable of delivering that protection. That belief is at odds with the traditional view of Stephen as weak and intensely disliked.

The king arrived in Lincoln by 6 January 1141, displaying his customary speed and vigour. The citizens welcomed the king into Lincoln, and he quickly laid siege to the castle. At some point in the commotion, Ranulf managed to escape from the castle and fled to Cheshire, where he set about raising Welsh troops to return with. The earl also took the opportunity to appeal to his father-in-law for aid, since his wife remained trapped inside the castle at Lincoln. Unfortunately for King Stephen, Ranulf's wife was Maud of Gloucester, a daughter of Robert, Earl of Gloucester. Ranulf pledged his considerable power to the empress's cause if Earl Robert would help him drive the king from Lincoln. Aside from any concern for his daughter, Earl Robert must have leapt at the chance to bring such a figure over to his half-sister's side. It might prove to be the tipping point that pressed their cause forward.

Robert gathered as many men as he was able and met Ranulf on the road to Lincoln. It was now the king's turn to be taken unawares by the rapid approach of a vast host. He only received news of their arrival when they were almost upon him. Some of those with the king advised him to leave, to take the opportunity to regroup and then assault the rebels when they could match their numbers. Perhaps aware of his father's reputation after his flight from Antioch, Stephen refused to withdraw or 'to sully his fame by the disgrace of flight',[3] and vowed to stand and fight Robert and Ranulf. Having tried for months to engineer an encounter with Robert, it is unlikely the king would have willingly passed up this chance. Robert was far from Bristol now, as exposed as he had been since his arrival in England and the two were within striking distance of each other at last. Aside from genuine concerns that he might look like a coward, Stephen may have believed he would never have as good a chance to defeat Robert again.

Several chroniclers recorded, with a heavy dose of foreshadowing facilitated by their power of hindsight, that the omens were not good for the king. On the morning of the 2 February, Stephen attended Mass, but as he processed with a lighted candle in his hand, as the service demanded on the Feast of the Purification, the flame blew out. The candle snapped, too, and had to be pressed back together and relit in the king's hands. Breakage and repair was the scheme the writers saw God working out for the king. As Bishop Alexander of Lincoln, now reconciled with the king, performed the service, the fastening that held the pix – containing the bread that would be transformed into the body of Christ – to the wall shattered. Crashing onto the altar, it confirmed that a fall was imminent. For all the enormity of these portents, Stephen remained resolute that he would fight.[4]

Earls Robert and Ranulf were near the city with a vast army. Stephen had brought only enough men to lay siege to the lightly defended castle. He was reinforced by locals willing to fight for him, but still, probably, hopelessly outnumbered. William of Malmesbury's account of the battle may have come from Earl Robert himself, and Henry of Huntingdon was a canon at Lincoln, so he may well have had first-hand knowledge of the fighting. Still, the precise details remain fragmented and hard to string together into a coherent account of the Battle of Lincoln on 2 February 1141. Most sources seem to agree that the fighting took place on the day Earl Robert arrived and that his army had been forced to traverse some obstacle to reach the city. The *Gesta Stephani* thought it was a ford that had to be crossed, while William of Malmesbury claimed that the River Trent was in flood and that Robert swam across, leading the rest of his army. Henry of Huntingdon describes it as 'a marsh which was almost impassable'[5], possibly a reference to the Foss Dyke, made swampy by a flood of the River Witham, a suggestion that aligns with the belief that the fighting took place on flat land just to the north of the city.

Henry of Huntingdon attributes the speech made to the royal army before the battle to Baldwin Fitz Gerald, who was forced to encourage the men because 'king Stephen's voice was not clear'.[6] Baldwin told those listening:

> All ye who are now about to engage in battle must consider three things: first, the justice of your cause; secondly, the number of your force; and thirdly, its bravery: the justice of the cause, that you may not peril your souls; the number of your force, that it may not be overwhelmed by the enemy; its valour, lest, trusting to numbers, cowardice should occasion defeat.[7]

The justice of their cause lay in the defence of God's anointed king and their own fealty to him. Baldwin assured them that when it came to numbers, they were not inferior in cavalry and outnumbered the enemy in infantry, though this seems at odds with other claims that the attacking army was larger. As for their valour, Baldwin did not doubt that it was beyond reproach as springing from men long trained for war. In addition to all of this, King Stephen himself, their anointed monarch, would stand amongst them 'in place of a host',[8] embodying the strength and valour of a thousand men in himself.

As Baldwin's speech drew to a rousing close, the enemy's approach could be heard. Stephen had been joined at Lincoln by William of Ypres, his trusty mercenary captain; Waleran of Meulan, Earl of Worcester; Simon of Senlis, Earl of Northampton; Gilbert de Clare, Earl of Hertford;

William le Gros, Earl of Albermale and York; Alan of Brittany, Earl of Richmond and Hugh Bigod, who became Earl of Norfolk during this year. Although five earls turned out for the king, they represented only around a quarter of the available peers, which might suggest a lack of confidence in Stephen. However, if their express purpose was to keep peace in their localities, then it would stand to reason that they would not all be gathered around the king, particularly when the arrival of the rebel army caught them by surprise. Most of those with Stephen were earls of relatively local regions, drawn in to deal with what looked like a local crisis.

The royal army was divided into the traditional three bodies; the vanguard, the centre and the rearguard. William of Ypres commanded the van, comprised of his Fleming and Breton mercenaries. Against them were arrayed 'a wild band of Welshmen' led by Meredith and 'Kaladrius', who might have been Cadwaladr ap Gruffydd, the third son of Gruffudd ap Cynan, King of Gwynedd, and younger brother of Owain the Great, later recognized as the first Prince of Wales. As the Welsh advanced, William of Ypres's men charged and routed their opponents quickly, only for Earl Ranulf's other men to attack William's cavalry and send them into disarray.[9] The vanguard was broken, and William of Ypres fled the field immediately. The *Gesta Stephani* bemoans that 'a great many, like the Count of Meulan and the famous William of Ypres, fled shamefully before coming to close quarters'[10] and Orderic Vitalis believed that this eagerness to escape emboldened the enemy, while also 'spreading panic in the ranks of their confederates'.[11]

Henry of Huntingdon believed that William of Ypres, rather than being guilty of cowardice, had seen the way that the battle was going and chosen to withdraw to avoid capture; that, 'perceiving the impossibility of supporting the king, he deferred his aid for better times'.[12] This is entirely possible and not unreasonable, though it appears dishonourable, at least on the surface. Warfare was still predominantly based on control of castles, and military action generally revolved around besieging and defending these fortifications. Open battles were generally avoided by any commander. They were unpredictable because even overwhelming numerical advantages offered no guarantees. Once two armies engaged, it became a matter of luck, or of God's judgement, and death was a real risk, more so than in the case of a siege where there was a recognized mechanism for bringing about a peaceful conclusion. Even if the battle was survived, being captured and taken hostage could ruin a nobleman with the extraction of a crippling ransom for his release. The common soldier had no such protection and was far more likely to be struck down dead, so few had any real desire to engage in pitched battles during the twelfth century. William of Ypres and the others who fled might well have had one eye to being free and alive to fight another day, preferably in another way.

For Stephen, it does not seem to have been an option. Orderic believed the king was 'mindful of the brave deeds of his ancestors'[13] but more than ever his father's reputation for cowardice must have been playing on his mind. With most of his men gone and all of his cavalry fled, King Stephen was left in the centre of the fighting that raged on in a confused, exhausting cacophony. Henry of Huntingdon described the gleaming flashes of swords and helmets, the clanking ring of metal crashing into metal and the reverberation of shouts and screams that bounced around the hills surrounding the fighting. The cavalry of the rebel army charged again and again at the resolute core of men around the king. Some were trampled by the horses, others struck down by sword blows, and still more were dragged away as prisoners. The fighting at close quarters was relentless as the circle was drawn tighter together.

The only place where there seemed to be any break in the fighting at all was around the king. Here, those trying to assault Stephen himself recoiled under the 'unmatched force of his terrible arm'.[14] Earl Ranulf, infuriated that Stephen was not only holding out against the odds but that the king was also winning so much glory, ordered his men to target the king with all their might. Although the precise details differ in the chronicle accounts, all tell stories of the ferocity with which Stephen fought. Henry of Huntingdon describes the king felling many men with his large battle-axe before it shattered under the weight of its work. Drawing his old sword, Stephen continued to defend his position until it too broke. Seeing the king suddenly unarmed, a soldier named William Dekains rushed in and grabbed the king by his helmet shouting, 'Here, here; I have taken the king!' so that others rushed in to help secure him. Orderic has a slight variation on the story in which Stephen fights with his sword and a Norwegian-style axe 'with which some youth had supplied him'.[15] It is possible that he heard a version in which Stephen's sword was broken, and he was then handed an old axe by one of the citizens of Lincoln fighting with him. In this retelling of the battle, fatigue overcomes the king, and he is forced to surrender himself to Earl Robert.

One thing on which all accounts agree is the king's brave ferocity. Robert of Torigni colourfully described the king facing his opponents 'like a lion, grinding his teeth and foaming at the mouth like a boar'.[16] Even William of Malmesbury was forced to concede the king's prowess before attributing the final victory to Earl Robert:

> The king himself, though he did not lack spirit in self-defence, was at length attacked on all sides by the earl of Gloucester's knights and fell to the ground on being struck by a stone. It is not known who dealt the blow. So, as all around him were captured or put to flight, he brought himself to yield for a time and be held prisoner.[17]

It is perhaps striking that Malmesbury attributes such a dishonourable attack as throwing a stone to knock the king out to one of the attackers, but he does not deny Stephen's admirable attempts to defend himself. Those who had advised the king to leave Lincoln and regroup were probably right. William of Ypres and others had seen the hopelessness of their situation, knowing the battle was lost before it began. Rather than being cowardly, their departure would prove vital in the months that followed. In the end, Stephen's pride and his need to overcome his father's legacy had got the better of his common sense. Fighting at Lincoln and refusing to withdraw might have been seen as bravery befitting of a warrior king, but instead has been viewed as signals of Stephen's vanity and even wilful stupidity. Had he chosen to run from Lincoln on 2 February 1141, he would doubtless have been remembered as a coward. Furthermore, it might have done the same irreparable damage to his reputation as it had to his father's, leaving his kingship in tatters and causing a haemorrhaging of support from his own cause to that of his cousin the empress. Others had the luxury of being able to leave and fight another day. For a king, it was never so clear-cut.

In the aftermath of the battle, Lincoln was sacked in punishment for its favouring of the king over Earl Ranulf. The victors ran through the city, chasing down the townsmen who had fought for Stephen as they ran for home. In the heat of their victory, they fell to plundering before setting fire to houses and churches alike, creating 'a piteous scene of devastation everywhere'.[18] William of Malmesbury becomes callous in his desperation to excuse Earl Robert of any culpability for this behaviour. Having portrayed his patron as an heroic paragon of chivalry, it becomes a stretch to explain the burning of houses and churches, but William simply offers that it was well deserved. The men of Lincoln were cut down, he insists, 'through the just anger of the victors and without causing any grief to the vanquished, since it was they who by their instigation had given rise to this calamity.'[19] Blaming the citizens of Lincoln for informing the king that Earl Ranulf had taken the castle by force as a justification for slaughtering them and burning the town seems cold, but William needed to protect his patron's reputation.

For the chroniclers seeking to make sense of this overturning of the natural order of things, the explanation for Stephen's defeat and capture could only lie in God's withdrawal of favour from him for a time. Thus it was the 'judgment of God on King Stephen'[20], though the writer of the *Gesta Stephani*, with the benefit of hindsight, suggested that there was hope for redemption in the fall because it was the will of God, 'who humbles a king for a time that he may afterwards exalt him to greater fame and power.'[21] The author seems to offer a parallel for Stephen with the biblical King David, whose sin, in David's case adultery, causes God to withhold His grace and costs David his throne until he returns later in peace to rule successfully and be succeeded by his son Solomon. King David is often held up as an ideal of kingship and his successor Solomon as an exemplar of wisdom, so the writer appears to offer great hope for the future in King Stephen's setback.

It surely cannot have felt that way for the king as he was transported as a prisoner to Gloucester where he was brought before his cousin Empress Matilda. Although reportedly treated with great respect and deference by Earl Robert, the empress appears to have had less sympathy for her cousin. From Gloucester, Stephen was sent to Bristol, and although his captivity began with a degree of freedom, it seems to have made some amongst the empress's faction nervous because it soon became 'close custody'[22] which was envisaged by most as being meant to last 'until the last breath of life'.[23] The fallout from the Battle of Lincoln was unprecedented. The King of England was a prisoner, and his place was to be taken by a queen regnant. Empress Matilda had to handle the moment with care. The trick would be to impose herself without behaving in a manner deemed so unbecoming of a woman that it cost her support. It was never going to be an easy transition, but just over five years since her father's death, Empress Matilda had achieved in England what her husband had been unable to in Normandy.

For Stephen, it was a waiting game in his cell at Bristol. He could only hope either that the empress would trip over her own desperation to capitalize on her unexpected victory or that those who had left Lincoln before it had gone so wrong would remain loyal and try to find a way to fight back. It is perhaps a comment on Stephen's kingship that many of the worst losses and outbreaks of lawlessness seem to have taken place while he was a prisoner. Either he had kept an effective lid on the worst of the troubles by his vigorous responses around the kingdom or the absence of certainty around the throne drew out the worst in people who saw an opportunity to create chaos. It must have been frustrating for such an active, driven man to find himself pacing in confinement with no idea what was happening beyond the walls of his enemy's fortress at Bristol. Whatever he thought, felt or feared, the fate of his kingship was now entirely out of his hands.

14

Empress Matilda

But still the greater part of the kingdom at once submitted to the countess and her adherents.[1]

Suddenly, the initiative and authority fell into the lap of Empress Matilda as a result of the unpredictability of battle. Having been presented with the unexpected opportunity, the job for her cause was to arrange matters around the empress to smooth her move into power and onto Stephen's throne. Part of the problem that the empress and her supporters faced is accidentally exposed by William of Malmesbury in his effusive praise of Earl Robert's conduct:

> Therefore the worthy earl of Gloucester gave orders that the king should be kept alive and unharmed, not suffering even that he should be the victim of any insulting language. Behold, he mildly protected in humiliation him whom he had just been furiously assailing when exalted in majesty, so that, controlling emotions of anger and joy, he both showed kindness to a relative and had regard, even in the person of a captive, to the splendour of the crown.[2]

Stephen was treated with kindness and reverence by Earl Robert, as a king, even though he was also now a captive. It is perhaps a signal of the empress's better understanding of the real situation that it is after the king reached her at Gloucester that his respectful detention became more severe and more like confinement at Bristol. Her case rested on Stephen having usurped Empress Matilda's throne but the long and constant recognition of Stephen as the rightful, anointed king, not least in Rome, would be a high hurdle to overcome. It was hardly helped by the empress's own half-brother and military commander treating him like a king.

The victory in England, even before it had been fully secured, had a devastating impact in Normandy. In some of Orderic Vitalis's last entries in his chronicle, which tails off when Stephen is still a prisoner as the elderly monk's health failed, he explains that Geoffrey, Count of Anjou stormed into the duchy on hearing of his wife's victory. Immediately after entering Normandy, Geoffrey despatched letters to all of the lords demanding that they surrender their castles to him and refrain from causing any trouble. Orderic had long lamented that the duchy had been deprived of a firm hand to keep it in line and though he does not offer his opinion on Geoffrey's demands, he might have been impressed with the decisiveness of his seizure of the opportunity. The Norman barons assembled at Mortain and tried to decide what they should do for the best. Their duke was a prisoner of the man trying to lay claim to their fealty, or at least of his wife, and there seemed little chance of his release.

The first instinct of the gathered barons was to turn to Theobald of Blois. It is a sign of their resistance to the idea of Angevin rule that they now went back to the man they had considered before Stephen rather than accept the apparent military and political supremacy of Geoffrey. Theobald was offered both the kingdom of England and the duchy of Normandy if he would stand up against the Count of Anjou. He refused. Subject to a few conditions, Theobald made it known that he was willing to cede all of his rights to either region to Geoffrey. He asked only for the handover of the city of Tours, which he claimed as part of his own county, for the release of his brother Stephen and the restoration to Stephen and his heirs of all the lands he had held under their uncle Henry I. The issue was not definitively settled and the Norman barons remained resistant to Angevin rule, but this moment was a decisive one for Normandy, more so than for England. Geoffrey had broken the back of the duchy's efforts to keep him out, and although it was not yet under his complete control, his foot was well and truly in the door.

The speed with which Geoffrey acted in Normandy can be contrasted with the response of his wife the empress in England. Her father had won power by snatching it quickly after the death of his brother William II. In 1135, Stephen had been so successful because he had taken the initiative and offered a fast resolution to the increasing lawlessness. Speed was demonstrably of the essence, yet Empress Matilda chose to take her time as she meandered east. On 17 February, more than a fortnight after Stephen's defeat and capture at Lincoln, Empress Matilda had only travelled as far as Cirencester. The leisurely style of her progress may be a signal of the shock of her new dominance, or that she wished to be seen to be taking her time rather than rushing at it as though it wasn't really hers by right. It is hard, though, to ignore the recent precedents for securing the treasury, the capital and the immediate support of the church and nobility. Giving them time to weigh their options rather than forcing their hand in the suddenly altered political landscape was perhaps an ill-advised course of action.

By the beginning of March, Empress Matilda was in negotiation with Bishop Henry to facilitate her entry into Winchester to secure the royal treasury and the crown jewels. There was still no sense of a headlong rush to impose the empress on England, but rather of a carefully staged and managed advancement to the throne. There is often a strong sense of Bishop Henry betraying his brother at this point. If the bishop is seen as resenting having been passed over for the See of Canterbury and as disapproving of some of his brother's decisions, then the possibility that he sought greater influence at the side of his cousin becomes more believable. However, it is far from certain that Henry had wanted the archbishopric, or that he would have been acceptable as a pluralist, a breach of the rules that had made him rich and which he would have been forced to give up. The question of Henry's agreement to some of his brother's policies and decisions cannot be answered sufficiently either. He appears to have been behind the advice to allow the empress to leave Arundel Castle and Stephen had followed that course of action. If the two disagreed, it was probably not on every matter and certainly no more than siblings or kings and ministers generally differed. Betrayal may not have been Bishop Henry's intention at all. In fact, the very opposite might have been the case.

If King Stephen's cause were to have any hope of survival and revival, he would need someone close to the centre of the new authority to facilitate that. Watching Bishop Henry's actions to try and determine his true motives is critical to understanding the events of the remainder of 1141, though they can only really be guessed at or suggested. The other aspect of his responsibilities as both bishop and Papal Legate was the need to restore and maintain peace. Lawlessness was not in the interests of church or state, and when conflict arose between Christians, the church took its role in bringing the two sides to terms seriously. For Bishop Henry, having secured an office that made him senior to the Archbishop of Canterbury, the weight of this expectation fell firmly on his shoulders. If he failed, he risked his own reputation and the loss of his legatine authority. Whatever his personal feelings and loyalties, his responsibilities must have also been at play as events unfolded.

At a meeting on 2 March at Wherwell, about ten miles north-west of Winchester, the final details of a deal were thrashed out. William of Malmesbury, who may well have had inside information, is clear about the terms of the arrangements on both sides. The empress agreed to place all of the important business of England under the control of the bishop. He would, in particular, have full control over the appointment of bishops and abbots and she would keep to their arrangement for as long as he maintained faith with her. That Matilda would, in the hot glow of victory and with Bishop Henry's brother her prisoner, hand over wholesale control of the kingdom to him seems unlikely. In Germany, she had seen the tensions between church and state and her own father had fought hard to maintain his privileges in the face of Rome's expansion of interest into the political and temporal. It is almost unthinkable that she would now willingly give away all of the authority she had won, and it seems equally likely that those closest to her, including the reliable Earl Robert, would have had something to say against such an agreement. The description of this settlement by William of Malmesbury perhaps contains an element of mischief, either his or his source's, to portray Bishop Henry as defecting from his brother entirely or to provide an explanation for the failure of their working relationship. If that is not the case, then Bishop Henry was surely duped into finding terms with the empress that were doomed from the outset.

In return, Bishop Henry agreed to receive the empress as 'lady of England', promising to stick to their agreement for as long as the empress did.[3] The term 'Lady of England' or 'Lady of the English' is oddly distinct from describing her as a queen. This leaves room to suggest that there was some uncertainty about the precise nature of the role Empress Matilda would assume: whether she would exercise power for her young son, Henry, until he was old enough to rule or even whether Geoffrey might have been meant to become king at her side.

However, the title had some precedent in England. Æthelflæd, the eldest daughter of King Alfred the Great, had ruled the kingdom of Mercia from 911 until her death in 918 and was known as Lady of the Mercians. The designation used in 1141 might have been intended to hark back to the fame and success of the Lady of the Mercians by extrapolating her title to a national level. The *Gesta Stephani* seems to be alone at this point in describing Empress Matilda as having 'made herself queen of all England'.[4] A queen was traditionally the consort of a male ruler, whose role was clearly defined and delineated from that of a king. A queen consort operated in the arenas of peacemaking and other activities supporting her husband's rule but was not a military commander or the ultimate decision-maker. If Empress Matilda had called herself Queen of England, it left room to believe that she was no more than her husband's consort. Adopting the style Lady of the English might, to a twelfth-century ear, have conveyed a much more definite impression of the precise role she was taking up. Matilda, Lady of the English would not rule as the wife or mother of another. She would be the ultimate authority in England in her own right. If she held power by virtue of any man, it was only her father, as his rightful heir. Far from sowing uncertainty, the title the empress now sought surely made it abundantly clear what the country could expect from her.

On 3 March 1141, Bishop Henry led the delegation that welcomed Empress Matilda into Winchester. He handed over the castle and royal treasury to her. A clerk named Turstin placed the royal crown into her possession. The *Gesta Stephani* is dismissive of the reception the empress received in Winchester, writing only that Bishop Henry 'bade the people, at a public meeting in the market-place of the town, salute her as their lady and their queen.'[5] William of Malmesbury focuses on a much more formal reception for the empress at Winchester Cathedral, where she entered in procession with Bishop Henry at her right-hand side and the Bishop of St David's on her left. There appears to have been some sense that most of the barons in England began to accept Empress Matilda, though if it was the case, it is not necessarily a comment on Stephen's popularity. For any but the most devoted to him personally, political realism must have played a part in their decision-making. Geoffrey was moving to take control of Normandy, and the empress appeared in complete command in England. For anyone keen to retain the lands and offices they held, who could see no likelihood of King Stephen's release and restoration, there must have appeared to be little option but to submit.[6]

It is from this point onwards that the manner in which Empress Matilda, Lady of the English behaved was to become a matter of notoriety.

Had any man, a king, wilfully asserted his rights and dealt ruthlessly with those who had opposed him for years, few would have criticized him, and many might have applauded the strength of his arm. For a woman to behave in the same manner was unfathomable. Men could not make sense of it. To rule, she needed to act like a king, restoring and enforcing law and order, making men loyal to her, by force if necessary, and she would need to be able to raise an army and put it in the field to defend herself and her people. A woman in the twelfth century, and for centuries either side of it, was not expected to behave in these ways: to act like a man. The challenge Empress Matilda faced was to find a way to balance need and expectation. If she behaved only in the way anticipated of a woman, she could not retain control of a kingdom. By assuming the role of a man, Matilda risked unnerving the men whose support she needed and driving them away. It is possible that the time she took to reach Winchester was spent trying to find a compromise that would make her acceptable to the barons of England whilst allowing her to keep a tight grip on the reins of government.

If the matter was given any thought, no workable solution seems to have been found. The direction selected by the new Lady of the English was to impose herself just as though she was a man: a king. The chroniclers are almost unanimous in their scorn for the demeanour of the empress in the wake of the victory at Lincoln and reception at Winchester. The *Gesta Stephani*, still favouring King Stephen, complained of the empress that

> she at once put on an extremely arrogant demeanour instead of the modest gait and bearing proper to the gentle sex, began to walk and speak and do all things more stiffly and more haughtily than she had been wont, to such a point that soon, in the capital of the land subject to her, she actually made herself queen of all England and gloried in being so called.[7]

The writer continued to bemoan her treatment of those who had been loyal to Stephen, some of whom 'she received ungraciously and at times with unconcealed annoyance, others she drove from her presence in fury after insulting and threatening them.'[8]

Henry of Huntingdon concurred that 'she was elated with insufferable pride at the success of her adherents in the uncertain vicissitudes of war, so that she alienated from her the hearts of most men.'[9] He clearly gave her no personal credit for the successes of her cause but blamed her for destroying the strong position that had been gained for her. The empress no doubt saw little need to compromise in the way that she behaved. Her father had been a ruthless and successful ruler, sometimes viciously punishing his opponents, and she knew that his model had worked, though he faced more opposition than he liked to admit. If she had been asked to consider how she would exercise her authority, she might have seen no reason at all not to behave precisely as her father had, and as any man would. Doing otherwise would expose her weakness and differentiate her from kings in a way that might have threatened her security. If it was a conscious decision, it was a bold one and a gamble that allowed only for total success or utter failure.

Theobald, Archbishop of Canterbury was conspicuously absent from Winchester on 3 March. He arrived a few days later after the business had been largely concluded and it is to be wondered whether his exclusion was a deliberate move by Bishop Henry in the power battle between the Legate and the archbishop. When Archbishop Theobald reached Winchester, he certainly set about taking back some control from a moral high ground. The archbishop refrained from offering his fealty to the empress 'as he thought it unbefitting his reputation and position to transfer his allegiance without consulting the king'.[10] In what must have appeared an open rebuke aimed at Bishop Henry, Theobald insisted that he be permitted to visit the king in his dungeon at Bristol before he would consider pledging fealty to the empress. Perhaps out of respect for his position, Theobald, a number of bishops and a group of laymen were given permission to go to the king. Having managed to obtain 'a courteous permission to change over as the times required'[11], the archbishop, bishops and others finally agreed to recognize Empress Matilda as Lady of the English. Stephen's agreement, if it was genuine, must be seen as a final signal of his acceptance both that his prospects were all but gone and that those seeking to survive in his kingdom now had to work with the new regime. It remains a chivalric concession nevertheless, and Stephen may have considered that keeping men who had once been loyal to him in power was preferable to their wholesale replacement by the disinheritated or Angevin men, which would cause any faint hope of a return to vanish altogether.

15

King Stephen

> In our time, also, Walkeline was bishop of Winchester; he was succeeded by William Giffard, a man of true nobility. Both these are dead, and have come to nothing. Their seat is occupied by Henry, the king's son, who promises to exhibit a monstrous spectacle, compounded of purity and corruption, half a monk, half a knight.[1]

Perhaps in response to the uncertainty Archbishop Theobald created, Bishop Henry called a Legatine Council to meet at Winchester, opening on 7 April and lasting until 10 April. Empress Matilda held her Easter court at Oxford in splendour that loudly proclaimed her new status, but she was given no time after Easter Sunday, 6 April, before Bishop Henry's meeting began. Perhaps the intention was that she should not be able to be at the council. William of Malmesbury attended the proceedings and recorded a full account of the deliberations there. On Monday, 7 April, Bishop Henry opened the council, reading out the apologies of those who had failed to attend. Next, he had a secret conference with the bishops who were there. Then the abbots were taken aside before the archdeacons were spoken to. William insists that none of the content of these discussions was made public, but that everyone was preoccupied with settling things down.[2] On the following day, Tuesday, Bishop Henry addressed the whole council. He recited the chain of events that had led to that day: his uncle King Henry dying without a male heir and having caused everyone of note in England and Normandy to pledge allegiance to his daughter Matilda. He then claimed, in a speech directly quoted by William, that Stephen had been permitted to rule because it had proven tedious to wait for Matilda to arrive from her home in Normandy. The bishop went on to express his regret at that decision:

> I am vexed to remember and ashamed to tell what manner of man he showed himself as king: how no justice was

> enforced upon transgressors, and how peace was at once brought entirely to an end, almost in that very year; bishops were arrested and compelled to surrender their property; abbacies were sold and churches despoiled of their treasure; the advice of the wicked was hearkened to, that of the good either not put into effect or altogether disregarded.[3]

Henry summed up his personal conflict in the matter by considering that 'while I should love my mortal brother, I should esteem more highly the cause of my immortal Father.'[4] It was an apparently visceral assault on his brother's character and kingship. The bishop explained his abandonment of his own brother by claiming that he had failed to uphold the promises made to Bishop Henry about the freedoms of the church and to uphold law and order. It is hard to discern whether Bishop Henry really believed what he was saying. It is possible that he did feel his brother had failed – after all, he was languishing in a prison cell at that moment – and that the empress, if not deserving of a chance, might, in fact, have had right on her side all along. The judgement of God was the best explanation for anything that happened and could not be easily explained. If God had seen fit to strip Stephen of his crown, then it was reasonable to look for the faults in him and his rule and to suspect that the failure to adhere to oaths made to Matilda was part of the source of the Lord's dismay.

As a political as well as ecclesiastical animal, Bishop Henry had to try and maintain his position under the new regime. He would be chief amongst those suspected of harbouring sympathy for Stephen and those culpable in his swift securing of Empress Matilda's birthright. If he was to avoid losing his Legatine power and his wealth, then he had to align himself to the new order. He had, if anything, orchestrated something of a coup by manoeuvring himself into a position of acting as the gatekeeper to Empress Matilda's accession. She had been required to go through him and to obtain his approval before arriving in Winchester. Still, he would have to distance himself from his brother if he was to retain any status under her rule. That meant he needed to explain his easy support for her and the equally smooth abandonment of his brother. It is here that the bishop might be seen at his most politically ruthless and his words gave rise to a suspicion that he may have favoured the empress's cause all along, particularly when he had worked for Matilda's release from Arundel Castle.

There is another possible explanation. If Stephen was to find a way to regain what he had lost, he needed men at the heart of power. If he was so willing to acquiesce to the requests of Archbishop Theobald and others to transfer their allegiance because he recognized that a sweeping clearout of the establishment would hinder his chances, then Bishop Henry had a part to play. By keeping himself the most senior figure in the English Church and near the centre of political power, he could help his brother to judge when the time might be right and help him take advantage of any reversal of the empress's fortunes. Some of Bishop Henry's words, reported by William of Malmesbury, may hint at what he was really up to. William was triumphant in his report that Henry told the council:

> 'Therefore, first, as is fitting, calling God to our aid, we choose as lady of England and Normandy the daughter of a king who was a peacemaker, a glorious king, a wealthy king, a good king, without peer in our time, and we promise her faith and support.'[5]

Before this offer of support to Empress Matilda, the bishop made another critical statement. He told the council that 'The case was discussed in secret yesterday before the chief part of the clergy of England, whose special prerogative it is to choose and consecrate a prince.'[6] This must have been what the separate meetings with bishops, abbots and archdeacons were about. Bishop Henry was positioning the church as the arbiter of royal titles with authority to elect a monarch. It was an attempt to move towards a more continental, Germanic style which he might have felt could be acceptable to the empress, though asking any ruler to give away their powers was unlikely to be a welcome request. Such a concession may have been part of the price of Bishop Henry's support, in which case he was furthering the interests of the church as he faced the new political realities in England.

Thc claim to authority might also havc bccn notcworthy if thc bishop was working to keep his brother's hopes alive. It would still represent a recognition of the church's power, but if they could deselect Stephen and elect Empress Matilda, then it would surely be possible for them to do the reverse at a later date. Bishop Henry created a legal situation in which the church was permitted to elect a new monarch and then consecrate that person, but he also created a mechanism, by those same powers, that might one day allow Stephen to regain his throne. If that fell

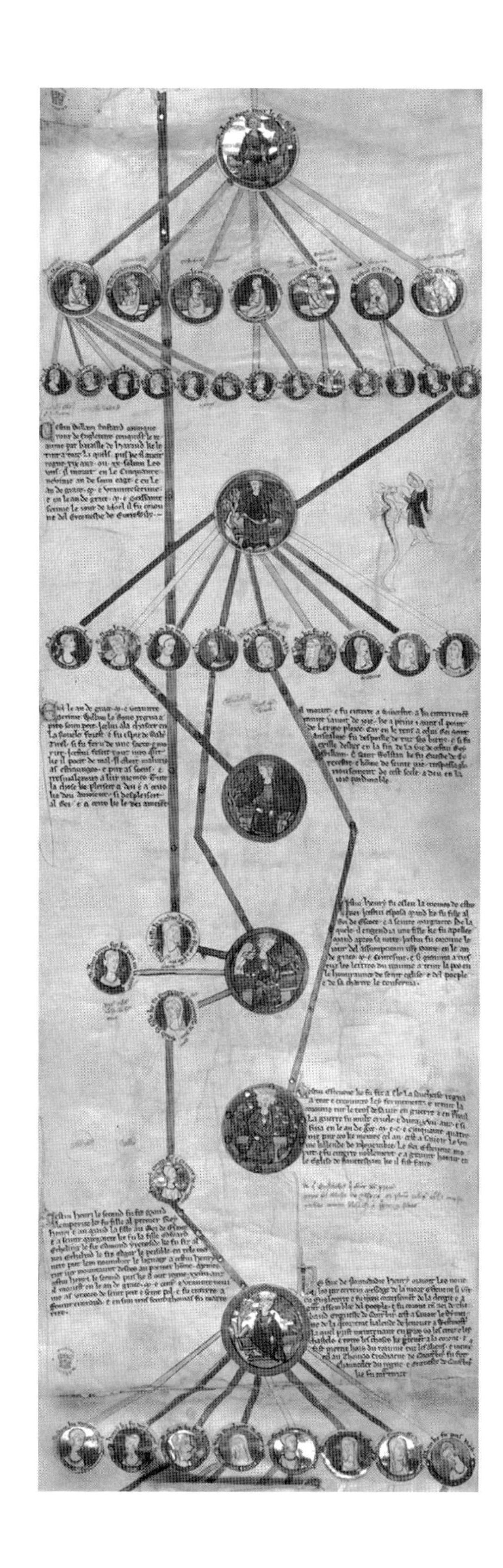

Descendants of Robert of Normandy to Henry II. (*via British Library Manuscripts*)

Above: Genealogy of Henry I showing his only legitimate children, William Adelin and Matilda, along with his first wife Matilda of Scotland. (*via British Library Manuscripts*)

Left: Henry I above an image of the *White Ship* Disaster. The death of William Adelin in the shipwreck sparked the succession crisis that followed Henry's death. (*via British Library Manuscripts*)

Empress Matilda at a feast with her first husband, Holy Roman Emperor Henry V. The union with Henry was prestigious for England and Matilda seems to have been happy in the Empire. (*via Wikimedia Commons*)

Genealogy of Adela of Normandy, daughter of William the Conqueror, showing her son Stephen in the bottom right. (*via Wikimedia Commons*)

A drawing of Malmesbury Abbey from 1807, where William of Malmesbury penned his chronicle of The Anarchy. (*via Wikimedia Commons*)

Empress Matilda and Holy Roman Emperor Henry V receiving their crowns. (*via Wikimedia Commons*)

Above: King Stephen on his throne with a hunting hawk. Stephen's accession left him open to charges of usurpation and oath breaking that led to civil war. (*via British Library Manuscripts*)

Right: Matilda of Scotland (c. 1080 – 11 May 1118), first wife of Henry I of England and mother to Empress Matilda. Also known as Edith or Edith Matilda, her possible position as a nun before her marriage was used to suggest that her daughter could not be legitimate and so could not inherit the crown of England. (*via Wikimedia Commons*)

Left: Enamel effigy of Geoffrey of Anjou from his tomb at Le Mans. The heraldic devices on his shield may offer an early hint of the three lions that later became the royal arms of England. (*via Wikimedia Commons*)

Below: King David I of Scotland with his successor and grandson Malcolm IV from a Charter to Kelso Abbey. (*via Wikimedia Commons*)

An image of Robert, Earl of Gloucester, illegitimate son of Henry I and half-brother of Empress Matilda, from the *Founders' Book of the Monks of Tewkesbury Abbey*. Robert's wife Mabel FitzHamon was the daughter of Robert FitzHamon, the founder of Tewkesbury Abbey. (*via Wikimedia Commons*)

Henry of Blois, Bishop of Winchester, younger brother of King Stephen, holding his bishop's crosier and ring, from the *Golden Book of St Albans*. Bishop Henry is often accused of switching sides frequently throughout the dispute between his brother Stephen and cousin Empress Matilda. (*via British Library Manuscripts*)

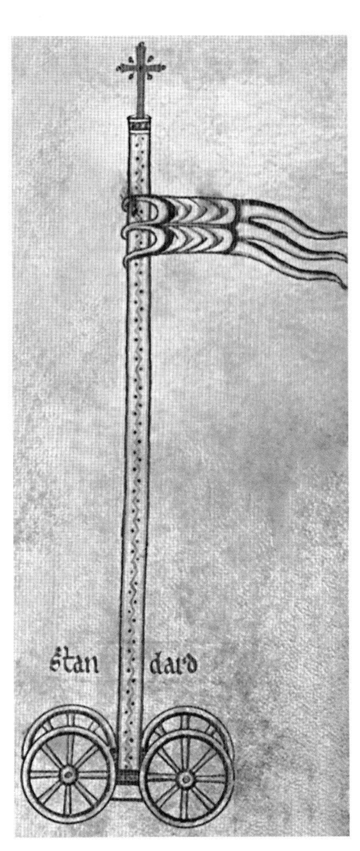

Left: A drawing of the Standard, after which the Battle of the Standard in 1138 was named. The sketch appears in the margin of Roger of Hoveden's Chronicle. (*via British Library Manuscripts*)

Below: An image of the Battle of Lincoln, 1141, from Henry of Huntingdon's *Historia Anglorum*. (*via British Library Manuscripts*)

Wall paintings of medieval knights riding into combat from Claverley Church, Shropshire. The wall paintings are stunning survivals of the Reformation. (*Author's Collection*)

Knights in combat on the walls of Claverley Church, Shropshire. Although the murals date from around 1220, they are believed to represent images of the legends of Charlemagne and Roland. (*Author's Collection*)

Chainmail, Norman shields and heraldry can be seen clearly in the wall paintings at Claverley Church. (*Author's Collection*)

A representation of Queen Matilda, wife of King Stephen, petitioning Empress Matilda for mercy for her husband and son after Stephen's capture at the Battle of Lincoln. (*via British Library Flickr*)

Above: Empress Matilda sends Queen Matilda away empty handed. The reaction caused a swell of sympathy for Stephen's cause, which may have been Queen Matilda's aim. She was consistently able to offer a more attractive and acceptable example of the behaviour expected of a medieval queen than the Empress could deliver. (*via Wikimedia Commons*)

Right: Part of the remains of Oxford Castle, from which Empress Matilda made her dramatic escape in the dark and snow in 1142. (*Author's Collection*)

Great Seal of King Stephen, showing him enthroned on one face and riding into battle on the other. Stephen spent much of his reign in harness and the image of him as a military leader was a stark contrast to the position of his cousin Empress Matilda. (*via Wikimedia Commons*)

Above left: Great Seal of Empress Matilda, who effectively ruled the south-west of England for over a decade before handing her claim to the throne to her oldest son Henry, later Henry II. (*via Wikimedia Commons*)

Above right: Great Seal of King David of Scotland, showing him enthroned on the obverse. David took control of a large part of northern England as Stephen and Matilda fought for the throne of England and brought peace and structure to the region. (*via Wikimedia Commons*)

Reverse of the Great Seal of King David of Scotland. English chroniclers were scathing of the number of times that David was driven out of England in armed conflicts. (*via Wikimedia Commons*)

Stained glass image of St Bernard of Clairvaux, a leader of the Cistercian Order and a campaigner for reform who frequently had the ear of various popes. Bernard disapproved of King Stephen's brother Henry of Blois because of his wordly wealth and political activity. (*via Wikimedia Commons*)

A manuscript depiction of King Stephen, often remembered as a weak king whose ambition led to The Anarchy. (*via British Library Manuscripts*)

Right: A drawing of Empress Matilda from the fifteenth century Rous Roll. (*Author's Collection*)

Below: Henry II and Eleanor of Aquitaine, right, were a power couple in medieval European politics. Empress Matilda passed her claim to the throne of England to Henry as her oldest son and he took up the fight against Stephen, though the two quickly arrived at terms. (*via British Library Manuscripts*)

A chronicle image of King Stephen and Henry II. The compromise reached by them brought an end to civil war, though it is uncertain how long it might have lasted had Stephen lived longer. (*via Wikimedia Commons*)

within the compass of the church, and Bishop Henry was still the most senior ecclesiastical figure in England, then he would be able to control his brother's return to the throne if that became feasible. Archbishop Theobald's insistence that Stephen's permission must be gained to transfer loyalties meant that there was also the apparatus to shift that fealty back again, even if it required Empress Matilda's consent. Perhaps Bishop Henry and Archbishop Theobald were not as far apart on some of these matters as it might seem they were.

Another action of the bishop's during this council, which he revealed during this speech, also suggests that he had not entirely abandoned his brother. It is necessary to recall the deal made between King Stephen and the citizens of London on his accession. The *Gesta Stephani* explained that 'a mutual compact was previously made and an oath taken on both sides, as was commonly asserted, that as long as he lived the citizens would aid him with their resources and protect him with their power, while he would gird himself with all his might to pacify the kingdom for the benefit of them all.'[7] Stephen had certainly played his part in the rapid subduing of threats after his accession. It seems likely that Bishop Henry now called this debt in on his brother's behalf. Bishop Henry sent messengers to London, providing safe conduct for representatives of the city to come to Winchester and attend the Legatine Council. Assuring those listening that the Londoners would arrive by the next day, he adjourned the proceedings, but not before he had described those coming as 'in effect magnates because of the greatness of their city in England'.[8] Bishop Henry gifted the citizens of London a seat at the table to make the decision on the future direction of the kingdom, and he must have remembered their pledge to Stephen and the affection they held the king in. The only reason he can have invited them was to allow them to champion Stephen's cause in a way that he could not.

Sure enough, the Londoners arrived in Winchester on Wednesday. They were presented to the council to offer their opinion but took care to explain that they had been sent by the commune of London. This was an important assertion because it implied a degree of freedom from centralized authority. Communes were becoming more widespread across Europe, though the firm, central monarchy in England had prevented them from taking hold. City states in northern Italy provided a model for free communes committed to protecting themselves, militarily if necessary. Monasteries and merchants' guilds were the closest England saw to communes, but London staked a claim to that status now. It is possible King Stephen had given the city commune status in 1135 as part of the deal to secure their support and that they sought to reassert that right now, or to threaten the empress with their willingness to maintain independence and to defend themselves.

They went on to assure the council that they did not bring 'contentiousness' with them, perhaps in an effort to mitigate any perceived threat.[9] The only demand that William of Malmesbury records the Londoners making was 'a request that their lord the king should be released from captivity'.[10] Bishop Henry gave an eloquent response, reiterating the sentiments of his speech the previous day to oppose the Londoners' request. If he had called on them precisely to give this support to his brother, then he had to remain opposed to their demand in order to keep his place at Empress Matilda's side. It is hard to know whether he hoped for more than he received from summoning the Londoners, but he had enabled them to make several points. Firstly, they were still openly loyal to Stephen. Secondly, they wanted his release. Thirdly, they viewed themselves as a commune with all of the associated implications that they intended to act independently to defend their rights. Finally, there was an unspoken acknowledgement of the fact that if Empress Matilda wished to gain control of the capital, where she would hope to undergo a coronation, she had a long way to go. Her path was not clear and would not be easy; the spectre of Stephen was not as yet entirely banished.

Next to arrive at the council was a clerk named Christian, who brought a letter addressed to Bishop Henry. The Legate took the note but refused to read it out before the gathering, so Christian took the message back and read it aloud himself. It was from Queen Matilda, and she begged the assembled clergy to restore the king to his throne. She singled out Bishop Henry in particular to insist that he should favour his brother's cause against the cruel men who owed the king their fealty but had now clapped him in chains. The meeting broke up the same day, though it is uncertain why. Empress Matilda does not figure in the accounts of the deliberations, but she can hardly have been pleased by the end of them. Although they had acknowledged her as Lady of the English, several hurdles had been placed in her way. Support for her was not universal, and she would evidently have trouble bringing the city of London and its people round to her side. Queen Matilda was still active on her husband's behalf, and her family contacts in Boulogne could prove bothersome.

Whether or not she trusted Bishop Henry, or was able to perceive his motives is as uncertain as what those motives might have been. Had he abandoned the king, or was he working to keep himself in a place from which to help his brother when the time came? Was the outcome of the meeting a disappointment to him as London failed to acquiesce and his sister-in-law pleaded for help or was it precisely what he had orchestrated?

A year or two later, Brian Fitz Count would write to Bishop Henry as part of a dispute over the seizure of food around Winchester by Brian's men. It is impossible to know how much of what was written matches Bishop Henry's own words in March 1141 and how much of it is simply a reiteration of Brian's own beliefs used to justify his men's actions. He insisted that 'You yourself who are a bishop of holy church, ordered me to support the daughter of your uncle King Henry and assist her to recover her right, which had been taken from her by force,' He continued that Bishop Henry should 'Be assured that neither I nor my men have done this for money or fee or land, either promised or given, but only because of your command and for my honour and that of my men' before listing those he could call as witness to his claim. They included Archbishop Theobald, ten bishops, King David of Scotland and a host of barons including Robert, Earl of Gloucester and Reginald, Earl of Cornwall.[11] Brian was neck deep in the empress's cause as soon as she had landed, so it is disingenuous of him to claim that he only backed the empress because of Henry's command after the Battle of Lincoln. He does, though, appear adamant and vehement that Bishop Henry convincingly portrayed himself as Empress Matilda's man at Winchester in March 1141. Perhaps Bishop Henry had played his part very well indeed.

Queen Matilda was still behind her husband's cause, not least because his fortunes directly impacted those of their surviving children, Eustace, now around eleven years old, William who was about six and Mary who was probably five. The queen offered a perfect example of how a woman could wield power when it was on behalf of a husband. Her impassioned pleading with the Legatine Council held by her brother-in-law was precisely the kind of negotiating and appeal to chivalric desires to protect a damsel in distress that would have resonated with the men of the kingdom. They knew how to react to this kind of activity. It was what they considered normal, proper for a woman. Whether she intended it or not, the queen was offering a direct, almost tangible comparison to the empress. If Queen Matilda was behaving as a woman was expected to, Empress Matilda was defying all of those rubrics. It gave the great men of the kingdom a diametrically opposed set of options. They could return to being ruled by a king, with a queen at his side who knew what was required of her office, or they could continue to follow a woman who behaved as though she was a man in a society with no blueprint for such a thing.

William of Ypres and other military men had not abandoned their king yet either. It is tempting to see Bishop Henry feathering his nest under the new regime after betraying his brother, to see the queen making a desperate plea for the impossible release of her husband, and to view those still willing to fight for Stephen as lacking a place in the new order and simply seeking to cause trouble. It is equally feasible that in the spring of 1141 there was still profoundly held loyalty to Stephen and the organization of a resistance to the empress's advances toward power that ultimately aimed for his release and restoration. In this scenario, Bishop Henry holds not only authority over the church but significant political power, as demonstrated by the empress's need to negotiate with him before being permitted to enter Winchester. Calling a Legatine Council was a reminder of that power, but also an assertion that he, as a representative of the church, held a right to choose and consecrate a monarch. If Empress Matilda acquiesced to that claim in order to win the throne, then it negated her entire cause in one fell swoop. In recognizing the right of the nation, or the church, to elect a ruler, she approved of their actions in appointing Stephen in 1135. Her case rested on an issue of illegitimacy and usurpation. Bishop Henry effectively undermined that argument whilst appearing to be trying to gift the empress the throne.

If Queen Matilda was in communication with her brother-in-law to help organize this resistance movement, then her letter, Bishop Henry's reluctance to read it and the clerk's dramatic recitation anyway become a piece of theatre. The queen behaved as those listening would expect of a woman, a queen presenting a contrast to the empress's haughty, manly demeanour. It offered comfortable certainty over radical change. All of the time, a military threat lay just behind the thin veil of political manoeuvring. Bishop Henry called the Londoners to Winchester on the pretence that their support would be needed if the empress was to be crowned, but he must have known of their affection for Stephen and their pledge to support him. If nothing else, their reservations slowed the pace of Empress Matilda's journey to the throne even more, buying time to organize their fightback.

There may have been no such unity of purpose amongst King Stephen's wife, brother and mercenaries. Bishop Henry could have thrown his lot in with the empress's cause in recognition of her victory, presuming it, as many others did, to be final. The queen might have been merely desperate to salvage something, hoping for pity for herself and her children if nothing else. Mercenaries, with no paymaster to keep them in check, could have been simply running riot, or waiting for the next chance of a windfall. It is impossible to know what each of these parties was planning and hoping for, but possible to see some coordination of their efforts to remove the heat from the empress's victory, to slow its progress, highlight its deficiencies and to set about creating the mechanisms by which Stephen might be restored to the throne when the time was right.

16

Empress Matilda

So difficult was it to reduce the Londoners to acquiescence that, though these proceedings took place, as I have said, immediately after Easter, it was not until a few days before the Nativity of St John that they received the Empress.[1]

The Legatine Council held at Winchester had broken up on 10 April, but, as William of Malmesbury lamented, it was not until almost the Feast of the Nativity of St John on 24 June that Empress Matilda was permitted to enter London. It must have been frustrating for the empress to be forced to enter into prolonged negotiations with her capital city just to be allowed to enter it. Control of London would be necessary for a coronation at Westminster Abbey, never mind the political need to hold the nation's capital. The Londoners were intransigent, though how long they could hold back the swelling tide is questionable. The delay might have been about extracting the maximum concessions possible from the empress while they still held some of the cards, or even about hoping for King Stephen's fortunes to change. Either way, it was embarrassing and maddening for Empress Matilda, who needed to secure her tenuous hold on authority by being consecrated as Lady of the English. It was this that had made Stephen's position unassailable, not least in the papal courts, and now she needed it too, as soon as possible.

While she waited for London to agree to her arrival, Empress Matilda was not idle. She emulated Stephen's policy of decentralization by creating her own set of earls to exercise local authority in her name. It is striking that one of Stephen's initiatives that has been condemned as desperate and backward was also enacted by the empress at this point. It may have been a recognition that the uncertain times demanded it, but equally, it could have been a popular and effective policy. The latter would explain Empress Matilda's willingness to adopt it rather than seeking to differentiate herself and follow policies more in line with those of her father. Baldwin de Redvers, who had been banished by Stephen and had attached himself to the Angevin cause almost immediately, was made Earl of Devon. William de Mohun was created Earl of Somerset, where his father had been High Sheriff. The troublesome Hugh Bigod became Earl of Norfolk, and Aubrey de Vere was made Earl of Oxford.

One of the most significant confirmations, rather than new appointments, was that of Geoffrey de Mandeville. Geoffrey had been created Earl of Essex by Stephen around May 1140, and the king had returned estates in that county which Geoffrey had been deprived of by Henry I. Geoffrey seems, like many others, to have quickly recognized the need to become conspicuously aligned with the freshly victorious Empress Matilda. In turn, she could see in him the key to gaining control of London. Like his father William before him, Geoffrey had custody of the critical Tower of London. He was swiftly forgiven debts that his father had incurred to the crown, partly the result of a huge fine imposed by Henry I after a prisoner escaped from the Tower. The prisoner was Ranulf Flambard, Bishop of Durham. A principal servant of William II, he had been arrested on Henry I's accession on charges of embezzlement in 1100. Bishop Ranulf was the first inmate of the Tower of London, and he would become the first to escape it, on 3 February 1101. Popular legend explains that friends smuggled a long rope in to the bishop and after he managed to encourage his guards to get so drunk they passed out, he lowered himself from the window of his cell. Flambard was forced to flee to the continent where he joined Henry's brother and enemy Duke Robert of Normandy. He was eventually stripped of all his property and his bishopric. William, suspected by Henry I of some involvement, or at least of incompetence, was punished for the lapse in security. It was hardly an auspicious start to the Tower's later dark and formidable reputation as a prison.

Like so many other central figures during this period, and during 1141 in particular, Geoffrey's precise role and his motives are difficult to untangle. One explanation of his actions is that he saw a chance to play the two sides off against each other in order to make the greatest possible gains for himself. Empress Matilda confirmed Geoffrey in the earldom Stephen had granted him, forgave his significant debts and also appointed him hereditary Sheriff of Essex, Hertfordshire, Middlesex and London. He had extracted a fabulous deal from his switch of allegiance, but like many others, he probably saw no real alternative as the summer of 1141 approached. Stephen was a prisoner, and Matilda was stepping ever closer to a coronation. Geoffrey placed himself at odds with the population of London, but perhaps did no more than make the best of the new political realities. Hindsight allows the suggestion that his actions were more cynical, that he understood his power in London and Empress Matilda's need for it, so he extracted all that he could before giving her aid. Even if that were the case, it is hard to blame him.

A coup fell into the lap of Empress Matilda when Waleran Beaumont, Count of Meulan and Earl of Worcester became a vassal of the empress. The Beaumont twins were core pillars of Stephen's rule, and Waleran's brother Robert would remain loyal to the king. It seems likely that Waleran was driven now by pragmatism rather than any genuine desire to abandon Stephen or promote the empress's cause. Robert's lands were primarily in England based on their father's earldom of Leicester, but as Count of Meulan, Waleran had significant holdings in Normandy that were coming under threat from Geoffrey of Anjou. His own English earldom lay jammed up against Empress Matilda's territories, and if he continued to oppose her, he would be on the front line of the fighting. Resisting her in England in the name of a king she held prisoner might be enough to see his Norman properties become the focus of unwanted attention from Count Geoffrey. It seems likely that the Beaumont twins divided their loyalties to keep a foot in each camp, relying on the ability of whichever of them had selected the winning side to preserve the holdings of the other when the dust settled. Nevertheless, a Beaumont twin, so central to Stephen's efforts to retain control of both Normandy and England, at the empress's side was a strong signal that her faction was on the very brink of victory.

King David of Scotland came south to join in his niece's triumph. He was confirmed in his own English earldom of Huntingdon, but the relationship seems to have soured quite quickly as Empress Matilda tried to establish her authority but managed only to appear aloof and haughty. The writer of the *Gesta Stephani* complained that 'she did not rise respectfully, as she should have' when King David, Earl Robert or Bishop Henry entered her presence. This was another peculiar issue of her sex and the perception that women should be submissive and subservient to men. No king would have been expected to rise when an earl or bishop came to see him. It was this kind of expectation that

Empress Matilda needed to find an alternative to, but which she seems instead to have railed and thrashed against. The same writer complained further that the empress 'no longer relied on their advice, as she should have, and had promised them, but arranged everything as she herself thought fit and according to her own arbitrary will'.[2] Such strength and determination to impose personal authority could be admired in a man. Emanating from a woman, it was a source of confusion, consternation and even fear. William of Malmesbury seems to have believed Earl Robert was increasingly excluded too, or else sought to excuse his patron from the approaching problems. He wrote that 'if other members of his party had trusted his restraint and wisdom, they would not afterwards have endured such a turn of ill-fortune,'[3] suggesting that there was some truth to the story that the empress was not listening to advice any longer.

Problems with the alliances Empress Matilda tried to forge began to show almost immediately, and she was forced to pick sides amongst her own adherents (or supposed adherents). King David asserted his right to appoint a new Bishop of Durham to the vacant see, claiming that Durham and the surrounding area fell under his jurisdiction. The King of Scots wanted the post for his own chancellor, William Cumin. The chapter at Durham was horrified and wrote to the empress and Bishop Henry for aid. The bishop immediately responded by supporting the right of the chapter to elect their own bishop and instructed William Cumin that he was not to take up the see unless he was legitimately elected. Empress Matilda immediately overruled Bishop Henry and ignored the chapter's objections. She recognized William Cumin as bishop-elect and began plans to invest him herself as soon as she had been crowned. Not only did the empress alienate a potentially vital ally, she outraged the entire church by refusing them free elections.

Furthermore, she effectively recognized the right of her uncle King David to control swathes of the north of England, something that was unlikely to be well received in the north and which smacked of abandoning a section of her people. In attempting to assert some dominance, the empress only managed to appear subservient to King David and an enemy of the church. It was not a good start. There was no such trouble with the appointment of a new Bishop of London. Empress Matilda wanted the post for her father's former Master of the Writing Office, Robert de Sigillo, who was now a monk at Henry I's foundation at Reading Abbey. Robert was put forward by the empress, duly elected and blessed by Theobald. Although Stephen later resented having the empress's man in such a position, he found himself unable to remove Robert because his election had been entirely proper and legal. Durham was evidently a very different matter in which the empress had tried to subvert a free election to mollify her uncle.

It may be significant that at this moment, Norman barons such as Juhel de Mayenne, Alexander de Bohun, Guy of Sablé and Pagan of Clairvaux began to appear as witnesses to Empress Matilda's charters at Oxford. Their presence suggests a degree of contact with her husband that must have sought to relay information about their respective achievements in England and Normandy. It is possible that Geoffrey of Anjou was trying to impose his will on his wife at this moment so that he might have some interest in the kingdom of England, though his actions and attitude seem to consistently display a spectacular disinterest in anything beyond Normandy. Count Geoffrey had taken a long time to make any headway in the duchy, and his latest and greatest success had come off the back of his wife and her half-brother's success in England. He was willing to take his time to get a firm grip on Normandy and may have felt that trying to support his wife in England was a step too far, that he would overreach himself and let what he had gained slip through his fingers. Indeed, he might have sent his wife on her way to England to indulge her and get her out of his way while he set about trying to subdue Normandy. If he had, then her success was an unlooked-for boon. Both Henry I and Stephen had gained control of Normandy by first establishing themselves as King of England. If the empress saw that well enough, Geoffery did not care. He did not wish to claim Normandy as an extension of the English crown or, in fact, in any way on behalf of his wife. He was not interested in being the duchess's husband, or the queen's husband. He wanted to be Duke of Normandy in his own right, and nothing would shake his focus from that goal.

Some final negotiations for the reception of Empress Matilda into London must have been made at St Albans, where she was warmly welcomed. Her proximity to the city suggests she had finally tired of waiting and decided to move closer to force the hand of the citizens. An agreement was reached, perhaps with the weight of Geoffrey de Mandeville placed firmly behind it. Around 21 June 1141, Empress Matilda, Lady of the English was welcomed into the capital city of her kingdom and began to prepare for a coronation that would secure her position. Almost immediately, the empress blew away any goodwill she might have gathered. This time it was not really an issue of her sex, but entirely one of her attitude. Rather than wait for her coronation to be completed before venting whatever frustration she felt against the Londoners, she seems to have believed her position already unassailable and the empress began to make unnecessary mistakes. These were undoubtedly the things over which William of Malmesbury thought Earl Robert was being disregarded.

The *Gesta Stephani* recorded that Empress Matilda arrived in London at the invitation of the city. She came with a large army, apparently with the consent of the citizens, who believed that 'they had attained to joyous days of peace and quietness and that the calamities of the kingdom had taken a turn for the better'.[4] Whether this is true or not is impossible to tell. The city may have realized that it had held out and slowed the empress down for as long as was possible without risking an attack. The power that Geoffrey de Mandeville was accruing in the empress's efforts to gain entry threatened the desired independence of the capital, which was claiming the status of a commune, and the citizens may have resented Geoffrey's promotions and realized they needed to cut their losses and make peace with the empress. In turn, Empress Matilda must have feared that the city still harboured some loyalty to Stephen which she expected them to demonstrate convincingly had been transferred to her. They had tried to demand Stephen's release at Winchester and had been uncooperative ever since, so any suspicion was not unreasonable. As her father had often done, she turned to financial punishments to secure loyalty and deprive her potential enemies of funds with which to oppose her.

Even as London seemed to rejoice in welcoming the new Lady of the English, the smiles, real or pretended, were wiped from the faces of the citizens. Matilda sent for the wealthiest men in London and ordered them to pay vast sums of money to her as a tax. She asked 'not with unassuming gentleness, but with a voice of authority',[5] to the shock of the gathered well-to-do of London. Those before her spluttered their objections: they had no money to give after all of the upheavals of recent years. They assured her that when the nation was in a more settled state, they would gladly provide her with whatever sums she demanded, but for now, the men protested, they simply could not afford it. Empress Matilda, her worst suspicions appearing to be true,

> with a grim look, her forehead wrinkled into a frown, every trace of a woman's gentleness removed from her face, blazed into unbearable fury, saying that many times the people of London had made very large contributions to the king, that they had lavished their wealth on strengthening him and weakening her, that they had previously conspired with her enemies for her hurt, and therefore it was not just to spare them in any respect or make the smallest reduction in the money demanded.[6]

The empress was enraged at the refusal and, if what the writer of the *Gesta* reports is correct, saw through their assurances of loyalty, fearing that they refused her because they still remained loyal to Stephen. There was feeling on both sides that she had blown it. William of Malmesbury complained 'behold, when it was thought that she was about to gain possession of the whole of England, everything was changed.'[7]

To make matters worse, Queen Matilda interjected, doubtless picking her moment to emphasize the differences between the two women and their approaches. The author of the *Gesta Stephani* interestingly describes the queen as 'a woman of subtlety and a man's resolution',[8] perhaps meant to mean that she represented everything that the empress was not. As she had done at Winchester, Queen Matilda demonstrated her own intricate understanding of how a woman could operate the levers of power in England just as the empress threw a wrench into her own. Messengers arrived in London from the queen to request from the empress the release of her husband from his terrible imprisonment, but not the return of his crown or indeed any of his possessions. All that she asked for aside from Stephen's freedom was the return to their son Eustace of his rightful inheritance in Boulogne, which he should have held through the queen from her father.

It was a layered request that can only have been designed to detonate at every level of Empress Matilda's cause, exposing her flaws and widening the cracks in her support. It was as devilishly clever as it was perfectly timed. The queen demonstrated to the men in London and around the empress precisely how a woman was expected to act, not shouting and demanding money, but interceding to find peace and resolution. This was a woman the men of power could understand and deal with. Her request to release Stephen was a plea for mercy from the empress. Making no mention of him returning as king did not preclude the possibility, but she implied that he would simply retire into obscurity. The empress could never agree to this petition; it would have been a death knell to her chances of reigning peacefully. Her father had kept his own brother imprisoned for twenty-eight years until the latter's death, so she can have had few qualms about doing the same to her cousin if it kept her throne secure. But a woman in power was supposed to represent and exercise mercy, to encourage it in her husband under more usual circumstances. The queen was forcing Empress Matilda to refuse to give mercy when it was asked for, pushing her even further from the accepted norms of behaviour for her sex.

Asking for Eustace's inheritance from her father, the County of Boulogne, and nothing else was perhaps the most ingenious trick of all. It was something the empress could agree to, but the queen must have gambled on her rejection of the petition wholesale. Queen Matilda did not demand the return of all Stephen's lands in England and Normandy which he had held under Henry I, nor did she even ask for these for her oldest son and heir. All she wanted was her father's county to pass to Eustace, from grandfather to grandson; after all, she had only been a custodian, her husband holding it in trust for their son, because she was just a woman. Queen Matilda must have known the empress was likely to refuse given the mood she was in, but denying a rightful inheritance was a dangerous precedent to set that placed everyone with property to leave behind them on edge. If the new regime did not adhere to the basic, accepted rules of inheritance, it would be hard for most to attach themselves to it with any certainty.

The final ticking bomb was the insinuation in the queen's plea that a woman could not rule. She wanted her father's inheritance to pass to her son, ignoring any rights she may have had. The notion perhaps mirrored a lingering preference for Empress Matilda's son Henry of Anjou to be the focus of her efforts. Some might have felt far more comfortable with the idea of Empress Matilda transmitting a claim to Henry from her father than the notion of her actually ruling. At the very least, it kept the empress's supporters discussing the merits of alternatives and the problems in her claim to a right to rule, dividing her support. As her personality began to become an issue turning many away from her, an alternative would increase in appeal. If Queen Matilda were able to demonstrate the ability to act impeccably on her husband's behalf, then Empress Matilda's behaviour would seem all the more jarring and unacceptable in comparison. Every aspect of the queen's brief and apparently desperate plea was designed to tear aware at the empress's support. And it worked. Spectacularly.[9]

The queen's messengers were harangued and offered only insults for their troubles. The empress refused to grant anything that the queen requested and sent her envoys away in a rage.[10] Bishop Henry seems to have backed the request that Eustace should be permitted to inherit Boulogne and he was angered by the empress's refusal. As at Winchester, it is tempting to see the queen and the bishop stage-managing the opportunity for the empress to expose her own flaws, her able to offer a contrast to the empress and him able to advise on the perfect moment to move. Bishop Henry withdrew from the empress's court, and William of Malmesbury saw this as the moment he became disaffected with her cause. He reportedly met the queen at Guildford, and they had a family summit to decide what to do.[11] It is perhaps naive to believe that they had not been in communication throughout the spring and summer, but William thought the empress had fatally wounded her own hopes after her arrival in London. He saw that 'all the barons of England had kept their faith with her but she had broken hers, being unable to show restraint in the enjoyment of what she had gained.'[12] It seems that even those who sympathized with her cause found her to be a poor winner.

17

King Stephen

> [Bishop Henry] resolved to make a pact of peace and friendship with his enemies for a time, that with peace thus assured to him and his he might quietly watch the inclinations of the kingdom and how they were displayed and might rise more briskly and with less hindrance to assist his brother if a chance were offered.[1]

If the author of the *Gesta Stephani* was correct, Bishop Henry had indeed been biding his time until he was able to help his brother. The bishop may have helped create that very opportunity by crafting with his sister-in-law a political trap for the empress, which she kindly sprung with little effort at all. If that was the plan, it relied on Empress Matilda reacting precisely as she did in order for the next phase to swing into operation. Even now, the queen was able to lay bare the critical difference between her position and that of the empress. There remained unanswered or unsolved the question of how Empress Matilda, as Lady of the English, would fulfil one of the most vital roles of a medieval ruler and take an army into the field to defend herself and her people. Delegating that to a man raised the question of whether he, whoever he might be, Earl Robert or Count Geoffrey, was really the de facto monarch, not Empress Matilda. As suddenly as her husband might have done, Queen Matilda appeared outside the walls of London with an army, raised in the names of her imprisoned husband and disinherited son, demonstrating precisely how a woman could put an army into the field: in support of her men.

As the queen's force, probably comprised primarily of Flemish mercenaries under the command of William of Ypres, camped in the south bank of the River Thames and casually attacked the opposite side, they exposed the empress's inability to defend London. Despite all of her threats and posturing, she could no more guard the city against attack than she could protect herself. The empress and her followers were just sitting down to a lavish feast, oblivious to what was happening outside until the city's alarm bells began to ring. In what must have been a stage-managed moment, the citizens of London unbarred all the gates and rose up themselves. Their target was the empress as they poured out of their homes 'like thronging swarms from beehives'.[2]

Realizing too late what was going on, the empress and those with her leapt from the tables and made for their horses, riding at full speed away from London just as the angry horde broke into their lodgings. The mob found ample plunder and plenty of food left behind in the desperate evacuation, and even as she was waiting for her coronation to take place, Empress Matilda was driven out of London. Bishop Henry was understood by many to have been aware of the plot, and by some to have been its instigator.[3] As the empress fled to Oxford, the bishop and others headed off in different directions, their break from Empress Matilda now clear for all to see. Bishop Henry no longer pretended to be the empress's man, had he been pretending to this point; her refusal to allow free elections in Durham might have been enough to turn him away from her cause if he had genuinely flirted with abandoning his brother.

As soon as he got back to Winchester, the bishop placed his own castle at Wolvesey, the bishop's palace just outside Winchester, in readiness for action and laid siege to the royal castle. Bishop Henry seems to have been able to predict Empress Matilda's moves at will, and her predictability was to compound her downfall as she reached for the very pinnacle of her achievements. She arrived at Winchester in short order with a large army on 31 July, to the shock of the populace. As the empress and her horde entered through one of Winchester's gates, Bishop Henry calmly mounted his horse and left by another, making for his palace at Wolvesey. The empress must have seen some parallel with the events at Lincoln a few months earlier. Stephen had been lured to a town by an assault on a royal castle only to be fallen on by a hostile army and captured. As she ordered her men to relieve the royal castle and prepare to besiege the bishop's palace, she also sent out summons to any loyal knights who could bring men to Winchester to join her building an army. She had, perhaps, seen too late that she had been enticed into a situation almost identical to Stephen's in February. Her fury may have blinded her until this moment, and might have kept her from still seeing it as her numbers swelled within the city walls. When the empress sent instructions to Bishop Henry to come to her without delay, he told the messengers 'I will get ready,' with no intention of attending on her.

Few seem to have come to the empress at Winchester. William of Malmesbury complained that many earls, 'for they were young and frivolous',[4] in fact saw an opportunity to revitalize the king's cause. The town was becoming a dangerous melting pot, and the heat was intensified as flames ravaged the buildings on 2 August. William of Malmesbury claims that the people of Winchester, remembering the oaths Bishop Henry had caused them to swear to the empress, remained loyal to her and so the bishop ordered firebrands thrown from his palace into the buildings around to deny her supporters shelter. In the ensuing chaos, a nunnery was burned to the ground, and Hyde Abbey just beyond the walls was engulfed. It was said that within Hyde Abbey was a likeness of the crucified Christ and a vast array of jewels, gold and silver, all given to the abbey by King Cnut. After it was destroyed, Bishop Henry reportedly ordered it stripped and dispersed the recovered contents, some 500 marks of silver and 30 marks of gold, as rewards to his knights.[5]

As the empress's army began to set a siege outside the walls of the bishop's palace at Wolvesey, Queen Matilda and William of Ypres pounced, encircling the attackers so that they were sandwiched between the garrison inside the castle and the army of the queen outside it. The whole thing rings of a carefully arranged and executed plan to lure the empress and her army into a trap. King David was still with his niece, as were Robert, Earl of Gloucester and the earls of Cornwall, Devon, Somerset, Hereford, Warwick and Chester, though William of Malmesbury complained that Ranulf, Earl of Chester was both 'late and ineffectual'.[6] The predominantly west-country basis of support for the empress's cause was plain to see, as were those still holding sympathy with the king. Queen Matilda arrived with not only William of Ypres but also the earls of Surrey, Northampton, Hertford and Essex, since Geoffrey de Mandeville had heeded the call to arms in Stephen's name. The queen also led a large contingent of Londoners, not satisfied with chasing the empress out of their city and willing once more to show their support for King Stephen. There were daily clashes for a while as the three forces jostled for supremacy, but Earl Robert soon recognized that their cause was weakening the quicker and was the more likely to fail first.[7]

On 14 September, Earl Robert seized the initiative. He made a feinting attack against the queen's army, distracting them while Empress Matilda and the rest of her force tried to conduct an orderly withdrawal from Winchester. There is some suggestion amongst the chroniclers, notably the *Worcester Continuation* and *The Anglo-Saxon Chronicle*,[8] that Bishop Henry was once more hedging his bets, meeting with the empress and Earl Robert and even ordering the city gates opened to allow them to escape. This accusation has echoes of the empress's release from Arundel Castle, and it is possible there is some truth to it, but it is also feasible that Bishop Henry was seen as having duped Empress Matilda and was deemed a fair target for scorn and slander for that piece of trickery alone. Brian Fitz Count would later complain of Bishop Henry that 'he had a remarkable gift of discovering that duty pointed in the same direction as expediency.' In answer to the bishop's complaints about Brian's betrayals, Fitz Count irreverently described himself as a man 'whose main offence consisted in refusing to change sides as often as himself'.[9]

Empress Matilda herself left the city in such a rush that she was forced to ride to Ludgershall astride her horse, like a man. Brian Fitz Count travelled with her, as did her half-brother Reginald, Earl of Cornwall. The *Worcester Continuation* says that they found no rest or security at Ludgershall and were forced to continue on to Devizes so that the empress 'once more mounted her horse, male fashion' before having to be transferred to a litter for the rest of the journey. Exhausted and almost certainly realizing the significance of news that was catching up with them, 'she was placed nearly half-dead, upon a hearse, and being bound with cords like a corpse, and borne upon horses, was carried, ignominiously enough, to the city of Gloucester'.[10]

Even the writer of the *Gesta Stephani* admired Brian's commitment to the empress:

> The Countess of Anjou herself, who was always superior to feminine softness and had a mind steeled and unbroken in adversity, was the first to fly, going to Devizes with only Brien and a few others to accompany her. But she and Brien gained by this a title to boundless fame, since as their affection for each other had before been unbroken, so even in adversity, great though the obstacle that danger might be, they were in no wise divided.[11]

The *Worcester Continuation* also describes how Miles of Gloucester, Earl of Hereford, 'being hemmed in by the enemy, threw off his armour and all his accoutrements, and, glad to escape with his life, fled in disgrace, reaching Gloucester, weary, alone, and half naked'.[12] King David fled back north, garnering the scorn of the chroniclers as he was sent scurrying out of England for the third time. As the stragglers made it back to Gloucester, so the news became more certain. One of their number had not escaped.

Robert, Earl of Gloucester had kept a few men behind with him to cover the retreat of his half-sister and the bulk of their force. As he made a slower, organized retreat, the queen's army caught up with him at Stockbridge, and after a scuffle, he was captured by the men of William de Warenne, Earl of Surrey. Earl Robert was placed into the custody of William of Ypres and imprisoned at Rochester Castle. For King Stephen's faction, the scales seemed finally to be balancing out. It did not escape the chroniclers that the two men had met almost identical fates, captured whilst fighting after the bulk of their army had left, the king taken on the Sunday of the Purification of Our Lady and now Earl Robert on another Sunday, the Exaltation of the Life-Giving Cross. William of Malmesbury was to hear stories of his patron's bravery in the face of this fresh setback. None would see the smile slip from Earl Robert's lips, nor would his spirits drop as he was taken away to Rochester. So effusive was William that he wrote, 'Such consciousness of his lofty rank did he breathe, that he could not be humbled by the outrage of fortune.'[13]

The immediate determination of King Stephen's followers seemed to be to arrange a prisoner exchange. When they tried to negotiate terms with Earl Robert, he calmly refused to conduct any discussions behind the empress's back. He remained unmoved in the face of both flattery and threats, though he seems to have allowed his captors to reduce their position to a straight swap of Earl Robert for King Stephen, with no other terms. They would then return to the lands they each controlled and defend them as best they could. England would be returned to the situation it had been in immediately before the Battle of Lincoln.[14] If the intention was to wipe the events of 1141 from the political slate, then it was a short-sighted and desperate plan. Things had changed beyond recognition in Normandy, and Stephen's capture had exposed the fragility of some loyalties to him. Perhaps that was little more than would be the case for any monarch in that unusual circumstance, but not all had to face the blatant realization of the sudden abandonment of their liegemen.

On reflection, Earl Robert reportedly decided that he would not agree even to this deal. He was almost certainly recounting the tale to William, so his portrayal as the calm and resolute prisoner should be taken with a pinch of salt. The earl was struck by the strength of his own negotiating position. An earl, he reasoned, was not of the same value as a king, so the empress should look for something beyond a mere exchange and gain some victory in Robert's release to help it match the setting free of a king.[15] Those representing Stephen's faction began to grow more desperate, as Earl Robert might have hoped, and they promised Robert the complete control of all of England, his political position lower only to the king as regards the crown, but the government of the country to be left entirely to the will of the earl. William recorded the earl's defiant reply, hoping that posterity would remember his patron's brave resolve. Earl Robert told his captors, 'I am not under my own control but in the power of others; my answer is that when I see myself my own master I will do whatever reason dictates with regard to your proposal.'[16] There may well have been a healthy dose of playing up his own part in Earl Robert's recollection of the episode, but it is also possible that the gist of what he related was accurate, since it falls into line with the final solution settled upon.

When the lure of power failed, Earl Robert was subjected to intimidation. Faced with threats that he would be sent to Boulogne, the earl reacted, according to William of Malmesbury, with an even calmness. He assured his captors that there was nothing he feared less than a trip to Boulogne, and threatened them in return that he had complete confidence in his wife and his men. If Earl Robert was sent to Boulogne, they could be confident that Stephen would be in Ireland in the instant that his countess heard of it.[17] Doubtless, in telling his tale of bravery under duress, Earl Robert meant to do his own reputation a great deal of good. In the process, he actually weakened Empress Matilda's entire cause. If the empress's claim relied on the illegitimacy of Stephen's kingship because he had broken his oath to recognize Empress Matilda and had usurped the throne, then the recognition Earl Robert offered him here only reinforced Stephen's claim to be the legitimate king. Robert might have served the empress better by holding a line that he was the more valuable prisoner, not Stephen since the king was just a usurping oathbreaker and Robert was a noble knight devoted to the fulfilment of the very promise Stephen had broken. As it was, Earl Robert proclaimed his own bravery but weakened the cause he fought for in the process.

The negotiations did come to involve the empress, and she too did little for her cause in the same manner as Earl Robert. She was so desperate to have her half-brother and senior military commander back at her side that she recognized King Stephen's status and value in order to secure Earl Robert's return. An elaborate set of checks was designed to ensure that both sides stuck to their agreement to release their key prisoner. Chivalry seems to have no longer been accepted, despite both King Stephen and Earl Robert maintaining an inviolable reputation for behaving correctly. On 1 November 1141, King Stephen emerged from Bristol Castle as a free man. He had agreed to leave his wife, Queen Matilda, and their son Eustace behind as hostages to guarantee his good faith. Earl Robert was brought from Rochester back to Winchester, and King Stephen made for the city with all haste. As soon as Stephen arrived at Winchester, Earl Robert was released, leaving his own son William to act as a hostage for the queen and her son. Earl Robert sped to Bristol, ordering the release of Queen Matilda and Eustace as soon as he arrived. Once the queen was back in Winchester, the earl's son was also released and the complex arrangement fulfilled on both sides.

It might appear that the year had ended with all sides in precisely the same position they had begun it, but such an appearance is deceptive. Empress Matilda had come within touching distance of the prize she had fought for six years to obtain, but ultimately she had let it slip through her grasp. Her sex presented complications, but there is a strong and unanimous sense amongst the chroniclers that it was her personality that scuttled her cause. The arrogance and unbending behaviour attributed to her might have been overplayed since it would appear exacerbated by the fact that she was a woman and presented those looking for one with an excuse to turn aside from her, but it seems likely to have grown around a grain of truth. The empress appears to have been a poor winner and to have begun to extract her vengeance before making certain that her position was secure and unassailable. The Angevin cause, at least in the person of Empress Matilda, had been irreparably harmed by her response to obtaining power and the threat that she had posed to London and many nobles previously loyal to Stephen.

The king, though now free to try and reestablish his authority, had similarly seen permanent harm done to his reputation. He had come out of his captivity still wearing his crown, and with some acknowledgement from his enemies of his de facto position as monarch, but he had come within a hair's breadth of being deposed. The sheen of majesty in which a king bathed, the illusion that they were chosen by God for the role, was tarnished forever. The author of the *Gesta Stephani* tried to draw comparisons with the biblical King David, but that could only ever paper over the crack in Stephen's kingship now. Furthermore, the chronicles, notably *The Anglo-Saxon Chronicle* and the *Worcester Continuator*, seem to point to the period of Stephen's captivity as the pinnacle of a breakdown in law and order: that this was the closest the civil war came to genuine anarchy. Although that offers some signal that Stephen was managing to restrain the worst of the lawlessness, the lid was now off the box and replacing it would always be harder than keeping it in place had been.

Normandy had been all but lost. The king could spare no time to leave England to try and repair the damage done there and must have been confronted on his release with the prospect of accepting, at least for now, Angevin control of his ducal lands across the Channel. Then there was the north. King David of Scotland had fled north after the Rout of Winchester, but he had already taken control of swathes of northern England, north of the River Ribble and the Pennines in the north-west and above the River Tyne in the north-east. His man, William Cumin, was still trying to force himself into the see of Durham, managing to get control of the bishop's palace even if the chapter continued to oppose his appointment. The empress had done nothing to prevent this expansion and, on his release, Stephen was presented with a fait accompli, with the prospect of having to conquer the region if he wanted it back. The populace even seemed willing to slide their feet comfortably under David's table if it meant settled rule and the room to prosper. The north was, for now, lost, even had Stephen not been the one to lose it.

Where there had once been one authority, there were now four. King Stephen could expect the south-east and some of the Midlands to remain loyal. Hugh Bigod in Norfolk could prove a problem in himself. He never seems to have become dedicated to Empress Matilda's cause, but nor was he entirely separated from Stephen, causing trouble much more for his own purposes than anyone else's. Across the Channel, while Count Geoffrey was tightening his grip on Normandy while England demanded focus, there was little hope remaining of winning lost territories back. Losses in Normandy also represented a threat to England because it had grown clear over the past seventy-five years that the Anglo-Norman barony preferred to keep one ruler across all of their territories to prevent a conflict of allegiance. It was precisely this kind of consideration that had caused Waleran Beaumont, once at the very core of Stephen's regime, to transfer his loyalty to Empress Matilda and Count Geoffrey. It was a grave warning to the king of the dangers inherent in letting go entirely of Normandy.

To the north, King David of Scotland, despite his protestations of loyalty to his niece the empress, had used Stephen's incarceration and the empress's attempts to gain control of the south-east and London in particular to grab land. Chunks of Northumbria and Cumberland had been subsumed into the Kingdom of Scotland and David based himself in these newly snatched areas to emphasize his presence and authority. The continued efforts to secure the see of Durham on the southern edge of his expanded realm demonstrate that David was keen to see how much further he could expand his borders, and that would present a significant problem for Stephen as he tried to reestablish himself on his release.

In the south-west and part way up the Welsh Marches, the empress's cause had a firm grip on the land, ruling it as an alternative state-within-a-state. The existence of this alternative had been key to driving England toward civil war: why respect the king's judgement if you disagreed with it when there was a more sympathetic ear also vying for your fealty? The return to that status quo at the end of 1141 only meant that the civil war, or the stalemate that had dominated the conflict until Stephen's capture, was likely to become even more entrenched and divisive. A king cannot control his barons if they feel free to attach themselves to a direct rival when they are chastised for their transgressions. The kingdom, therefore, could never be brought to peace while both factions maintained what they considered their rightful claim to the crown. Although it appeared that the sides had merely returned to their stand-off as it was before the Battle of Lincoln, matters had altered radically. The weaknesses of both factions had been exposed without destroying the strengths which would keep them clinging on. The political landscape was fundamentally different. Stephen had his crown back, but his kingdom had shrunk and been altered by his captivity so that his scope for income generation was decreased and the threats around him were pressing in ever closer.

Stephen began 1142 in ill health, possibly a result of his imprisonment, but it prevented any immediate attempts to dominate the new political scenery. It remained to be seen whether his trademark vigorous and energetic response could ever be enough again: if he still had it in him as he moved beyond his mid-forties.

18

Empress Matilda

The boy is called Henry, recalling his grandfather's name,
and would he may some day recall his prosperity and his power.[1]

There is a strong possibility that Empress Matilda also began the year 1142 in ill health. A truce was agreed between her and King Stephen in the opening months of the year, and the tense stalemate persisted. As it extended into Lent, for anyone waiting to see who would gain the upper hand after the tumultuous events and drastic reversals of 1141, it can only have served to heighten the edgy anxiety gripping a country that held its breath, waiting for a new war to erupt.

During March, in early Lent, Empress Matilda called a council of all her supporters to meet at Devizes. They were trying to find the best way forward when the truce expired, and hostilities might begin again. The fragility of their own position is highlighted by the decision that the best hope to move their cause forward was to appeal directly to Count Geoffrey for military aid. This was no small choice to make. To date, Empress Matilda had been trying to wrest control of England from Stephen entirely in her own name and by her own efforts. She was ably supported by Earl Robert and others, of course, but the drive was hers and in her own name. It seems she wanted it made plain that she did not come to England as Count Geoffrey's wife, but as the legitimate heir of King Henry I. For his part, Count Geoffrey seems to have been utterly devoid of interest in the conquest of England, perhaps regarding it as a dangerous overreaching of his resources. He was apparently content with his slow and solid acquisitions in Normandy, which had reached a tipping point in 1141, while Stephen was a prisoner of his wife so that the duchy stood on the brink of falling completely under his control.

The precise arrangements between Empress Matilda and Count Geoffrey remain a mystery. Had the count packed his wife off to England to keep her out of the way and busy while he conquered Normandy? If nothing else, the presence of the empress and Earl Robert would be a distraction for Stephen that could only benefit Geoffrey's plans. If the count intended to become Duke of Normandy in his own right, claiming it for the Angevin line rather than in the name of his wife, then it served his purposes to have her out of the duchy altogether. The waters in Normandy could not be muddied by her standing at his shoulder. Besides, he may have felt that if she happened to have some success in England, he would share in it as her husband anyway, without necessarily having to share his own gains in Normandy. Alternatively, the plan may have been for a two-pronged attack on Stephen all along. By dividing their forces between Normandy and England, they had opened up two fronts and Stephen would be forced to select one of them to fight on, unless perhaps he could delegate some of his responsibilities. A recognition of that need may have been behind his policy of creating earls with regional and local military authority and duties.

Empress Matilda's arrival in England may have been entirely of her own choice and initiative. If Geoffrey was consumed by Normandy, which was generally considered the lesser prize and could reasonably be expected to fall in consequence of a victory in England, the empress might have decided to take the bull by the horns herself. If she was to stake a claim in her own right rather than as her husband's wife, or by hiding behind his sword and shield, then England was the obvious focus for her attention. She could even upstage Geoffrey by winning both England and Normandy in one fell swoop, snatching victory from right under his nose. It perhaps depends on how much of the old, volatile rivalry still burned between them after more than a dozen years of marriage and three children. She probably turned forty in February 1142, and Geoffrey was not yet twenty-nine, so their relationship had possibly settled and mellowed a good deal, but it might equally have remained bitterly competitive. It remains impossible to discern whether they were working together in their separate ventures or in competition with each other.

Whatever the truth, recognizing that she had to ask her husband for assistance cannot have been easy for Empress Matilda. William of Malmesbury knew that much business was conducted in secret at the council held at Devizes, but the only outcome that was made public was that her advisors approved of sending to Geoffrey for aid, 'it being his duty to maintain the inheritance of his wife and sons in England'.[2] The appeal was meant to be to the count's sense of duty as the empress's husband, and it must be wondered quite how happy she was with being forced to adopt this course of action. Had she meant to try and secure the throne of England for herself by herself, then calling on Geoffrey was something of an admission of defeat. It may also have been a recognition that she had mishandled their victory the previous year and that she needed Geoffrey's help if she was going to bring about a final victory.

Interesting too is the return to references to her sons, last prevalent during debates about the precise aims of Henry I's settlement plans. This may mark the point at which the empress, perhaps convinced by her advisors, began to let go of her intentions to ensure that she was crowned Queen of England or Lady of the English. It may have been a tactic to appeal to Geoffrey as both a husband and a father, particularly if the empress felt he might not respond to his duties as the former, but Matilda may have begun to realize the enormity of the task before her. She had almost grasped the crown in 1141 and might never have another chance. Whether because of her sex, her personality or other problems less personal to her, it was abundantly clear to all that she had let victory slip through her fingers. Involving her sons at this point was probably not only meant as a reminder to Geoffrey, but also the nobility of England. She may not be the ruler they wanted, either because she was a woman, she had shown herself insufferable as a ruler, or because some were unable to get beyond the general, and papal, acceptance of Stephen as king, but Empress Matilda had an ace card.

She was already willing to look to the next generation of this struggle. Her oldest son Henry was a grandson of Henry I and offered a return to her father's line without any of the problems that she had encountered unless his personality proved the match for hers. The empress might already have turned one eye to promoting her son's inheritance of the crown, even if she could not win it, showing that the claim of Henry I's blood was not going away. It is intriguing to wonder whether Empress Matilda had learned some valuable lessons from her cousin Queen Matilda during the previous year. Queen Matilda had been able to leverage the allegiance of men to her husband by positioning herself as a protector of their titles and inheritances. She did not act in her own name, and that allowed men to follow her onto a battlefield and fight for her, something the empress had conspicuously struggled with.

It had been the plaintiff petitioning for her son's inheritance in Boulogne that had appeared to create a well of sympathy for the queen that was turned to revulsion with the empress's refusal to recognize that right. Whether consciously or not, Empress Matilda now used the very same tactic to appeal for her own son's inheritance: his grandfather's throne in England. Not only was she now fighting for her individual rights, but to protect those of her sons. That was something the men around her could recognize and knew how to respond to.

The men sent to Normandy to visit Count Geoffrey were carefully selected to try and garner a positive response. It soon became clear that one of the couple was far better at playing politics to get what they wanted than the other. It was three months before the envoys returned, coming before the empress at Devizes on 14 June 1142. They relayed the news that Count Geoffrey had seemed cautiously positive about her request for help, but had been made uncertain by the fact that he did not know any of the men sent to petition him, so was unsure whether to trust what they said and unwilling to deal with them. He would, the count told his wife, be only too happy to discuss the matter more fully with the one man in her company whom he did know well: her half-brother, Earl Robert. If Robert would travel to Normandy, Geoffrey intimated that he would be willing to do all that he was able to assist his wife.[3] Of course, what he was able to do, or not, was nowhere detailed.

Earl Robert was, perhaps unsurprisingly, disinclined to leave the empress's side. After the shock victory of the last year, had come a startling reversal brought about, if the chroniclers are to be given any credence on the issue, by the frosty attitude of the empress and her reticence to accept counsel when in the ascendant. Although the pieces had been roughly reset to their positions at the beginning of 1141, the playing field had radically altered. As the truce between the two sides came to an end, it was hardly an auspicious time for the empress to be divested of her most influential supporter and primary military commander. If the tension had been building around who might move first and how the struggle might re-erupt, then Earl Robert can not have been happy about being asked, at that very moment, to leave the empress and visit her husband to negotiate for help.

There must have been mounting pressure on the earl to make the visit. Count Geoffrey had made it clear that he would only discuss the matter with Earl Robert, and the empress's advisors had decided that

Geoffrey's help was needed were they to progress their bid to unseat Stephen once and for all. It was a trap, and Geoffrey had laid it perfectly. Robert finally succumbed to 'the unanimous wish of all'[4] that he should sail to Normandy and bring back men and money for the cause. Before he would leave, though, Earl Robert demanded hostages from the most senior men around his half-sister. These detainees would act as sureties both for the empress and for Count Geoffrey, but probably for Robert more than either of them. They were likely to be the sons and heirs of those who had anything to lose being left with the empress. Earl Robert took them to ensure that they would keep faith with his half-sister and guard her in his stead. Empress Matilda was to stay at Oxford Castle while Robert was away, and those who had provided hostages were to be at her side at all times.[5] This done, Earl Robert sailed from Wareham, though he may still have had strong reservations about the trip.

On his arrival in Normandy, Earl Robert may have thought his concerns had been misplaced. Count Geoffrey was quick to come and meet him, full of greetings and enthusiasm.[6] He willingly listened to his brother-in-law's explanation of the situation in England and heard the plea for help, which seems to have extended to asking Geoffrey to come to England in person.[7] Any hope of swift and willing assistance was soon washed away by the tidal wave of excuses Geoffrey offered. The count played his part very well. He did not discourage optimism on the part of Earl Robert, but instead set out the obstacles that had to be overcome before he would be able to provide the military aid the empress requested. If there was still some frostiness in the couple's relationship, Geoffrey must have enjoyed toying with his wife's hopes. He could see she was desperate simply by her appeal to him. After all her haughtiness in their earlier relationship, which may have lingered as part of her personality as shown by her response to victories in 1141, then the count may have measured out some satisfying vengeance for himself here. She had left him and forced him to ask her father to send her back. Still, after fourteen years of marriage and three children, she would not take his title. His own wife would not identify herself as Countess of Anjou but clung to the imperious title dubiously acquired from her first husband because it placed her above her second spouse. Now here was a chance to make the most of her desperate petition.

If Geoffrey set about enjoying his wife's enforced bout of meekness, then he would not lose sight of business in his quest for a little fun.

He had turned her first embassy away, but not without hope. His demand that Earl Robert should come to him to personally handle the negotiations had been agreed to, which can only have demonstrated quite how anxious Empress Matilda was at the moment. The insistence on Earl Robert's attendance in particular and in person was not just about draining every drop of recognition of Geoffrey's own status from his wife by having her most senior advisor sent: there were tactical reasons in Normandy that Geoffrey wanted his brother-in-law there, and the empress's desperation helped him realize them. The first problem that Geoffrey complained prevented him going to England to support his wife's cause was the sheer number of castles that were still being held against him. Normandy was simply not secure enough to leave.

Robert took the bait. He accompanied Count Geoffrey on a prolonged campaign to reduce Norman resistance to Angevin rule. Robert remained a powerful landowner and well-respected magnate in Normandy, so Geoffrey had probably lured him across the Channel with this very end in mind. Their joint efforts were strikingly successful. Ten castles, at Tinchebrai, St Hilaire, Briquessart, Aunay, Bastebourg, Trévières, Vire, Plessis, Villers and Mortain fell into Count Geoffrey's hands with Earl Robert's assistance. The last of them, Mortain, was King Stephen's own possession, the county that had been his, and it must have been a symbolic victory when it fell under the weight of the Angevin advance. Geoffrey's slow, patient conquest was finally paying dividends. Although it was not yet complete, the balance of power in the duchy had tipped and, unlike his wife in England, Count Geoffrey was both determined and able to take advantage of it.

It was probably now that Earl Robert realized the extent to which he had been duped and used. William of Malmesbury, perhaps echoing his patron's complaints, noted of the capture of these ten castles that 'by this service he accomplished almost nothing towards the object of his mission. For the count of Anjou invented fresh pretexts, when the first were removed, as excuses for not coming to England.'[8] It must have quickly become abundantly clear that the count never had any intention of coming to England in person, and might not be induced to offer any help at all. However, some hope was sparked in Earl Robert by the final proposal the count offered. It is not recorded how much effort it took on Earl Robert's part to secure this concession, but the fact that William of Malmesbury does not paint it as a diplomatic victory for the earl would seem to suggest that it was not one, and perhaps that it was Count Geoffrey's idea. Robert was permitted to take the oldest son of the empress and the count back to England with him.

The boy, Henry of Anjou, sometimes referred to as Henry FitzEmpress in reference to his mother's, rather than his father's title, was nine years old. His father may have seen in the expedition to England a chance to introduce his heir to the problems of government and even expose him to some military campaigning. If so, England might have offered a somewhat gentler training ground than the continent. The Normans prided themselves in their often brutal response to attackers, having willingly burned their own homes and property more than once to stop it falling into Angevin hands. In this same year, 1142, the dispute that rumbled on between King Stephen's older brother Theobald, Count of Blois and Champagne and his feudal lord King Louis VII had turned terrifyingly ugly. The root of the quarrel seems to have lain in Louis' giving of permission for his seneschal, Raoul, Count of Vermandois to repudiate his wife and marry one of the sisters of Louis' wife instead. The problem was that Raoul's first wife had been Eleanor of Blois, a sister of Theobald. The count had taken the slight to his family's honour seriously and had chosen to take the side of the pope against Louis in a dispute over land. The tension resulted in a military attack on Champagne by Louis during which the French king ordered the burning of the town of Vitry-en-Perthois, including the church there, with 1,300 people locked inside. The disgrace of this episode played no small part in eventually causing Louis to withdraw and hand Champagne back to Theobald.

It is striking that, for all the famously poetic and dramatic passages penned by chroniclers in England, there was no comparable incident during nineteen years of civil war. No senior figure was killed on a battlefield or during a siege. Towns such as Winchester had been torched when they were the focus of action by both sides, but all that was recorded in Bishop Henry's city was that a church was burned that had been full of treasure. That is entirely different from one with 1,300 people locked inside to perish in the flames. The Anarchy draws its name from the sense, created by the commentators at the time, that England was lawless, vicious and savage during the period with no stability provided by a government and pernicious barons free to behave as outrageously as they wished. Yet there is no single event on a par with King Louis' actions at Vitry-en-Perthois, and in 1142, Count Geoffrey was happy enough to send his nine-year-old son and heir to England. If it were anywhere near as bad as it has been described in the nine centuries that have followed, it would have seemed madness for Geoffrey to let little Henry travel there. In some respects, it appears as though England might have been seen as a safer, more gentle introduction for the boy than anything that was going on in Normandy, Anjou or France. Count Geoffrey and Earl Robert must have been confident that the boy would be free from the serious risk of harm, a certainty that seems at odds with the chroniclers' description of a dystopian nightmare gripping the country.

In England, King Stephen had been trying to make the most of Earl Robert's absence. Just as the earl had feared, the removal of him as the empress's second-in-command had been seized upon as an opportunity to damage her cause. With a return to his lightning movements, Stephen appeared utterly unexpectedly at Wareham. The port, just west of Bournemouth and sheltered in a natural harbour that is protected to the south by Corfe Castle, was regularly used by the empress's supporters as a safe route from their west-country base to the coast and across the sea. It was from here that Earl Robert had departed and Stephen looked to take an opportunity to slam the door behind him. William of Malmesbury explains that Stephen came so suddenly that he was able to set fire to the town and take the castle with no resistance at all. There may have been a secondary purpose to this strike. As well as removing the safe port from the empress's hands and making Earl Robert's return to England more difficult, an attack into the region of the empress's power would cause fear amongst her followers. She was still at Oxford, but it would soon become clear that those who had provided hostages as surety of their pledge to remain at her side had left her. It seems feasible that the assault on Wareham served the dual purpose of shutting Earl Robert out of England and luring those about the empress at Oxford back west in fear for their own lands.

As September drew to a close, King Stephen appeared outside Oxford, and finding it only lightly protected set about taking control of, and perhaps burning, the town.[9] William of Malmesbury claimed that the empress was at Oxford with no more than her household knights. The implication is that the other men who had sworn to remain at her side were no longer there, and as they frantically began to gather at Wallingford to work out how to rescue the empress, it becomes more clear that they had abandoned her. Whether this was because of the fear that Stephen was looking to grab back swathes of the west country while Earl Robert was absent and they were all in Oxford, or whether they had been sent away is not clear. The author of the *Gesta Stephani* is keen at this point to recall that the empress was 'always breathing a spirit of unbending haughtiness'[10] and it is not impossible that she had dismissed the men lingering and fussing around her in Robert's absence. For someone trying to project the image of a ruler with a court operating about them, it would seem counterproductive to send her followers away without reason. The attack on Wareham was perhaps the cause of many leaving, possibly with the empress's blessing, to counter the king's new offensive.

Empress Matilda found herself quickly blockaded in at Oxford Castle as Stephen settled in for a siege. The king was reportedly adamant that 'the hope of no advantage, the fear of no loss should make him go away, unless the castle had been surrendered and the empress brought into his power'.[11] It seems that Stephen saw at Oxford an opportunity to enter the end game. Empress Matilda was isolated. Oxford had been well fortified with earthworks by Earl Robert before he had left,[12] so having easily taken the town, Stephen was able to defend his position as well as besiege the castle. Brian Fitz Count seems to have led the muster of the empress's absent followers at Wallingford, and his presence there gives some credence to the notion that Stephen had lured her supporters away with his attack on Wareham and that they had left with the empress's blessing. Brian's devotion to Empress Matilda is universally recognized as unwavering, so he seems the least likely to have wilfully abandoned her, yet he was outside Oxford now desperately trying to find a way to free her. Those gathering at Wallingford seem to have accepted that they were unable to directly attack the king at Oxford, in part because Earl Robert had made the place so defensible, but it could also suggest that their numbers were woefully lacking in comparison to Stephen's. They were left kicking their heels and desperately trying to work out how to break Empress Matilda out of Oxford Castle.

News of the fresh plight of his half-sister was quick to reach Earl Robert in Normandy. Doubtless one of the paths taken by those congregating at Wallingford was to send desperate messages to the earl across the Channel. In the absence of the empress, it was to Earl Robert that they would turn for direction and leadership and, as ever, he was not slow in providing it. Whether Count Geoffrey was a willing donor to the cause or was pressed to offer more help by an increasingly agitated Earl Robert is impossible to tell, as by when he set sail from Normandy, the earl brought with him not only his young nephew. Henry FitzEmpress was now embarking on an adventure to rescue his mother, accompanied by more than 300 knights in fifty-two ships. The earl may have been able to raise some of these from his own Norman lands, but it seems likely that such a fleet had been not prepared and equipped without the active involvement of Count Geoffrey. Whatever amusement he had gained at the expense of his wife and her need to ask him for assistance, it was a different matter to find her besieged and under genuine threat. Geoffrey could not ignore the chivalric imperative to protect his wife in the face of such direct action. It perhaps made the decision to send young Henry a little harder, but neither Geoffrey nor Robert can have felt the personal danger to the boy was too great, even now.

There is one more intriguing insight offered by William of Malmesbury before the earl and his nephew set out for England. When recording the decision of Count Geoffrey to allow his son to travel to England, William noted the count would 'allow the boy's uncle to take to England his eldest son by the empress, so that on seeing him the nobles might be inspired to fight for the cause of the lawful heir. The boy is called Henry, recalling his grandfather's name, and would he may some day recall his prosperity and his power.'[13] There was apparently some sense from Geoffrey that young Henry was the one behind whom the cause should now muster, at least in England. There might have been some final mischief in the count's mocking of his wife's chances, pointing out that their nine-year-old son had a better chance of success than she did. If Geoffrey was not quite so malicious, he could genuinely have believed that Matilda had irreparably destroyed her own cause by the end of 1141 and as autumn chilled the air of 1142, she was trapped within Oxford Castle. Introducing Henry now served several purposes, as well as providing an unspoken 'I told you so' if Geoffrey had always held that his wife was overreaching herself in England or would mismanage the business.

Henry offered a new focus for those around Empress Matilda if she had proven herself ill-suited to power. Rather than alienate those who had remained loyal, and in the hope of being able to attract some support away from Stephen, the boy would provide a refreshing element to his mother's cause in England. The introduction of such a young boy also served to make it clear that the empress's claim, which also became an Angevin claim in Henry's person, was not going away. There was another generation being prepared to keep up the fight, and Henry had two younger brothers as well, should anything happen to him. The next generation would not face the same problems their parents had either. If Empress Matilda's sex and personality were proving too much to overcome and Geoffrey's Angevin blood made him appear an unwelcome invader, then Henry offered solutions to all of these problems: he was male, a grandson of Henry I, and great-grandson of William the Conqueror. He had Norman blood, but also Angevin roots that brought a new scope to the potential of his rule. He offered, at least on the surface, the perfect antidote to all of the poisons, solving every issue, except that Stephen still occupied the throne.

Henry I might have envisaged, perhaps believing he would live longer than he did, that his grandson would take the throne after him. In that case, Matilda and Geoffrey were only ever meant to protect that inheritance for him, and promoting little Henry's claims now served to offer those conflicted about oaths given to Empress Matilda and to King Stephen who gave thought to the fact that Henry I might really have meant a clean slate. Of course, all of this presumes that the wishes of a king who had been dead for seven years still had any bearing on English politics, but time has a knack of adding a rose tint to the spectacles used to look back across it. More than that, those who had anything to lose would gain little from the prolonged stalemate, and however it was dressed up and served to them, they were hungry for a resolution that could be accepted by all. The belief that barons and magnates thrived on the uncertainty of war and the lack of supervision provided by an anarchic state is at odds with everything that can be discerned of most medieval noblemen. Some must have made the most of the confusion in 1141 to snatch what they could, but that does not mean all indulged their less noble inclinations, or that any wanted such lawlessness to prevail in the longer term. The attitude of some of the most significant magnates in England would become increasingly important, given their traditional reputation for revelling in the free hand The Anarchy gave them to dive into terror and bloodshed. For the moment, though, the arrival on the scene of the nine-year-old Henry of Anjou, FitzEmpress, brought a new dimension to the conflict that might have been as welcome to some as it was concerning to others.

Earl Robert seems to have toyed with the idea of landing at Southampton, a city that supported Stephen and seemed a suitable place to begin wreaking vengeance. The influence of a family named Veal appears to have stayed his hand. They were a prominent family of burgesses and seafarers whose relatives might also have been amongst Earl Robert's Norman tenants, and they successfully convinced the earl not to target Southampton for his landing.[14] Instead, the fleet arrived back at Wareham, Earl Robert hoping to tempt Stephen away from Oxford with the threat of the port's recapture. A siege was set, and after a short time, the garrison sought terms. As was traditional, they were permitted to appeal to King Stephen for help and, if it were not forthcoming by an appointed date, they would surrender the castle to Earl Robert.[15] Aside from the growing impatience of waiting for that date, it suited Robert either to lure the king away from the empress and thus relieve her situation, or else to regain Wareham and claim a swift victory against Stephen on his return. True to his word, King Stephen would not be moved from the walls of Oxford Castle until the siege was won, so Wareham was given over to Earl Robert and his young nephew, who was already learning valuable lessons.

In short order, the force from Normandy, as yet unsupported by any English knights, took a castle that the king's men had erected on the Isle of Portland just west of Wareham. They then quickly won Lulworth Castle, which stood between Wareham and Portland.[16] The victories were swiftly and easily earned, but none drew the attention of the king away from Oxford. Earl Robert called a muster at Cirencester on 29 November to gather what forces he could add to his 300 knights from Normandy and launch a rescue attempt to free Empress Matilda. King Stephen was rumoured to have had something like a thousand knights with him so Earl Robert can have been under no illusions. He would need every fighting man he could get. When he had a sufficient number of men at his disposal, Earl Robert marched out of Cirencester for Oxford as December began and winter bit hard. He did not get far.

At Oxford, the snow had begun to fall, blanketing the countryside in a crisp white covering, but the bitter cold was matched by the chilling siege. Things within the walls of the castle were becoming as bleak as the pale winter sky as food and water began to run out. King Stephen remained resolutely outside the walls, protected by the earthworks his foes had provided and battering the castle relentlessly with siege engines. It was doubtful that the garrison would hold out much longer and as the weeks had turned into months and the temperature plummeted, it must have become plain to all inside that help was not coming. They could hardly know that Earl Robert had just left Cirencester with a vast force that trudged through the snow towards them, even as they began to despair.

It was at this moment that Empress Matilda took a decision that was one of her most famous and defining choices.[17] Just as the castle appeared on the brink of capitulation, the empress took a bold and daring step that would not only ensure her personal position in the history books, but which also made certain that her cause, and that of her sons, was kept firmly alive. As the snow thickened, the River Thames outside the castle froze over. During the darkness of the freezing cold night, the empress and three knights selected to accompany her slipped out of the castle. In some accounts, they were lowered down from windows with rope, but others hint that they used a postern gate to escape. The company of four wore white cloaks to offer some camouflage against the heavy snow and made their way on foot across the frozen Thames. They picked their way through the pickets and encampments of the king's besieging army, managing to go entirely unnoticed as men shouted and trumpets blared. They walked six miles on foot through the snow, a draining experience in the disorientating darkness through a landscape concealed by crisp white snowfall. They reached Wallingford before morning and, exhausted and freezing cold, entered the sanctuary of that castle's walls.

It was the news of this miraculous turn of events that reached Earl Robert as he marched on Oxford. William of Malmesbury's narrative sadly ends at this moment. Although full of bias in favour of Earl Robert, the patron he ceaselessly admired, his *Historia Novella* is packed with critical information on the period and his voice will be missed as the story continues. William had heard no details by the time he set down his version of events and could only offer that 'I should certainly be pleased to add the manner of the empress's escape if I had sure knowledge of it, for it is a manifest miracle of God.' He concluded his manuscript by offering that 'I am, however, disposed to go into this more thoroughly if ever by the gift of God I learn the truth from those who were present.'[18]

The writer of the *Gesta Stephani* wished to imbue this moment with some biblical, Christ-like meaning. He pointed out that the river had been high when Stephen's army had been forced to cross it, yet now the empress and her companions walked across the same path, the lady herself reaching the other bank dry footed and without any dampness on the hem of her dress. The chronicler was almost at a loss to explain why it had happened: it was obviously divine intervention. What mystified the author was why God had chosen to facilitate Empress Matilda's escape that night. It was, he thought, either so that her fame might be magnified throughout later generations, as it indeed has been, or it was a sign that God had not finished punishing the kingdom and meant the civil strife to continue by aiding the empress's flight.[19] Either way, there was no small amount of admiration for the empress's daring in making her audacious bid for freedom.

19

King Stephen

> Seeing that the enemy had assembled in great force and advanced from the city, that some, with only the river in between, were provoking himself and his men with insulting language, and some were doing very grievous harm to his men from the other side of the river by vigorous archery, on being shown an old, extremely deep ford he most gallantly plunged in himself among the foremost, swiftly made his way across by swimming rather than wading, furiously charged the enemy, and compelling them to retreat to the gates of the city joined battle with them with the greatest spirit.[1]

This was how Stephen arrived in Oxford on 26 September 1142: all anger, vigour and determination. When the news broke that the empress had slipped out of Oxford Castle during the night more than two months into the siege that was nearing its conclusion, hope and determination must have given way to frustration and despair. Stephen, though, was never one to wallow in his misfortunes and perhaps despair never entered his mind, merely leaving space for annoyed regret at such a good chance lost. The empress had evaded his grasp for the moment, and there was nothing to be done about that. As he considered the merits of pursuing the siege into which he had invested so much time and money now that the main aim was out of reach, the garrison broke and offered to surrender the castle. With the empress gone they risked only their own necks by holding out against the king, who might vent his failure to capture her on those left within if they tested him. On the bright side, the *Gesta Stephani* noted that Stephen quickly placed his own garrison into Oxford Castle and 'exercised absolute authority over a very wide tract of country in that region'.[2] It had not been a complete loss, and he had not been faced with another army led by Robert, Earl of Gloucester. Yet.

King Stephen spent Christmas 1142 at Canterbury in what must have been a gesture of thanks for that region's resilience and loyalty under the leadership of Queen Matilda and William of Ypres. The year had not gone well despite his best efforts to re-establish himself. Illness, no doubt a lingering price of his imprisonment, had robbed him of part of the year in which he might have launched a refreshed bid to restore his authority. The empress had slipped through his fingers at Oxford when the castle had been on the very brink of falling. Earl Robert had been absent in Normandy for months, but in remaining entirely committed at Oxford, Stephen had not been able to capitalize on the lack of leadership everywhere else. Had he succeeded in taking Empress Matilda into his custody, it would have proven a worthwhile investment that might have changed the course of the struggle, but her escape made the whole affair look like a giant waste of time and money and a conspicuous failure. As the regions that remained loyal to him shrank, so did the king's ability to raise money, and as the deep well of cash bequeathed by Henry I began to run dry, Stephen would find it harder and harder to pay the mercenaries he relied on.

As Lent began in 1143, King Stephen set about probing the borders of his authority, looking for weak spots. He set up a small, highly mobile force that could move almost undetected through the countryside, scouting castles and reconnoitring their defences, even burning crops and disrupting supplies where it was simple to do so. It was not an army equipped or expected to conduct sieges but might well have been designed to identify the softest targets to help Stephen calculate his next moves. When they arrived at Wareham and found it well defended, the strike force retired north a little, towards Salisbury, and sent word to Winchester that a large army would be needed to retake the port. It must have been Stephen's primary objective because the king did gather his forces and arrive at Wareham soon afterwards to try and snatch back the castle once more. Cutting off the empress from overseas aid was even more critical now that Count Geoffrey appeared to be taking a more active interest in England and as he tried to reimpose himself, Stephen could not let the losses he had suffered in remaining focused on Oxford go unopposed any longer. When he got to Wareham, though, the king found the castle far too well defended to provide an easy victory. Stephen fell back to Wilton just west of Salisbury and decided to strengthen the castle there, probably to use as a base of operations against the empress's faction. He had succeeded in driving them firmly back to their West Country heartland and perhaps saw Wilton as the perfect launchpad to keep pressing them into submission.

When Earl Robert understood what King Stephen was attempting to achieve he ordered all of those loyal to the empress to make for Wilton to offer battle to the king's army there. The earl must have been aware that their cause was firmly on the back foot and that if they allowed Stephen time at Wilton, he might craft himself an unassailable base from which to keep them pinned back indefinitely. When news reached Wilton of the approach of the empress's army, led by Earl Robert, Stephen arrayed his own knights on the outskirts of the town to meet them. Undaunted, Earl Robert marched right up to the king's lines on 1 July 1143 and deployed his own men into three battles ready to fight. There is some uncertainty as to whether there was actually an armed confrontation at Wilton. The author of the *Gesta Stephani* certainly believes that there was, stating that Robert 'carefully divided those he had brought with him into three bodies of men closely packed together and heavily charging his opponents with the greatest resolution compelled the king to give ground.'[3]

King Stephen, perhaps twice shy after being bitten at Lincoln, retreated from Wilton with all possible haste. Bishop Henry, back at his brother's side, joined him in flight and it is possible that Stephen this time surrendered to counsel that he should not risk a pitched battle again. It would be hard to argue with such advice after the disasters of Lincoln and the repercussions. The still sympathetic author of the *Gesta Stephani* believed it was the right course of action, concerned that had the king stood and fought he would 'most discreditably have fallen into enemy hands a second time.'[4] William Martel and his men remained behind and gave battle as well as they could. It is not clear whether they refused to withdraw or offered to stay behind to cover the king's retreat, but many of them, including William Martel himself, were captured. With the monkish disapproval typical of his class, the writer of the *Gesta Stephani* grumbled that Earl Robert and his men torched Wilton, a traditional charge if not a traditional tactic, adding that they broke into churches and nunneries in the area to drag men out.

Earl Robert was quick to capitalize on the victory, albeit without a fight, over the king. William Martel held Sherborne Castle in Dorset, which sat almost halfway between Yeovil on the south coast and the earl's stronghold at Bristol to the north. With his prisoner in tow, Earl Robert went directly to Sherborne and was quickly able to take the castle. It is hard to know what people made of news from Wilton. King Stephen was not a captive this time, but he had run away from Robert, so the garrison might legitimately have questioned whether they were now required to remain loyal to King Stephen. There was little need to explore the tricky question too far. Earl Robert demanded Sherborne as the ransom for William Martel and Stephen quickly agreed to secure the freedom of one of his most trusted men. The author of the *Gesta Stephani* betrays some of the narrow and intensely local interests of himself and his various colleagues writing chronicles during this period by describing Sherborne Castle as 'the master-key of the whole kingdom'.[5] If the writer was the Bishop of Bath or someone close to the bishop, then Sherborne, a royalist outpost between Angevin dominions lying just south of Bath, might have appeared a critical property in the struggle to control England, but it was not.

Sherborne must have held local significance for Earl Robert to be keen to grab it back, and it doubtless helped secure the corridor from the south coast to Bristol and the lands held in the empress's name. The chronicler recognizes its importance too, whilst perhaps over-egging the pudding a little. The truth of Sherborne's worth lay not only in a safe line of communication and travel but in the firm message that the fight was back on. Earl Robert had returned, bringing his nephew with him. Stephen had fled, and the empress's men were taking back castles from him. If the *Gesta*'s writer overestimated the national value of Sherborne, he was right enough in his assessment that Earl Robert and his allies 'made the kingdom subject to them far and wide'. His assertion that they, 'without any resistance from anyone put almost half of England, from sea to sea, under their own laws and ordinances'[6] sounds like another exaggeration. The land is narrow in the west country, and Bath was certainly in the process of being swallowed up by the expansion and consolidation of the region nominally under the control of Empress Matilda. Nevertheless, with Normandy almost lost, much of the north of England above the River Tees all but subsumed into the Scottish crown's lands and the empress controlling the south-west and pushing outward, half of Stephen's territory was no longer what it had been before the Battle of Lincoln. The comment is perhaps a signal of the perceived hopelessness of the situation.

The author of the *Gesta Stephani* cannot quite bring himself to abandon King Stephen and his cause just yet, though. He acknowledges that peace appeared to settle on those lands controlled by Earl Robert (never conceding that they were in the empress's power). Robert 'greatly adorned' his reputation by this restoration of order, except that as he tore down some castles and built new ones, the writer claims that the earl extracted forced labour from those in the region, also compelling them to fight for him when necessary. Nothing, the chronicler wryly noted, vexed the people more than being forced to work not for their own gain but for someone else's. More soberly, the writer described what settled in the south-west as a 'shadow of peace but not yet peace complete', because the people forced to demolish some castles and build other new ones were not oblivious to the fact that their enforced labours meant they were working towards the continuation of the strife that they wanted an end to.[7]

Wilton represented another setback for Stephen. If Lincoln had been in part a result of his desire not to repeat his father's mistakes at Antioch, at least in the sense that his retreat had permanently scarred his reputation, then at Wilton he had been forced to face the realities of his father's decisions in the Holy Land. That it remained better to escape and fight another day was an inescapable reality of a military system still predicated on siege warfare and the avoidance of pitched battles. Stephen had only been released in 1141 because those keeping his cause alive had managed to capture Earl Robert. He could not expect such providence a second time, and capture at Wilton might well have marked the end of his kingship. Aside from issues of his captivity and the efforts of the empress to establish herself again, having learned from her mistakes in 1141, few would continue to follow a king who kept trying to fight battles and kept losing. It was against this background that Stephen took his next controversial step, one that has been compared to his arrest of the bishops in June 1139.

Geoffrey de Mandeville had abandoned Stephen after the Battle of Lincoln, but with no more haste or apparent pleasure than most others facing an altered political reality. He stood out because he had managed to secure his own position at the same time, but he is hardly to be blamed for that. By the time of the Rout of Winchester, Geoffrey was back fighting for the king in Queen Matilda's army so he might appear far more committed to the royalist cause than that of the empress. Nevertheless, as he had done with the bishops in 1139, Stephen convinced himself, or allowed himself to be convinced, that Geoffrey still meant him harm. As Earl of Essex and castellan of several vital fortresses, including the Tower of London, Geoffrey remained a man with a great deal of power focused tightly within what was now Stephen's heartland. As in 1139, it is hard to unpick whether there was genuine concern from the king and those around him based on evidence, whether paranoia caused Stephen to see threats where there were none, or whether the scheme was merely an invention to excuse the confiscation of critical tactical properties. The reason for Stephen's actions is crucial to understanding his personality and style of rule, yet it remains frustratingly elusive. If there were any genuine doubt about Geoffrey's intentions, then it would be foolish of the king to ignore it, particularly as it affected the region that remained most loyal to him. If it were the creation of a devious, frightened mind, then it would expose the king's weakness and a willingness to break the rules that governed noble society which would alienate many from him.

Although the *Gesta Stephani* praises Geoffrey de Mandeville as 'a man alike remarkable for the ability of his shrewd mind and to be admired for the firmness of his unbending courage in adversity and his excellence in the art of war', the chronicle also tells of rumours about his loyalty.[8] Stephen was warned by those around him that Geoffrey secretly favoured the empress's cause and planned to improve his own position by being the man who secured the throne of England for her. His control of the Tower of London, in particular, made him well placed to make this offer, and it had been the reason the empress had courted him before trying to take control of London in 1141. Geoffrey's changing allegiances that year no doubt provided colour for the accusation, but were not out of line with the actions of a good many of his contemporaries. A whispering campaign was begun, and Stephen was warned that Geoffrey meant to betray him and counselled to brand the earl a traitor and seize his castles to improve the king's security. William of Newburgh considered that Stephen had conceived a determination to destroy Geoffrey after the latter had imprisoned Constance of France in the Tower during 1141.[9] Constance had been married to Stephen's son Eustace the previous year and, as the daughter of King Louis VI of France, she represented a significant alliance, and Stephen had been exposed as unable to protect her, risking his friendship with Louis. The author of the *Gesta Stephani* may have hit a nerve when he hinted that

Stephen's jealousy of Geoffrey might have added to the problems, not least by making rumours that he planned to join the empress all the more threatening. The writer noted of Geoffrey that 'everywhere in the kingdom he took the king's place and in all transactions was listened to more eagerly than the king and received more obedience when he gave orders.'[10] The reasons for Stephen's decision to turn against Geoffrey must have been complex, and it is doubtful that it was an easy choice.

When the king's counsel met at St Albans for Michaelmas 1143, a scuffle broke out between Geoffrey de Mandeville and some of the other barons, presumably those close to Stephen who had advised him to deal harshly with the earl. It was an almost precise repeat of the brawling that had led to Bishop Roger's arrest in 1139, and in the arguing, Geoffrey was openly accused of treason. The earl laughed off the charges; he gave them no credence and so offered no defence, treating it as though it were a joke. His response was taken as a sign of guilt, though almost certainly an effort to defend himself would have been too. Geoffrey was arrested along with his retinue in breach of the safety he was entitled to rely on at the king's court, though if he were guilty of breaching the peace or evidence of treason existed, then the move would have been more reasonable. Instead, King Stephen has since languished in disdain because of the belief that he engineered both incidents as an excuse to arrest first the bishops, and now Geoffrey. It is that kind of sneaky, underhand and dishonourable trick that is at odds with the more general perception of Stephen not only in some quarters as a weak man but in most as one with much, perhaps too much, respect for the rules of chivalry that governed a knight's behaviour. The very fact that he chose to behave in the same manner again, knowing the problems it had caused in 1139, points either to belligerent stupidity or some substance to the charges against the men in both instances. Bishop Roger in 1139 and Geoffrey de Mandeville in 1143 are generally considered the innocent victims of Stephen's ruthless trickery, but it is as likely there was some substance to at least the suspicion that they were up to something.

The price of Geoffrey de Mandeville's release was the handover of the Tower of London and his castles at Saffron Walden and Pleshey. Their locations in and around London placed them at the heart of Stephen's remaining power base and so it is easy to see a baseless scheme to take them from Geoffrey in the king's actions. Stephen must have been aware that he would be irreparably fracturing his relationship with Geoffrey and either he deemed these three fortresses worth driving such a wealthy, powerful and militarily experienced man into opposition, or he genuinely feared Geoffrey was already too far along that road anyway. If it was the former, then he risked handing the empress a significant and well-placed ally and cannot have been blind to that fact. Disciplining barons was notoriously fraught during a civil war because they had another hearth at which to warm their feet rather than waiting out in the cold until their penance was complete. In arresting Geoffrey de Mandeville, Stephen knew precisely what he was doing, though it is almost impossible to tell now whether that was wilfully and spitefully making an enemy for a quick gain of castles, or nipping a genuine threat in the bud. On this point, Henry of Huntingdon notes the whiff of some genuine threat. Although he believed the arrest was 'an act more fitting the earl's desserts than public right, more expedient than just', he is also very clear that 'if he had not taken this step, the king would have been driven from the throne'.[11]

Predictably, as soon as he was released, Geoffrey flew to arms and began to 'rage everywhere with fire and sword'.[12] What may have concerned Stephen was that he did not head west into the welcoming bosom of the empress's faction. Instead, Geoffrey went to the Isle of Ely, perhaps with the blessing of Bishop Nigel, who had experienced Geoffrey's pain in 1139 and where the earl might have known he would receive some sympathy. Bishop Nigel had been restored by the empress in 1141 after falling from favour with Stephen in the wake of his uncle Bishop Roger's death. Stephen had been at Huntingdon in November 1143, where he had put pressure on Walter, Abbot of Ramsey to resign because of his sympathy for the empress. The king had installed a monk named Daniel, who was suspected of being the man who had led the king through the marshes to assault Ely a few years earlier. The appointment was, therefore, his reward, but the king had ignored the canonical right of election and Daniel's arrival was not welcomed. Walter launched an appeal to Rome, and it was only eighteen days after Daniel's appointment that Geoffrey de Mandeville arrived at Ramsey. It was widely assumed that he had come to drive Daniel out and restore Walter, imposing order on the region as chaos threatened to erupt, but instead, the earl added to the disorder.

Stephen may, had his intentions been genuine, have begun to fear that he had misjudged Geoffrey and made a mistake. There was no declaration of support for Empress Matilda, even if the Abbey of Ramsey was suspected of favouring her, but Geoffrey was now firmly in opposition and preparing to make war against Stephen. From Ely, Geoffrey took control of the nearby Abbey of Ramsey, just to the west, where he drove out the monks and set about fortifying the church, 'turning the house of God into a den of thieves'.[13] Geoffrey vented his anger on the surrounding countryside in another episode that, however brief, has given body to the idea that Stephen's entire reign was awash with terror and blood. The earl secured several satellites around Ramsey, at Wood Walton in the south-west and Benwick and Chatteris to the north-east, which kept a line of communication with Ely open. He also held Fordham and Mildenhall and managed to sack Cambridge. Hugh Bigod, another man frequently disaffected from Stephen without being necessarily pro-Matilda, seems to have joined Geoffrey in causing trouble and the Abbot of Bury St Edmunds, who was a loyal servant of the king, reported much distress on his lands during this period.[14]

It may be a direct result of this incident that one of the most famous lamentations on the period was added to *The Anglo-Saxon Chronicle* at Peterborough, just thirteen miles north-west of Ramsey.

> I neither know nor may tell all the horrors and all the tortures that they did to the wretched men in this land. And it lasted the nineteen winters while Stephen was king; and ever it was worse and worse. They laid gelds on the villages from time to time and called it 'Tenserie'; when the wretched men had no more to give, they robbed and burnt all the villages so that you might well go a whole day's journey and you would never find a man occupying a village or land being tilled. Then was corn dear and meat and cheese and butter; because there was none in the land. Wretched men starved of hunger; some went seeking alms who at one time were rich men; others fled out of the land.
>
> There was never yet greater wretchedness in the land; and never did heathen men worse than they did. For too frequently they did not even abstain from churches and churchyards, but took all the property that was therein and afterwards burnt the church and all together. Nor did they abstain from bishop's land or abbot's or priest's, but robbed

> monks and clerks; and every man another who anywhere might. If two men or three came riding to a village, all the township fled before them, supposing them to be robbers. The bishop and clergy cursed them ever, but it was naught to them; for they were all accursed and forsworn and lost.
>
> Wheresoever men tilled, the earth bare no corn, for the land was ruined by such deeds; and they said openly that Christ and his saints were asleep. Such and more than we can say we endured nineteen winters for our sins.[15]

It is perhaps striking, though, that at the same point, the writer of the *Gesta Stephani*, with his focus usually reserved for the south-west, chose to paint an equally bleak picture. It is entirely possible that his sorrowful tone is a result of news from Peterborough. The ease with which such tidings seemed to travel, as will become more clear later, is difficult to understand if the entire countryside was filled with vicious bandits and no one was safe in their own home, in a church or on the roads. Nevertheless, the author complained that:

> At this time England began to be troubled in many different ways; on the one hand to be very hard pressed by the king and his supporters, on the other to be most violently afflicted by the earl of Gloucester; sometimes to endure the furious attacks of one party, sometimes the unbridled rage of the other; but always and everywhere to be in turmoil and to be reduced to a desert … You could see villages with famous names standing solitary and almost empty, because the peasants of both sexes and all ages were dead, fields whitening with a magnificent harvest (for autumn was at hand) but their cultivators taken away by the agency of a devastating famine, and all England wearing a look of sorrow and misfortune, an aspect of wretchedness and oppression. To crown all these evils there was the fact that a savage crowd of barbarians, who had swarmed to England in a body to serve as mercenaries, were affected neither by bowels of constipation nor by feelings of human pity over sufferings so many and so great, but everywhere in the castles they conspired with one mind to commit crime

> and outrage, were increasingly occupied in pillaging the goods of the poor, devoted all the zeal of their evil hearts to encouraging hostility on both sides and murdering men in every quarter.[16]

Stephen rushed into East Anglia to reduce the increasing unrest there, but found Geoffrey de Mandeville evasive and could do nothing to bring the earl to battle. Much as the Welsh had always done, and as Miles of Gloucester had learned to do, Geoffrey relied on guerrilla tactics to strike soft targets quickly and make sure he was gone before the royal army could arrive. Even the energetic and agile Stephen found himself chasing shadows. It was increasingly frustrating since it tied Stephen up in expensive manoeuvres but also made him appear incompetent. Geoffrey had the upper hand, and Stephen could think of only one response, however inadequate and undesirable it might be: he encircled the fens around Ely and Ramsey and placed garrisons into castles, though it is not clear how many of these were existing structures and how many were newly erected for the purpose. Each stronghold required a garrison, and so Stephen's forces became suddenly stationary. The king was robbed of his preference for mobility to greet threats, but he had not been able to draw this one out or catch it up.

Awareness of a perception of his immobility might have been behind Stephen's decision around May 1144 to try and lay siege to Lincoln. Ranulf, Earl of Chester had taken control of the castle there again, and the king arrived to begin the process of forcing him out. The siege was short lived, and Robert of Torigny claimed that this was because during the construction of the siege machinery, a section of it collapsed and killed eighty men.[17] Henry of Huntingdon says eighty of the king's men were suffocated in the trenches, suggesting that they were digging either defensive works or to undermine the castle when a collapse occurred.[18] Stephen was so upset, perhaps also taking the incident as a bad omen, that he packed up and marched straight out of Lincoln again. It was not a place he was likely to wish to linger if things were going badly. The king moved next to relieve a siege on Malmesbury Castle, where he was successful, but when he tried to assault Tetbury Castle in Gloucestershire he withdrew quickly when Earl Robert appeared with an army and offered battle. Stephen's taste for risking all on the throw of a die in a pitched confrontation had well and truly soured.

In the king's absence, Geoffrey had returned to harassing the garrisons left behind and trying to bring anyone else who considered Stephen an enemy into allegiance with him. Still there was no sense that he was acting in open favour of Empress Matilda, but only in opposition to Stephen, a sentiment he shared with Hugh Bigod. In August 1144, Geoffrey and his men were in the process of laying siege to Burwell Castle in Cambridgeshire, south-east of Ramsey, when the earl was injured. Henry of Huntingdon relates that Geoffrey was the only one hurt in the incident when he was struck by an arrow from a common soldier. The earl laughed off the wound,[19] but it must have turned septic because, on 16 September 1144, he died. Even then, his problems were not over. Bishop Henry had seen to it that Geoffrey had been excommunicated when he had rebelled, encouraging his fellow clergymen to make use of this ultimate sanction where required. Geoffrey made it easy by grabbing the abbey at Ramsey and using it as if it were a castle, but dying whilst languishing in a state of excommunication was the worst possible fate for Geoffrey's soul. Henry of Huntingdon pointed to another case that occurred at the same time in which Robert Marmion, who had seized and fortified a church in Coventry and was also excommunicated, sallied out with his men and was the only one killed, despite being surrounded by friends. 'Dying excommunicated, he became subject to death everlasting.' 'See here the like just judgment of God, memorable through all the ages!'[20]

The *Gesta Stephani* crowed that 'as in his lifetime he brought confusion on the church and turmoil on the land, so for his confusion the whole Church of England united, because he passed away stricken by the sword of excommunication and unabsolved, and as guilty of sacrilege he could not be put in the earth.'[21] The church refused to accept Geoffrey's body for burial in holy ground. His family had it encased in lead, and it was eventually accepted by the Templars for burial in the Temple Church in London, where Geoffrey's son paid for an effigy of his father to be placed on the floor. It is likely that Geoffrey had been accepted into the Templars on his deathbed and provided them with valuable endowments in Essex to procure their help for his soul. His coffin was initially kept in unconsecrated ground in the Old Temple but when he was absolved by the pope, his remains were translated to consecrated ground at the New Temple in 1163, where the effigy his son commissioned can still be seen.[22] In many ways, this episode represented a return to form for Stephen and a solid victory. Had Geoffrey been defeated more quickly, it might well have constituted a perfect campaign. The rebel earl, when he could not be caught, had been encircled to restrict his activities until he was killed. The king had the backing of the church and was seeking to punish an excommunicated dissident who had violated ecclesiastical property so that he was not only defending his own rights but the position of God's church too.

The relatively swift and well-executed victory is to be compared to Stephen's years of failure to deal decisively with his cousin the empress. Geoffrey de Mandeville was no fool. He had been an immensely powerful man, a wealthy magnate and his military ability was respected alongside his political skill, yet Stephen had been able to crush his revolt with little real trouble. His inability to deal with Empress Matilda and Earl Robert in the same way demonstrates either the strength of their position, which is usually deemed lacking, or some blockage on Stephen's part, perhaps preventing him being ruthless with a family member, a woman, or even someone whose claims he could not ignore in good conscience. Whatever had really happened in 1135, Stephen knew that he had previously given an oath to uphold and protect the rights of his cousin and that he had then reneged on that promise. Did that knowledge restrain him to some extent? Or was the military situation of the empress's faction stronger than it is generally given credit for being? Earl Robert was proving impossible for Stephen to defeat and the king was now actively avoiding engagements with the earl. With their solid, apparently unassailable block of power in the south-west, they might simply have become too strong to be defeated, even if they were not able to take the fight to Stephen and break his kingship. It created a stalemate that benefitted no one.

It is worthy of note too that Nigel, Bishop of Ely was actually absent from his see throughout this episode. Geoffrey may have travelled there because Bishop Nigel was sympathetic, but it might equally have been because there was a vacuum in the area that Geoffrey could exploit. During 1142, Stephen seemed to have relied on Geoffrey de Mandeville to counter the threat of Bishop Nigel, in particular keeping the bishop and Hugh Bigod apart to prevent them from cutting Stephen off from Norfolk and the East Midlands. That might mean that Geoffrey did not seek out the Bishop of Ely as an ally, but sought out his lands as easy pickings. Bishop Henry had used his legatine powers to summon Bishop Nigel before him and accuse him of inciting sedition, giving church lands to knights and depriving a priest of his church.[23] Unable to argue his case against the legate, Bishop Nigel was required to travel to Rome to explain his conduct to the pope and seek his forgiveness in 1143.

The king made sure the journey was neither quick nor easy. When Nigel arrived at Wareham to sail across the Channel, he had reportedly already met with the empress. He was greeted near Wareham by a band of Stephen's soldiers, perhaps the same mobile strike force that had been roaming the region examining enemy defences before retiring towards Salisbury to await the king's army. They robbed the bishop, and he was forced to return to Ely to get more money before setting out again. Bishop Nigel did not arrive in Rome until 1144, and the letters of forgiveness that he received from Pope Lucius II were dated 24 May 1144. It is possible that Bishop Henry was able to ensure that Nigel's case snagged in the Papal court and took as long as possible to reach Lucius. The Bishop of Ely did not return to his see until 1145, by which time the episode involving Geoffrey had reached its conclusion, so the precise relationship between Geoffrey and Nigel is unclear. By the end of the following year, 1145, Stephen would make his peace with the Bishop of Ely so that Hugh Bigod remained the only significant thorn in his eastern side. By reducing these threats, he would be able to focus his attention better on the real problem in the west. In that sense, 1144 had proven a reasonably successful year.

20

Empress Matilda

> Philip son of the Earl of Gloucester, a man of strife, supreme in savagery, daring in what should not be dared, in fact a perfect master of every kind of wickedness.[1]

As King Stephen's attempts to firmly re-establish his authority appeared to be gathering momentum, Empress Matilda's seemed doomed to stutter and splutter, never quite moving convincingly forward. William de Pont de l'Arche, who held the royal castle and treasury at Winchester, fell out spectacularly with the king's brother Henry, Bishop of Winchester. There were armed men in the streets, but William found himself frustrated in attempts to get the better of the bishop, who was well provided for in soldiers, legal expertise and the backing of the church. William had managed to avoid suspicion of his loyalty that would have been natural given his closeness to the empress's father, yet as his feud with Bishop Henry grew, he chose that moment to write to Empress Matilda to ask for her help.

The empress and her advisors were ecstatic when the request arrived. William would be a valuable man to turn to their side and might offer access to Winchester and the royal treasury. It would be an added bonus if they could break the authority of Bishop Henry too, and there was a sense that William was better placed to achieve that end than they had been. However, the empress found herself unable to send the knights and captain William desperately requested, and that must have stung her. It showed that, unlike the king, she was still unable to put large numbers of men in the field and that her support base was both narrow and ill-equipped to help her. The best that she could do, anxious not to pass up the opportunity that had fallen into her lap, was to send a band of mercenaries under the command of one Robert Fitz Hildebrand. Although of low birth, he was a proven military man, even if the *Gesta Stephani* complained that he was also 'a lustful man, drunken and unchaste'.[2]

Robert Fitz Hildebrand duly arrived at Winchester Castle to a warm welcome. He became fast friends with William and soon had the freedom to come and go as he pleased in Winchester. Robert's baser instincts then got the better of him. The mercenary captain seduced William's wife and hatched a plot with her that saw William seized and placed in chains within his own dungeon as Robert enjoyed his castle, his money and his wife. The pair then made their peace with the king and Bishop Henry, but their victory was short-lived. The *Gesta Stephani*, applying the typical monkish flourish of divine retribution, took some pleasure in recounting Robert's death. Soon, 'a worm was born at the time when the traitorous corrupter lay in the unchaste bosom of the adultress and crept through his vitals, and slowly eating away his entrails it gradually consumed the scoundrel, and at length, in affliction of many complaints and the torment of many dreadful sufferings, it brought him to his end by a punishment he richly deserved.'[3] Robert Fitz Hildebrand had little to recommend him to a religious man, so his fate was divine punishment, justly delivered for the sins he had revelled in committing.

The episode made plain just how short of reliable support the empress was, but there was worse to come before the year was out. Miles of Gloucester, who had been made Earl of Hereford by Empress Matilda in 1141, began to run short of money to keep paying the troops he maintained in the field. Miles had been one of the empress's earliest and most committed supporters in England, and she seems to have viewed the man, who was perhaps a decade her senior, as something of a father figure. It was to his city and castle at Gloucester that she had gone when she needed a base of operations. Miles had been central to efforts to establish Matilda as Lady of the English in 1141 and had never deserted her cause. In his desperation to keep up this support, he began to extract ever harsher taxes across the lands he controlled until he came up against Robert de Bethune, Bishop of Hereford. Miles insisted that Bishop Robert make a significant contribution, but the bishop declared that the money belonged to the church and could no more be demanded or used to pay soldiers than the ritual objects that adorned the altar.

Miles was enraged and set about pillaging the bishop's churches and lands to gather the money he needed. Bishop Robert excommunicated the earl and maintained the sentence so strictly that throughout Miles's territory, no church service could be conducted, no baptism given and no funeral or burial performed. The interdict worked quickly, and Miles offered to repay all that he had taken, pleading with others, often clergymen, to act as guarantors. When all was agreed, the excommunication was lifted, and Miles began to pay back the money, but on Christmas Eve, 24 December 1143, Miles was struck by a stray arrow fired by a hapless knight whilst out hunting, and he died of the wound. He left several churches burdened with repaying the money stolen from the bishop since he had convinced priests to act as sureties for his debt, but the *Gesta Stephani* suggests that such a blatant display of God's swift justice discouraged many other rich men from targeting church money to line their own pockets with.[4]

Across the Channel, things were going better for the Angevin cause. Count Geoffrey's slow and patient campaign finally paid off. In 1142 he had won control of Avranches, Coutance and most of the Cotentin region so that the west of Normandy was under his control. Cherbourg, at the northern tip of the Cotentin Peninsula, fell in 1143 along with Verneuil and La Vaudreuil further east. In January 1144, Count Geoffrey crossed the River Seine and marched up to the walls of Rouen, the duchy's capital city. The inhabitants opened the gates to him on 20 January and the count set about laying siege to the castle. The citadel was garrisoned by William de Warenne, Earl of Surrey, a great-grandson of King Henry I of France and second cousin to Louis VII whose daughter Isabel would marry Stephen's younger son William. William remained loyal to Stephen, despite the vacillations of his half-brothers the Beaumont twins, and he held out with his men for three months. The castle finally surrendered on 23 April 1144. Count Geoffrey was almost immediately invested as Duke of Normandy, ceding Gisors and the Vexin to King Louis VII in return for the French king's recognition of the Count of Anjou as the new Duke of Normandy.

The final success of her husband in Normandy had several impacts on Empress Matilda in England. In a number of ways, it bolstered her otherwise stagnating cause. Any of her followers who abandoned her now would face the inevitable loss of any lands they had in Normandy. The lingering preference for a single ruler by those who owed allegiance for properties in England and Normandy meant that the empress became a more attractive and viable prospect as her husband tightened his grip on Normandy. Stephen was in no position to even try and regain what Geoffrey had assiduously gathered for himself, so many barons were faced with the prospect of trying to juggle fealty to King Stephen and his enemy Count, now Duke, Geoffrey or suffer the loss of their lands and titles on one side of the Channel or the other. Geoffrey's advances also counteracted the stalemate in England, since the Angevin cause began to appear the only party making real headway against the other.

The benefits of Duke Geoffrey's victory did not come without problems for his wife. More than ever, it was hard to see how Empress Matilda would fit into any final settlement. It was abundantly clear that Geoffrey had not conquered Normandy for his wife or in her name. The Duchy of Normandy was now firmly an Angevin possession. For those with lands on both sides of the Channel, it still begged the question of who would rule England if the empress was successful: her, or her husband. If the fiery couple were to fall out again, with perhaps their marriage even being annulled, what would then become of the two regions and the hope of a single ruler? Furthermore, Stephen was compelled to accept that Normandy was lost and beyond recovery and although he might never have hoped for such a loss, it meant that he was free to focus all of his efforts in England. The steady progress the king had made during 1143 and 1144 might have been in no small part due to his release from further concern about the fate of Normandy. That made Stephen a more dangerous opponent with less to worry about.

Another question that was raised by Duke Geoffrey's victory was the future role his son and heir Henry of Anjou might play. The duke appears to have possessed an almost prophetic vision of the boy's impending prominence, at least on the continent. The lad was back with his father by March 1144 at Angers, perhaps with a view to training for the more likely situation that he would take some responsibility in Normandy or Anjou soon. Geoffrey's own father had handed over the county of Anjou to the sixteen-year-old Geoffrey so that he could go to Jerusalem and now, Geoffrey might have felt it was right to begin his eleven-year-old son's real apprenticeship. The boy had had an adventure in England, but it is likely Geoffrey viewed all of that as a distraction, though it helped his aims in Normandy by tethering Stephen to England. In 1145, Duke Geoffrey wrote a letter to his son asking him to show favour to the monks at Vendôme and suggesting the great things that awaited Henry.

> Since, God willing, I believe that you will succeed me in the governance of my land, I ask you to protect the abbey of Vendôme by every means in your power … For our

> predecessors founded this house and have defended it vigorously up to now. I for my part have never failed to provide help and counsel when need arose. So I bid you, who by the grace of God will surpass me and all my predecessors in power and dignity, to take the monks of Vendôme into your protection, and see that they suffer no wrong.[5]

Henry FitzEmpress arrived in England with his uncle Earl Robert with the suggestion that he might become a renewed focus for his mother's efforts. He had made no real impact and left again to return to his father. The problem was that the waters had been muddied and no questions had been answered. Was Henry now to be the figurehead of efforts in England? Did the empress accept that she would never become queen and that her best hope was to promote her son as the next king? Did Henry's recall to his father mean that the effort in England was being abandoned or sidelined? If nobody knew what was happening, then it was all the more difficult for them to make up their minds who to back.

Malmesbury Castle, just to the east of Bristol, had remained a royal fortress since Stephen had confiscated it from Bishop Roger of Salisbury in 1139. Despite its proximity to Earl Robert's impenetrable heartlands, it had for years held fast for the king against all attempts to besiege or assault it. A chance to win a tactically significant victory came in 1145 when William Peverel of Dover, the empress's castellan at Cricklade Castle just thirteen miles north-east of Malmesbury, managed to capture Walter de Pinkeney. Walter was Stephen's castellan at Malmesbury and was trapped whilst outside the castle. Taken before the empress, Walter was threatened with torture and death unless he handed over the vital outpost, but he stoically refused. Even had he been inclined to respond to the intimidation, it is unlikely he would have been able to actually effect a surrender. On hearing of Walter's capture, King Stephen had swooped in to reinforce Malmesbury, clearly unwilling to risk losing such a valuable asset. Infuriated, the empress ordered that Walter be chained up in a dungeon and 'delivered him to torment',[6] fulfilling her threat to have him tortured. Just like Stephen, Empress Matilda was finding it hard to win victories even when opportunities presented themselves.

Soon after this episode, William Peverel abandoned his post at Cricklade Castle, apparently struck by sudden remorse at the 'woes and sufferings that he had pitilessly brought on the people'[7]. It is tempting to wonder whether the empress's torture of Walter had been enough to make William decide he no longer wished to follow her. Whatever his reasons, William set off to join the Second Crusade where he was eventually killed fighting for the church, and thus 'he died a blessed death'.[8]

He was replaced at Cricklade by Philip, one of the sons of Robert, Earl of Gloucester. The author of the *Gesta Stephani* had nothing good to say about this 'man of strife, supreme in savagery, daring in what should not be dared, in fact a perfect master of every kind of wickedness'.[9] Philip began at Cricklade with ruthless aggression, conceiving a particular rivalry with William de Chainai, the king's man at Oxford. The two frequently engaged in armed scuffles and Philip ravaged the land in the region to such an extent that the writer of the *Gesta Stephani* claimed 'they left nothing in that region but a spectacle of strife and woe.'[10]

Philip soon suggested to his father that they would be able to take Oxford if they pressed harder and built castles in a few suitable locations that would restrict the garrison's movements. It was a similar tactic to that employed by Stephen to break Geoffrey de Mandeville's rebellion, and Earl Robert willingly agreed to support his son's scheme. In particular, Earl Robert built a new fortress at Faringdon and placed within it some of his best men to keep the king's forces pinned back at Oxford. William de Chainai felt he had little choice but to appeal to King Stephen for immediate aid. Stephen dropped what he was doing and rushed to Oxford, where he spent several days calling in reinforcements until he had enough of an army to march against the enemy. Preparing for a long siege at Faringdon, Stephen ordered the construction of a stockade and ramparts to protect his own force from a sudden attack. So, the castle built to oppress Oxford at Faringdon was now suppressed by a counter-castle of its own.

Stephen's men set up siege engines and encircled the castle with archers, so that it was bombarded relentlessly. Those within defended Faringdon Castle with resolution until, unbeknownst to them, their commanders made terms with the king and arranged the surrender of the new fortress. Not long afterwards, Earl Robert's son Philip suddenly defected to the king in something of a coup for Stephen but a blow to the empress and her half-brother. It was rumoured that Stephen had granted Philip vast amounts of land and castles as well as expensive presents to lure him over, but it is possible that the fall of Faringdon played a part in the break. The plan had been Philip's, and if he had appealed to his father for support that had not come, then he may have become bitter and disaffected. Although it is nowhere confirmed, it is possible that Philip was amongst those in command at Faringdon, and he had asked his father for help when Stephen surrounded them, but Earl Robert had ignored his plight. If that were the case, it would have been a sharp contrast to the king's response to the appeal of his men at Oxford and it might have been enough to make Philip punish his father by defecting to Stephen. He proved incredibly active in the service of his new liege lord after doing homage to the king.

Empress Matilda was finding the effort in England hard going during these years. Her husband had finally achieved victory in Normandy, but there was no sign of England falling in the wake of that gain. In fact, it might have made things worse for her because it was now evident that Normandy belonged to Geoffrey by right of conquest, not to Matilda by inheritance. Young Henry had been spirited back to his father's side, giving the appearance that Normandy and Anjou were where the serious business was being conducted. What was more, if Earl Robert could not even keep his own son on his side, others might be encouraged to abandon the empress in favour of a resurgent king, and those wavering from the king would be discouraged from rebelling by his show of strength and resilience. The deadlock was maintained, but it now looked as though the king was in the ascendant and that Empress Matilda was struggling to keep afloat.

21

King Stephen

> Then, after the earl had thus been freed, when he should have followed peace and kept the faith he had promised, he followed his inclination and flew to arms, and breaking the promise that bound him and disregarding the virtue of his oath he resolutely girded himself and his men to stir up strife against the king.[1]

Stephen was less frequently surrounded by his earls as his reign went on. Often seen as a sign that either they stayed away because their loyalty was no longer reliable or that he had lost trust in them, it is just as possible that they were kept busy in the regions. If Stephen had created them deliberately to provide military representation across the kingdom, then their absence is merely a signal that they were working as required. Names of new men began to appear more regularly as signatories of the king's charters. After 1142, men like William Martel (181 charters), Robert de Vere (142 charters) and Richard de Lucy (135 charters) were prominent, and others, such as Richard de Camville (sixty-three charters), William de Chesney (twenty-two charters) and Henry of Essex (thirty-seven charters) appeared frequently.[2] In those years, 74 per cent of all Stephen's charters were witnessed at London,[3] demonstrating his focus on the capital as an administrative centre but also a secure place where loyalty was not in doubt.

The year 1146 saw the return of an old, familiar, moustachioed face. In reality, Ranulf, Earl of Chester had never gone away. In 1140, the earl had fallen out with the king and had sought out his father-in-law Robert, Earl of Gloucester for assistance in the dispute centred on Lincoln. Ranulf's flirtation with the empress's cause had very little to do with his belief in her claim and everything to do with getting back what he believed was his. The plight of Earl Robert's daughter, trapped inside Lincoln Castle by the king, was natural leverage to use in trying to move her father and a new, mighty magnate appearing to show interest in the empress's cause was too tempting to turn away from. As Empress Matilda edged to power in 1141, Earl Ranulf must have begun to feel uneasy in her fold. A large part of the reason the earl had become disgruntled with the king was the concessions Stephen had made to King David, which Ranulf felt infringed on his own rights. What he had failed to foresee was that any regime under the empress would have even closer ties to Scotland and her uncle. Since 1141, King David had not been checked but had gained more territory in the north, pressing against Ranulf's lands in the north-west. The earl just might have realized that what Stephen had done had been to give a little to protect a lot, whereas the empress was allowing David to take what he liked. Having abandoned Stephen in a rage, the king began to seem more and more like the natural harbour for Ranulf's allegiance.

The desire, or need, for a man such as Ranulf to find a home for his loyalty is striking in the context of what is called The Anarchy. Barons are generally considered to have run amok, unfettered by central control and free to wreak havoc, rob, pillage and torture as they pleased. Earl Ranulf, in particular, was no minor nobleman. According to some contemporary estimations, he was in possession of around a third of Stephen's kingdom.[4] Although that might sound like an exaggeration, given the shrinking of the area that can be considered, even nominally, under Stephen's control by this point, the swathes of land in Cheshire and in the Midlands around Lincoln that Ranulf could claim dominion over made up a significant land mass. Ranulf might be amongst those most likely to act in the way tradition ascribes to nobles of The Anarchy. He had abandoned the king, yet was not really committed to the empress's cause. Why, then, did he not just go it alone, stay on his lands and rule like a tyrant in his own miniature kingdom, or even launch a bid for a crown of his own in part or all of England?

Answering that question is key to understanding what was really going on during the civil conflict that revolved around the crown of England in the twelfth century. Monks would have us all believe that the country spent nineteen years living in terror, famine and constant warfare. The writer of the *Gesta Stephani* still insisted that at this time, 'all alike had one end of misfortune and wretchedness in view, to stretch forth the unbridled lust of their tyranny against the people, to break the peace and destroy the covenant of tranquillity and arouse the turmoil of strife.'[5] Although there were undoubtedly moments, flashpoints, when such horrors were unleashed, they were quickly caged again; fighting was not the norm, however much devastation to local people, lands and crops, and breaches in the peace it might have caused. If magnates had an interest in carving out autonomous power for themselves, then the splintering of Stephen's realm would have suited them, and it might easily have seen a return to something like the old Anglo-Saxon kingdoms. King David was pressing further into the ancient kingdom of Northumbria, the empress held a portion of what was Wessex and Stephen remained in control of the south-east, where once there had been the kingdoms of East Anglia (though Hugh Bigod continued to cause him trouble there), Essex, Kent and Sussex. Ranulf's lands were not that far from the old boundaries of Mercia, and if a move away from central, monarchical authority was what some desired, they had the perfect opportunity to try and achieve it after 1141.

In that sense, it is striking that Ranulf was, in fact, desperate to find a home for his loyalties, a hearth to warm himself before. The most straightforward explanation is that this was the way Ranulf and his contemporaries understood the world to work. He was a nobleman, and demanded his due in that regard. He would fight tooth and nail to preserve his patrimony and would seek to add to his lands wherever possible, but he had no illusions that he might be a king. As Stephen and Matilda both struggled to break the stalemate, no other claimant threw their hat into the ring at any point. The crown was something separate and sacred. Ranulf wanted to make all that he could as a nobleman but had no pretensions to royalty. Even Earl Robert, who was the illegitimate son of a king and was probably encouraged, at least in 1135 if not continually afterwards, to make a bid for the throne, gave the idea no credence. The monarch, appointed by God and approved by the pope, was elevated above all others and it was not a position just anyone could seek out.

Nobles made their money at home by peace, not war. A bit of pillaging might bring some short-term cash, but it would likely bring trouble in return. The men who fought would often be those who also worked the land and made it profitable for their masters, so each one killed in a raid represented a long-term loss to the lord too. Well-managed, peaceful estates that returned bountiful harvests and filled the coffers were what pleased barons. Unnecessary fighting disrupted that easy, comfortable flow. If disputes erupted, it was in the interests of almost all parties to restore calm and peace as quickly as possible and with minimal damages. Although the chroniclers try to tell us the exact opposite, nineteen years of warfare was in nobody's interests. If some of the nobility began to distance themselves from Stephen, it was no more than they did from Empress Matilda too. It was clear that neither was strong enough to win or weak enough to lose and nailing your colours to either side's standard risked ruin if they failed.

In early 1146, peace talks had again been arranged between the two factions. During the truce to facilitate this, Earl Robert's son Philip, now in the service of King Stephen, had captured his own uncle, one of the empress's other half-brothers, Reginald, Earl of Cornwall. It is interesting that when Reginald protested that he had been relying on the truce to keep him safe, King Stephen ordered Philip to release him. All sense of honour and decorum was not lost to either side. When the two parties met, Empress Matilda insisted on her right to the crown and Stephen utterly refused to discuss giving it up, so they parted with nothing resolved. For the nobles, it was further confirmation that the impasse was unbreakable, at least for now.

The detachment of the nobles is more a signal of the intractable and irresolvable nature of the struggle between the king and the empress than their own desire to make hay in the absence of royal authority. In fact, literally making hay on their lands was what they really wanted to see done, and fighting did not help that. Besides, royal authority was nowhere absent. It differed across the country at the time rather than residing in one monarch and centring on London, but it could still be felt in its various forms. David brought peace to the north, and there was no real effort to dislodge him by the inhabitants who had fought so hard at the Battle of the Standard in 1138. It was as though accepting David allowed the north to opt out of the squabble between Stephen and Matilda, and their preference for making sure they had food to eat each winter was sufficient to override any affection for King Stephen or desire to be English.

Instead of driving the fighting onward, there would soon be a growing movement amongst the nobility to agree to keep peace between themselves. It began to matter little who won the crown, if either of the claimants ever would. Day to day, what was important was making sure that the fields could be worked, the mills could turn, and markets could operate freely and safely. That was how noblemen got richer and secured the loyal service of those under their control and protection. If nothing else, the fight between the two cousins for the throne proved the danger of failing to secure general acceptance, loyalty and affection. If the crown could fall into an unsolvable dispute that disrupted the kingdom, so might any baron's patrimony. Their lands were effectively kingdoms in miniature, but without the hallowed status, in which they were responsible for keeping law and order. If the sacred nature of the crown was not enough to protect the king, what hope for his nobles if they allowed the division to run rife on their own lands? Undoubtedly some, particularly mercenaries and those wishing to leap up the ladder of society, could and would exploit uncertainty for their own ends, but in general, the nobility, and particularly the more senior magnates, had more of an interest in peace than civil war. As the crown failed to ensure its delivery, they set about doing it themselves, not because they wished to be kings or because they despised King Stephen or Empress Matilda, but because it made sense, it kept them secure, and it preserved their wealth. For now, it is significant enough that a man like Ranulf, Earl of Chester felt that he needed someone to give his fealty to.

The precise date on which Earl Ranulf came to King Stephen is uncertain; it may have been in 1145 or 1146, though the latter seems more likely. Encouraged by the king's increasing successes and disillusioned by the empress's adherence to her uncle, Ranulf's rival, King David, the earl sought to make peace with Stephen and return to his allegiance. For the king, it was another moment of immense encouragement. He was not only beginning to win military victories against the empress, but key figures were actively seeking him out. Earl Robert's son Philip was already at his side and fighting vigorously for him, and now, Earl Ranulf wanted to warm his hands at the king's fire again. As one of the most powerful magnates in England, it was another coup and a step forward for Stephen. If, that is, terms could be agreed, and Ranulf could be trusted.

When the two men met at Stamford, ninety miles north of London and forty-five miles south of Lincoln, it was neutral territory. They agreed on a pact with little difficulty. Neither was required to provide hostages, and the king's central compromise was to allow Ranulf to retain Lincoln Castle until he could regain all of his lost lands in Normandy. As that seemed increasingly unlikely, Lincoln Castle, the real bone of contention between king and earl, would remain in Ranulf's hands, but if he were to give it up, it would only be after obtaining ample compensation. The settlement was either a sign of Stephen's desperation or his skill as a diplomat. The king's captivity had been the result of his commitment to recovering Lincoln from Ranulf, but he was now willing to give up on it to gain the earl's friendship and support. Given the recent upturn in his fortunes, Stephen was probably not as desperate as he might once have been, in which case the agreement was a shrewd one. If Stephen had, when dealing with King David, given up a little to gain a great deal more, the same logic applies with Ranulf. They could fight endlessly over Lincoln, taking and losing it ad infinitum, consuming men, time, money and effort without any real victory, or Stephen could allow Ranulf to keep his prize, albeit with a mechanism for its eventual return to royal hands. In that way, the king had one of his most significant magnates back at his side, extended his personal authority and could take his eye off Lincoln altogether to focus on more critical issues.

In return, Ranulf took up his homage to Stephen again and promised him military assistance in his escalating campaign. The agreement was not without its complications. Many of the men around Stephen, who had remained, had lost lands to Ranulf. Notable amongst these were William de Clerfeith, Gilbert de Gant, Earl Alan of Richmond, William Peverel of Nottingham, William d'Aubigny (known as Brito) and John, Count of Eu, and these men could hardly be expected to be pleased when Ranulf returned to the fold. If he was the king's man again, then they could not try and reclaim their lands from him. It is likely that, as well as seeing Ranulf's reappearance as compounding their losses, these men were suspicious of the earl's motives. Ranulf let it be known that he hoped for the king's help on a campaign into Wales, since 'he and his men would very soon be driven beyond the borders of his earldom if the king did not promptly give them the speediest help by that personal intervention with which he aided the others.'[6] In other words, he tried to suggest that it was in Stephen's own interests to help restrain the Welsh from probing across the border. Although there is a whiff of flattery to the earl's appeal, there was also plenty of truth to it. Stephen was recorded by all commentators as responding with unbelievable speed to new threats, often arriving before his enemies thought it possible, to deprive them of the chance to establish themselves anywhere. As the king's successes mounted, Ranulf could again see himself serving a king who would be able to protect the earl's lands as he was defending those of others.

The new alliance immediately bore fruit for the king. Ranulf's military support saw Stephen recover Bedford from Miles de Beauchamp and Ranulf then provided 300 knights for a fresh assault on the empress's outpost at Wallingford. The castle still refused to fall to the king, and something soured the relationship between King Stephen and Earl Ranulf again. What precisely caused the new rift is not recorded, but it is possible that Ranulf was becoming impatient for the king's assistance in Wales. Stephen, perhaps naturally, focused his efforts on central England, notably Bedford and Wallingford. If he ever intended to go to Wales as Ranulf had requested, it was sure to be low down his list of priorities. For his part, if the earl felt he had received assurances from the king that were now being reneged on, he might have begun to wonder if his knights appearing at Wallingford was all Stephen was really interested in.

Then, there were the inevitable rumours. Stephen's counsellors began to grumble about the prospect of leading an army 'by way of precipitous hills and tangled forests into ambushes that the savages had laid everywhere about'.[7] There was never food or water to be found in Wales to support an army, and there was no assurance of victory even if they managed to sustain the campaign. Besides, there were enough problems in England to occupy the king without going looking for more in Wales. The counsellors also pointed to the folly of being lured into Earl Ranulf's lands when his newly discovered allegiance to the king was far from established. He had given no hostages or sureties for all his assurances of loyalty so that it would be both rash and reckless to enter his territory. What, they whispered in the king's ear, was to prevent Ranulf taking him captive or assassinating him once he was in the earl's domain?

Following the pattern of other such spiralling relationships in the past, when Ranulf was at court in Northampton, a quarrel erupted between the earl and some of the king's men. These counsellors insisted that Ranulf should return to the king all of the king's property the earl held and provide hostages as an assurance of his good faith. It is generally assumed that Stephen was behind this but whilst it is impossible to clearly ascertain, it seems unlikely. In the case of the bishops and Geoffrey de Mandeville there was, amongst the chroniclers and commentators, some sense of a degree of truth to the accusations of treason but in Ranulf's case they are more shocked and see less tangible reason for the king to act. If Stephen had moved against Bishop Roger and Geoffrey de Mandeville in an effort to cut off their power and take their wealth for himself, then it is possible he saw an opportunity to do the same with Ranulf. Another explanation is that the king was easily duped and led by his counsellors, who played on his fears to turn him against men they wanted out of the way. If that is true, then the king was a gullible fool rather than a malicious schemer, and it is hard to know which is worse.

In this instance, Stephen had just achieved the propaganda and tactical victory of securing Earl Ranulf's fealty. He had left Lincoln in the earl's possession with little fuss and seen the benefits Ranulf could offer, not least in the 300 knights he brought to the king's side. In that display of strength, too, lay a threat of the dangers of crossing Ranulf. Having settled a problem that left him free from concern in Lincoln and the East Midlands, and which also provided him with a buffer against further encroachment by King David, which Ranulf was sure to actively oppose, it would seem folly to throw all that away on a whim. Perhaps the relative ease with which Geoffrey de Mandeville had been defeated gave Stephen confidence that he could do it again, but it had taken a year of castle building, skirmishing and sieges to achieve that end. Stephen may have been willing to invest another year in doing the same with Ranulf, but it seems an unnecessary waste of time if there was no real threat from the earl and with greater challenges in the west that Ranulf could be used to overcome. After the previous incidents, Stephen can have been under no illusion that if he elected to move against Ranulf now, it would end with another rebellion that he would be forced to face. Maybe it was worth it, perhaps Stephen even relished the challenge as one he could complete, unlike defeating the empress, but it would be risky, particularly if Ranulf were pushed back into the waiting embrace of his father-in-law, Earl Robert. An active desire to cause a breach with Ranulf made little sense in 1147, but that doesn't necessarily mean Stephen didn't plan it.

Ranulf was enraged by the demands made of him at Northampton. He insisted that he had not come to court to address these matters and had received no notice that they were to be discussed. The argument grew increasingly heated until Ranulf was openly charged with treason, a claim he vehemently denied, though he went red-faced, perhaps with rage, but giving the appearance of embarrassment, not least over his previous disloyalty to Stephen. When he tried to change the subject, it was taken as an admission of guilt so that Ranulf was arrested, chained and thrown into a prison cell. The king set the price for the earl's release as the return of the keys to all the castles he held from the king, including Lincoln. Ranulf agreed but can hardly have been pleased. His men were already up in arms on his properties ready to fight for him even before Stephen let him go. Here it is possible to see the king's attachment to honour and chivalry as causing him immense problems. Whether he believed in Ranulf's guilt or did not care, releasing him was asking for trouble, but still, however cruel the chroniclers paint the time as, there was no room for murdering prisoners. Whatever his motives and beliefs, Stephen might have been better served had Ranulf met a sticky end in custody rather than been set free.

To nobody's surprise, Ranulf immediately rejoined the empress's cause and flew into rebellion against Stephen. Whatever assurances the earl had offered the king about his future behaviour, Ranulf plainly felt able to point to Stephen's breach of their pact to excuse his own failure to now stick to terms. Ranulf's first target can have been no surprise. 'In front of Lincoln, which he had restored to the king for his freedom, in which also the king had stationed the flower of his troops, he made frequent raids with an armed force and sometimes experienced the spiteful caprice of Fortune, sometimes favoured with success by her smiles, won a glad and glorious triumph over the king's men.'[8] Ultimately, Ranulf lost a great many men and was forced to withdraw from Lincoln. He moved on to Coventry, some eighty miles south-west, but Stephen appeared quickly to relieve the town. The king was injured, though not seriously, during the effort to drive Ranulf away, but Stephen was victorious again and the earl was forced out of the city.

The idea that Stephen had orchestrated the move against Ranulf as an excuse to take his castles and attack the earl was given colour by the arrest at this point of Gilbert Fitz Richard, Earl of Hertford. Gilbert had been created earl by Stephen in 1138 and had shown no signs of disloyalty. Gilbert's uncle, Gilbert de Clare, known as Strongbow (though his son Richard is the more famous bearer of that nickname), had been made Earl of Pembroke around the same time and had briefly joined Empress Matilda after the Battle of Lincoln before returning to Stephen before the end of 1141. Gilbert Fitz Richard's principal offence seems to have lain in being Ranulf's nephew. Gilbert's mother, Adeliza, was Ranulf's sister and that appears to have been enough to precipitate his arrest. Again, the king demanded that Gilbert hand over all of his castles to secure his release. The move seems to have become something of an obsession, perhaps born of paranoia, genuine evidence of treason or of Stephen's sense that he was on the cusp of final victory and was becoming untouchable. Gilbert was threatened with banishment until he agreed to surrender the castles, but as soon as he was released, he sped into the camp of his Uncle Ranulf. When the Earl of Pembroke demanded that Stephen give him all of his nephew's confiscated properties, the king refused, and the earl joined the rebellion too, though he would be reconciled with the king quickly enough. If Stephen was playing a game, it was a perilous one.

The *Gesta Stephani* suggests that the king had harboured doubts about the earls of Hertford and Pembroke, so was quick to believe that they might join Ranulf, though his actions drove them there anyway. The incident of Gilbert's arrest, release and flight is the only time the writer reports direct speech, suggesting that he might have been present when the king made his decision and could remember the reasoning:

> 'And it is wrong,' he said, 'that the man to whom I have granted such great and varied wealth, whom I took when he was a poor knight and raised in honour to the dignity of an earldom, on whom again and again I have bestowed possessions in lavish abundance, according to his own heart's desire, it is wrong that he should now appear to be taking up arms so suddenly and so rashly and aiding the cause of my enemies against me. Where is his faith, his honour, where is the man who should have kept his faith to me unshaken and reckoned any swerving from his devotion to me a brand of infamy? He neither keeps faith to me, his one and only lord, nor, while doing this, does he in any wise avoid the shame of public disgrace. But let us now press closely on him as he flees and, not suffering any of his plans to ripen, let us bring to nought, by hastening our pursuit of him, whatever he has devised against us.'[9]

The wording might suggest that Gilbert's rebellion came before any arrest or seizure of castles, since there was amazement at his abandonment of the king, but commentators assert that the arrest came first. Stephen gave chase to Gilbert, capturing three of the earl's castles with ease and almost grabbing Gilbert himself, but the earl escaped in disguise, and the king carried on to take Pevensey Castle too.

It soon became clear that Stephen's mind was moving to the future of his dynasty. His oldest son, Eustace, whose date of birth is so unknown that he might have been anywhere between twelve and twenty by 1147, was knighted by his father. After endowing his heir with plentiful lands and possessions, the king provided Eustace with an impressive retinue of his own knights before finally bestowing in him the title Count of Boulogne, which was his maternal inheritance.

The *Gesta Stephani*'s author saw much to admire in Eustace at this point. Though young, he was 'of noble nature', 'of settled character, eminent for soldierly qualities, and notable for inborn merit'. The writer saw great things in young Eustace's future: 'He showed himself extremely gentle and courteous; everywhere he stretched forth a generous hand in cheerful liberality; as he had a very great deal of his father's disposition he could meet men on a footing of equality or superiority as occasion required.'[10] The knighting and gift of a county were the preludes to a coronation for Eustace. It had become common practice amongst the French royal family to have an heir crowned during their father's lifetime to help ensure a smooth succession and facilitate a gentle transfer of power. Stephen was acutely aware that his status as an anointed king and the backing this brought from the pope and the church in England had been the key to keeping him on the throne for so long, shielding him against the empress's claims. Now, he was hoping to pass that security on to his son. Stephen was heading into his early fifties, and he must have begun to realize that he would not be able to keep up his vigorous military activity indefinitely, never mind the fact that death was slowly creeping ever closer. Empress Matilda had tried to display her dynastic strength by drawing her son Henry into the conflict in England, and Stephen now did the same. If she would threaten to prolong the struggle into the next generation, then Stephen would call her bluff and set his own son up to be in the best position possible to win. The prospect of an enduring stalemate was frighteningly real.

22

Empress Matilda

When the Earl of Gloucester, with three other earls and his whole army in countless numbers, had planned to bring in supplies of food for them and destroy the bishop's castles the king, on being summoned by the bishop, arrived suddenly, put the earl and all his men to flight in panic, and when the castle was surrendered to him delivered it over to the bishop.[1]

Before the end of 1147, Brian Fitz Count tried to take a castle called Lidelea. The identity and precise location of this fortress remain a mystery, but it had been erected by Bishop Henry to restrict raids on his lands in the area. One of Brian's men managed to gain control of the castle by trickery, and they settled in, using it as a base to rob the bishop's surrounding properties. Bishop Henry refused to take the assault lying down and brought his own men to lay siege to the castle, building two counter castles from which to operate. The blockade began to bite, but as hunger took hold within, Earl Robert and his allies approached to try and relieve the castle, only for the king to arrive with his usual haste, causing the empress's men to flee. For Matilda, the fight was beginning to look like a lost cause. Giving up, though, was nowhere to be found in her nature.

On the other hand, the earls of Chester, Pembroke and Hertford had been driven into her camp by the king's heavyhandedness. Perhaps cncouraged by these developments, the fourteen-year-old Henry FitzEmpress burst back onto the scene in England. There is an interesting change of pace and tone in the *Gesta Stephani* at this point which may suggest a different author, or that the original author's views were softening and changing. He describes now the arrival of 'Henry, the son of the Count of Anjou, the lawful heir and claimant to the kingdom of England'.[2] The words seem carefully constructed to describe Henry as the lawful heir before mentioning his claim to England. They could, then, be interpreted to mean that Henry was his father's lawful heir, in Anjou and Normandy, and held out a claim to England too, whilst they appeared to suggest Henry was the legitimate heir to England. This perhaps marks a point in the conflict at which many were hedging their bets rather than nailing their colours to a mast. Either that, or the writer was teasing the lad, but he keeps up the balancing act in the remainder of his narrative.

Young Henry's arrival sent shockwaves through England. He had come with a vast army, numbering thousands, with thousands more waiting to cross behind him. He was weighed down with money and treasure to disperse and had set about ravaging any lands that opposed him. It was terrifying to the king's adherents. Except that none of it was true. Henry had come with a handful of knights and a smattering of mercenaries. He had no money and planned to pay his men from plunder he assumed he would win. It was a display of youthful exuberance and overconfidence, but it was not a well-planned campaign. As soon as the king's followers realized the truth, they recovered from their terror, which had made them appear 'as though cowering beneath a dreadful thunderclap',[3] regained their previous resolution at the king's increasing success and set about fending off the boy from Anjou.

Henry made his way to Cricklade Castle, just east of Malmesbury, and attempted to cut off the king's castle there from reinforcements. His insufficient numbers were quickly driven away, so they moved a little south to Purton Castle but were again repulsed, this time in a state of panic. After that, disheartened, hungry and unpaid, Henry's knights and mercenaries began to drift away and return home. The young man had been unable to retain the loyalty of his men when things started to go badly and had learned the dangers of failing to lay down sufficient funds for a campaign. He must have been disappointed too that the nobility of England had not come out to meet him and join his cause, but he had failed to understand that they would no longer take such a risk unless they were certain of victory, even if they favoured his cause. Henry could offer no such guarantee. It was a painful lesson for a fourteen-year-old boy, but it was about to get worse.

Bereft of money and most of his knights, but not of hope, Henry appealed to his mother for financial assistance. He still needed to cover the costs he had incurred so far and honour demanded that he pay his men. Finding the empress lacking in ready cash herself, Henry found no succour where he might best have hoped for it. Undaunted, he went next to Earl Robert to seek the money he needed. Surely his uncle would understand the military necessity of pressing their cause and finding wages to take the fight to King Stephen. Henry could not persuade Earl Robert to help either and found that his uncle, 'brooding like a miser over his moneybags, preferred to meet his own requirements only'.[4] In an astonishingly bold, or desperate, move, Henry sent secret messengers to the king to plead for his help as a kinsman. Given that the lad was in England to try and take Stephen's crown, it was an audacious appeal, but one with a basis in the code of chivalry that Stephen adhered to and Henry, an idealistic young teenager, might have respected too.

It worked. Stephen sent Henry all the money that he asked for, allowing him to pay off his men and leave England. It had been a premature attempt to assert his own claims. His mother and uncle clearly thought so and refused to help, suggesting that he had acted without their sanction and perhaps even trodden on his mother's toes by appearing to ignore her rights in favour of his own. Whether Henry realized it or not, his appeal to Stephen and the king's generosity probably changed the course of the years that followed. Some criticized Stephen's foolish, even childish willingness to help an intractable enemy who was determined to drive him from the throne, but others saw some logic and good judgement in the king's course of action.[5] Aside from fulfilling a chivalric duty to a family member, and a fourteen-year-old boy in some trouble, Stephen could consider that there were few better ways to soften an enemy's resolve than to offer them friendly aid in a time of dire need. Henry would surely be less likely to be cruel and vindictive to Stephen when the latter had shown him such compassion. The author of the *Gesta Stephani* certainly considered that the king would 'so overcome evil for good that by good well bestowed upon his enemy he might heap coals of repentance and reformation upon his mind.'[6] If nothing else, Stephen was feeling confident enough that a few coins to see the future hope of the Angevin cause scurry away from his shores with his tail between his legs and his wings clipped was a small price to pay. By 29 May 1147, Henry was being received at Bec-Hellouin, firmly back in his father's Norman territories.

Empress Matilda had been seen less and less in the activities of her cause since the failures of 1141. She may never have recovered from coming so close to her ultimate goal only to fail because of her personality. Even if she blamed her sex, or the fickle nature of the nobles, or the intransigence of the upstart citizens of London, none of those had changed, and some could never be caused to. The empress was not seen at the front line and had refused to help her son and heir in his efforts to keep her cause alive, or to replace it with his own. Although it is impossible to see at this distance, there is a suggestion of melancholy or depression about her withdrawal from any semblance of leadership. Her problems and sorrows were to be compounded before the end of 1147.

On 31 October, whilst actively planning further manoeuvres, Robert, Earl of Gloucester suddenly and unexpectedly died. Robert had been Matilda's rock ever since the public denouncement of his fealty to Stephen and must have been in her corner in private long before then. He had been the source of most of her victories, and though William of Malmesbury undoubtedly added flourishes to make his patron appear flawless, there can be little doubt that he was an incredibly capable politician and general. The Battle of Lincoln had been won by Robert, gifting his half-sister an almost clear path to the throne. When it went wrong, whatever the reason and wherever the fault lay, it was Robert who had covered Matilda's escape and allowed himself to be captured in the process. The highest signal of her need and probable affection for him was in her agreement that he should be exchanged for her own prisoner, King Stephen. An earl for a king, as Robert had tried to point out, was hardly a fair swap, but Empress Matilda believed her brother was worth the loss, worth a king.

Robert was approaching sixty when he died, but like the king, had remained incredibly active. He and Stephen perhaps had a lot more in common than either might have liked to admit, though mutual admiration must have existed too. Much of what William of Malmesbury admired in Robert can also be seen in Stephen, and both men were dedicated to the notions of chivalry that guided their conduct, particularly in war. Whatever the claims of the monks in the cloisters, this civil war was very much a gentleman's war. Siege warfare was much preferred to open battle, garrisons were allowed to go free if they followed the accepted structures of a siege, no major nobleman or senior figure on either side was ever killed fighting in the rare confrontations or at sieges. Prisoners were more often than not treated with respect and ransomed rather than executed. Much of this civility is owed to the attitudes of

Robert and Stephen. The empress was willing to be harsher and to resort to torture if she felt it was warranted, but Robert had been a restraining influence. He had been worth a king, and might have made a great one himself. Robert could, had he chosen, have tried to overcome all of the problems of Matilda's claim by replacing it with his own. He was a man, a great magnate, wealthy, and a son of Henry I. Illegitimate, maybe, but a son nevertheless, and hadn't his grandfather William the Conqueror been a bastard son too? It is to Robert's credit that he dismissed such talk out of hand and never looked back on it.

For Empress Matilda, it must have been a hammer blow. She had lost Miles of Gloucester, Brian Fitz Count was all but in retirement now, her cause was faltering in the face of Stephen's increasing confidence and success, and her oldest son had embarrassingly botched an invasion. The loss of Robert was probably the hardest of those setbacks to bear. If he had not landed with her at Arundel and moved to establish what had proven an unassailable base at Bristol, she might never have got further than her stepmother's hospitality. Robert had built the military arm that sought to enforce her legal claim, and it was his firm hand at her back that had kept her moving forward through all the problems they had faced. Her desperation to get him back at her side in 1141 amply demonstrates that she needed him and probably that she loved him dearly. More than any other, Robert, Earl of Gloucester had kept the flame of Empress Matilda's claim to the throne of England burning through the dark nights and swirling winds. It was thanks to him that her son Henry had any hope at all of continuing the fight because the questions of legitimacy and oath-breaking had been continually dragged to the front of everyone's mind in England by Robert for a decade.

That the death of Robert was both devastating and decisive can be seen in Empress Matilda's response. At some point in the early months of 1148, she left England and never came back. If she was already feeling some degree of depression or was no longer willing to carry the fight, then the loss of her unfaltering proxy was probably the last straw, and the hopelessness of her situation could no longer be brushed away by her brother's cheery refusal to be disheartened. Matilda went back to Normandy after almost nine years of trying to win the throne of England. In June she went to Falaise, and an alteration in her attitude towards affairs in England can be seen immediately. Jocelyn, Bishop of Salisbury had been actively campaigning for the return of Devizes

Castle, rebuilt and previously owned by his predecessor Bishop Roger but secured by Empress Matilda and used as one of her bases in England. He also wanted Potterne Castle and Canning Castle returned to the possession of the diocese and had taken his case to Rome.

Pope Eugenius III had issued a bull on 26 November 1146 demanding the return of the three castles to the Bishop of Salisbury. Refusal would result in excommunication for anyone holding the castle after three warnings.[7] Matilda was not about to allow herself to be sentenced to excommunication. The Papacy had not been sympathetic to her claims, but to some extent, the hands of successive popes had been tied by the earlier formal recognition of Stephen. Risking the loss of any hope of future support in Rome for her or her children was too much, so she tried to find a compromise by offering compensation, buying herself time in the process, but her offers were not accepted. The increasingly urgent need to complete the handover of these critical castles might have contributed to Empress Matilda's decision to leave England, whilst also making it clear that Rome was still firmly in Stephen's corner.

On 10 June, Matilda was at Falaise to make her peace with Bishop Jocelyn before Hugh, Archbishop of Rouen. The empress confessed her own sin in wrongfully seizing control of the church's possessions and gave them back, promising to prevent any of her adherents from entering any of the castles ever again to seek to deprive the bishop of them.[8] This is a considerable change in Matilda's attitude. Gone is the haughtiness and stern devotion to what she considered her rights. It is hard to see whether this alteration was merely the result of papal intervention in this specific matter or a symptom of her loss of conviction in or motivation for her entire cause. When Duke Geoffrey granted a charter to the Abbey of Mortemer on 11 October 1148, the document referred to the consent also obtained from Empress Matilda and their three sons, Henry, Geoffrey and William.[9] That would suggest that the whole family were together, and it might have been here that the future shape of Angevin efforts might have been debated and decided. Within a few months of this, Arnulf, Bishop of Lisieux would write to Robert, Bishop of Lincoln and towards the end of his letter he tantalizingly referred to Henry FitzEmpress as '*ducem nostrum*' – our duke. Although Henry was not using the title in his own charters yet, there is a hint that his father was preparing him to take over in Normandy and perhaps to turn his eye back to England.

Matilda must have resigned her own interest in the pursuit of the throne of England, at least in her own name, though she would remain devoted to her son's efforts to attain the rights she transferred to him. It is impossible to know whether she had to be convinced by her husband that a decade of failures, during which time he had won and subdued Normandy, proved that it was time to shift focus to their son, or whether she willingly shed the weight of the mantle she had borne. Henry was, by late 1148, approaching his sixteenth birthday and if Matilda had aimed to keep the conflict alive for him, even if she could not win it for herself, then the time was coming when he would have to be ready to make his own way. Henry had learned under his father, and although it seems Matilda and his uncle Robert had not approved of his attempt to invade England aged fourteen, he would soon be old enough to press his claims himself.

The situation in England had been changing significantly around the empress and King Stephen. Although their prolonged struggle might well have had an impact on what was happening, it was probably only one factor. In 1146, a Second Crusade to the Holy Land had been preached across Europe, including England. There was no sense from Rome that England was a no-go zone where nobles were so engrossed in enjoying their cruel warfare that they could not be tempted away. In fact, the opposite might have been true. Bernard of Clairvaux, who had become the self-appointed conscience of successive popes wrote in support of the crusade, and his words must have resonated in England:

> What is this savage craving of yours? Put a stop to it now, for it is not fighting but foolery. Thus to risk both soul and body is not brave but shocking, is not strength but folly. But now, O mighty soldiers, O men of war, you have a cause for which you can fight without danger, a cause in which to conquer is glorious and for which to die is gain.[10]

Many prominent men in England answered the call, perhaps only too happy for an excuse to get away from the unending troubles at home. On crusade, they were free from uncertainty about where their loyalties lay, their lands at home were protected by the pope so could not be seized in their absence as they might be in their presence, and if they died there, their place in Heaven was secure. For anyone unsure which side to take, who might eventually win and whether they had broken an oath to Stephen, Matilda or both of them, they would find freedom from such cares and forgiveness for their sins on crusade. The risks and discomfort might have seemed worth it, or even a welcome relief. Waleran of Meulan, Earl of Worcester, one of the Beaumont twins now straddling the civil war, took the cross. William de Warenne, 3rd Earl of Surrey would die during the Second Crusade. Others who departed England included Roger de Mowbray, Walter Fitz Gilbert of Clare, William Peverel of Dover and his successor at Cricklade, Philip, the son of Robert, Earl of Gloucester who had defected to Stephen. Even Roger de Clinton, Bishop of Coventry and Lichfield travelled to the Holy Land.

The following year, 1147, had also seen a large number of Englishmen depart to give aid to Lisbon and to try and free it from Muslim control. This well-organized and coordinated force was striking for its complete lack of noble leadership. Men from Norfolk and Suffolk were led by Hervey Glanville. Simon of Dover was in command of the men of Kent. William and Ralph Veal, of the seafaring family that had prevented Earl Robert from attacking Southampton, led the contingent from that city and a group of Londoners followed a man only known as Simon.[11] It would be surprising that such a dispersed array of men would be able to organize themselves across the whole south-east to make the necessary arrangements and hire transport to all set off for Portugal if England was torn apart by a vicious civil war that made roads impossible to travel. Their adventurous drive might hint that there was a desire to leave England, but it also demonstrates that the country was settled enough to allow them to arrange to do it efficiently and effectively. The writer of the *Gesta Stephani* persisted in painting a bleak picture throughout these changes:

> And though the vigorous youth of the whole of England, all who were pre-eminent for a gallant heart and a steadfast mind, flocked together most eagerly to take vengeance for these things, so that you would have thought England was empty and drained of men when so many, and of such importance, were everywhere setting out; yet did not strife and plunder, the sword and the enemy give any respite in England, because as some departed others took their places, the more zealous in doing evil the more recently they had come to it.[12]

The struggle in England, even if it was not as relentlessly brutal as chroniclers would have us believe, was not over. Empress Matilda had decided, for one reason or another, to set aside her own ambitions, but not her belief in her ability to pass a legitimate claim to the throne to her son Henry, hoping that he might fare better for all of the reasons of gender or personality that she had failed. The conflict was entering a new phase rather than petering out. The Matildine War was over, but the Henrician War was just beginning, and the empress was never far detached from the efforts of her oldest son.

23

King Stephen

> The pope conceded to the archbishop of Canterbury, who had won great favour in his sight, that he might absolve all the guilty bishops and abbots of England, or leave them under sentence as he thought fit.[1]

King Stephen, like the empress, began to experience problems that were in no way of his own making. A significant portion of the strength of Stephen's position came from his relationship with the church. Although it was rocky on occasion, he could generally rely on his brother's support and with that came the broad backing of the church in England. Bishop Henry had managed to secure a position as Legate between 1139 and 1143 that had made him senior to Theobald, Archbishop of Canterbury and it is striking that his stint in such high office coincided with some of his brother's darkest and most difficult days, through which Henry was able to guide the king's cause. The pre-eminence of the Cluniac order, to which Bishop Henry belonged, had facilitated the bishop's own rise, but the tide was turning.

Bishop Henry had been unable to secure an extension of his office or a reappointment later, and that was in part because of the new rising influence of the Cistercian order that was sweeping away Cluniac dominance. Bernard of Clairvaux was one of the major driving forces of the new primacy of his order. Later canonized as Saint Bernard, he spent eight years during the papal schism after the death of Honorius II in 1130 touring the continent to try and resolve the breach. He was eventually central to the recognition of Innocent II as the legitimate pope; historian R. H. C. Davis considered that Bernard 'had adopted the role of perpetual pricker of the papal conscience, demanding the condemnation of theological views he thought to be erroneous, and appealing against episcopal elections of which he disapproved.'[2] In 1145,

Bernardo Pignatelli was elected Pope Eugenius III, and a jubilant Bernard wrote to congratulate his former student and fellow Cistercian, assuring Eugenius that the church had 'confidence in him such as it had not had in his predecessors for a long time past'.[3] In the same letter, Bernard set Eugenius the challenge of tackling Bishop Henry in England in terms that made his disapproval of the worldly power the bishop wielded plain to see: 'When you have time, deal with them according to their works, so that they may know a prophet has arisen in Israel.'

A prolonged dispute over the election of a new Archbishop of York following the death of Thurstan in 1140 threw the church in England into years of disarray as the king, Bishop Henry and Bernard all tried to intervene. Bishop Henry attempted to secure the post for his nephew Henry de Sully, who had been appointed Abbot of Fécamp as compensation when his uncle had been unable to obtain for him the see of Salisbury. Now offered the senior post of archbishop, Henry de Sully refused to give up his abbacy, believing that, like his uncle, he could hold both positions. His nomination was quashed by Pope Innocent II on the grounds of pluralism. Many of the monastic reformers in the region looked to Waltheof, the Prior of Kirkham, as their preferred choice, but the king vetoed the idea because Waltheof was a stepson of King David and had been raised at the Scots king's court. His appointment would have provided David with more leverage to creep his borders south, and that was not a threat Stephen was adequately equipped to deal with.

Bishop Henry's next preferred candidate was his half-sister's son, William Fitz Herbert, who was treasurer to the church in York and so a familiar face. In January 1141, William was elected by the chapter at the instruction of the king and under the watchful eye of William le Gros, Earl of York, but within weeks the Battle of Lincoln had turned things upside down. Although William Fitz Herbert managed to retain the office, he was not consecrated until 26 September 1143, and his appointment caught the watchful eye of Bernard of Clairvaux. Bernard did all that he could to have William stripped of his archbishopric because the election had not been canonical, but completed under pressure from the king. There was some personal animosity between Bernard and Bishop Henry that stemmed from their juxtaposed positions and beliefs. Henry was everything that Bernard despised in a monk: rich, politically active, a nepotist, a pluralist, a builder of castles and fine houses for his own use and a monk who had stepped away from the cloister. To Henry,

Bernard represented a naivety that the church and state were separate entities and not entwined, and that religion could not be perfectly well served by taking a leading role in directing politics. The two were on a collision course. Bernard's outrage reached a peak in 1144 when he wrote to Pope Lucius II:

> Behold! Here, here I say is the enemy, here is the man who walks before Satan, the son of perdition, the man who disrupts all rights and laws. This is the man who has 'set his face against heaven', who has repudiated, reprobated, rejected and renounced the just judgment of the apostle, confirmed, consolidated, promulgated and clearly defined in solemn conclave. … I leave it to your judgment to decide how far the prestige of Rome has suffered in this matter. Would that the song in which they sing that Winchester is greater than Rome could be silenced on their lips![4]

The bitter feud over York lasted throughout the papacies of Celestine II and Lucius II, with Bishop Henry managing to employ all of his worldly guile to stay one step ahead of Bernard's righteous indignation, tying the complaint up in the Papal Curia and making sure it never found a conclusion. When his former protégé was elected Pope Eugenius III, Bernard wasted no time in telling him:

> I am importunate, but I have reason to be, and my reason is the apostolate of Eugenius! For they are saying that it is not you but I who am pope, and from all sides they flock to me with their suits. … And now I have another reason for importunity and one no less compelling, for it is in a very good cause. My pen is again directed against that idol of York, with all the more reason because my other attacks with this weapon have not gone home. … Let me speak more clearly: it belongs to the Roman pontiff to command the deposition of bishops, for although others may be called to share his cares, the fulness of power rests with him alone.[5]

In early 1147, Bernard's persistence paid off, and he finally caught up with Bishop Henry's games. William Fitz Herbert was deposed by the pope. A fresh election was ordered. When the chapter failed to return a unanimous verdict Pope Eugenius personally intervened to block Stephen's preferred choice and install Henry Murdac, Abbot of Fountains, and a fellow Cistercian. On 7 December 1147, Henry Murdac was consecrated by the pope himself, the first archbishop in England since the Conquest to be elected and consecrated without the approval of the king. A clerical feud was undermining Stephen's authority in England, and there was nothing that he could do about it.

When Pope Eugenius sent summons to a meeting of the entire church at Rheims to be held in March 1148, Stephen forbad any of his archbishops or bishops to attend, demonstrating his frustration at papal interference in England. The king selected bishops Robert of Hereford, William of Norwich and Hilary of Chichester to travel to Rheims and give the apologies of Archbishop Theobald and others.[6] Archbishop Theobald was aware of what was going on and although he had been something of a political nonentity up to this point, perhaps cowed by the confident authority projected by Bishop Henry, he began to step into the limelight. The Cistercian victory over the Cluniac Bishop Henry might have been the catalyst, but Theobald was to astound everyone. Having secreted a small fishing boat in a hidden bay for just such a reason, Theobald boarded the rickety, ill-equipped vessel and took his chances crossing the Channel with less than a dozen men in his company, 'rather as a survivor from a shipwreck than in a ship'.[7] When Archbishop Theobald arrived at Rheims, apologies having been given for his absence, it was a wondrous surprise to all, and he was received with great honour.

Outraged, Stephen began to impound Theobald's lands, ignoring the threat of an interdict against the kingdom. Theobald had perhaps been wary of being seen to give more weight to Stephen's prohibition than to the pope's summons, and he saw, or wished to find, a way to balance the competing demands. When Robert, Bishop of Hereford died while the council was in session, Eugenius moved quickly to appoint Gilbert Foliot, the Abbot of Gloucester and a man sympathetic to the empress, to the diocese. Gilbert was a Cluniac but was close to Theobald rather than Bishop Henry, and there must have been some sense that the pope, in appointing him, was offering a glimmer of hope to the empress's cause in England, even if only to spite Stephen. Theobald sent to England for three bishops to come and assist in the consecration of Gilbert, but all refused to so blatantly disobey the king. Instead, Theobald called on three French bishops to support him, and the consecration took place anyway. Gilbert was required to swear an oath that he would not formally acknowledge Stephen as King of England in another move that can only have encouraged Empress Matilda. Gilbert returned to England as Bishop of Hereford and immediately paid homage to Stephen, probably on the grounds that it was not his place to cause strife in England or to fail to recognize a king previously confirmed by Rome. If he felt the pope was playing games with the crown in England, he perhaps knew better than many, from his base at Gloucester, the harm that this would cause in prolonging the war or igniting a new, bloody episode and chose not to be party to it.

On the final day of the council, Pope Eugenius rose to excommunicate King Stephen by name for his intransigence. Those arguing Stephen's case could make no more headway. The candles were lit and the ceremony to enact the ultimate sanction of the church against a Christian was begun. Then, to the shock of all, Archbishop Theobald rose to plead for mercy for his king.

> Dumbfounded, not to say thunderstruck, by the boundless charity of this man, the pope at first meditated in silence and then, sighing, spoke as follows: 'My brethren, behold this man who enacts the gospel in our own time by loving his enemies and never ceasing to pray for his persecutors. For although the king has by his effrontery deserved our wrath and the wrath of God's church nevertheless we cannot but commend such love or refuse to hear his prayers. Yielding to his entreaties we now suspend the sentence and grant the king three months delay to give satisfaction. If he fails to do so by that time, the sentence shall then fall on him and his kingdom with heavier damnation than before.'[8]

Eugenius instead suspended Bishop Henry and the archbishops of Mainz and Cologne by name before adding more generally all those who had failed to heed his call to the council. Count Theobald of Blois and other nobles intervened at this point to secure a relaxation of the sentence on his brother Bishop Henry to enable him to appear before the pope to obtain his forgiveness.[9] Eugenius also granted Archbishop Theobald, 'who had won great favour in his sight', the power to absolve the bishops and abbots of England affected by the sentence as and when he saw fit.[10]

When Theobald landed back in England, he was met by Richard de Lucy and William Martel, representatives of the king, though they were sympathetic to Theobald too. The archbishop was warned to turn around immediately and leave again. Stephen was furious that Theobald had ignored his instruction not to travel to Rheims, apparently oblivious to, or unmoved by, the fact that the defiance had saved Stephen from excommunication. Theobald retired to St Omer, seemingly under the protection of William of Ypres, Stephen's loyal mercenary captain. He tried to negotiate with the king, but to no avail so that the interdict was finally imposed on England. Perhaps to the surprise of those watching from across the seas, the sanction had little or no effect. Church services, now prohibited by Rome, continued unhindered as bishops, perhaps reflecting Gilbert Foliot's view, preferred to nurse the peace that they could find rather than inflame the country.

At St Omer, Theobald became 'beloved by all for his upright character and dignified bearing, but above all for his gentleness and care for the poor, which made him seem a perfect example of kindness and generosity'.[11] The archbishop sent messengers to the pope, whom they caught up with at Brescia, to explain the developments. Eugenius, doubtless astonished to find his mercy thrown back in his face, immediately wrote to all the bishops of England, both individually and as a group, instructing them to admonish King Stephen for confiscating Archbishop Theobald's property and ordering them to see it restored and compensation provided. The bishops were to enforce the interdict at the pope's insistence if Stephen did not comply and warn the king that Eugenius would personally excommunicate him at Michaelmas if he refused to fall into line.

Although this sounds like the papacy was willing to go hard on Stephen, it was probably no more interference than other rulers were feeling as Rome sought to expand its influence, not least to try and make a success of efforts in the Holy Land. The Holy Roman Empire had a far more rocky relationship with the papacy than Stephen. In fact, it is evidence of Stephen's authority over the church in his country that by this point, he had successfully excluded both the archbishops of Canterbury and York from their offices. Not only that, but he had secured the loyalty of Gilbert Foliot despite his promise to the pope not to give it and his bishops were confidently ignoring an interdict imposed by Archbishop Theobald, relying on the king's protection against their ecclesiastical superior.

Stephen held to his course in his dealings with the church. He was even campaigning in Rome to secure the assistance of several cardinals 'who as he knew could be drawn through the mire of any disgrace at the mere gleam of a rusty purse'.[12] Archbishop Theobald persisted in summoning his supplicant bishops to come before him at St Omer, but they continually declined, pleading that they were unable to leave the country without the king's permission, and he would not give it. Rome sent no further help, so Theobald, continuing his newfound proactive confidence, got back into a boat and sailed to England to sort it out himself. He sailed from Gravelines and landed at Framlingham in Suffolk, where Hugh Bigod welcomed him and helped him establish a makeshift court where Theobald began to receive the bishops deprived of their excuse to fail to come before the archbishop.

Theobald had called the king's bluff, and it worked. Seeing the archbishop in the company of a man like Hugh, who was nominally still supporting Empress Matilda, raised the dreadful prospect of the whole church in England transferring to the empress's cause. It was not something Stephen could risk, given that his brother was no longer in the position he had been and the papacy was on the brink of a serious break with the king. In quick order, Theobald was reconciled with King Stephen. His lands were returned, compensation paid for the affront and new charters provided by Stephen to safeguard the church's privileges.[13]

York proved a slower problem to resolve. Henry Murdac, still unrecognized as archbishop by Stephen, tried to gain entry to York in 1148 and though he was welcomed at Beverley, the city of York refused to allow him through their gates. Henry Murdac moved to Ripon, lodging next to Fountains Abbey, where he was still abbot. The pope and Bernard of Clairvaux seemed willing to turn a blind eye to this particular example of pluralism whilst condemning others for the crime. Henry Murdac placed York under an interdict, but William le Gros, Earl of York and the treasurer of York Minster, Hugh du Puiset, managed to work together to see that the sanction had no effort. In a fury, Henry Murdac excommunicated Earl William and the treasurer, so Hugh excommunicated Henry back. King David offered his backing to Henry Murdac, which only served to harden Stephen's opposition and further transformed the ecclesiastical dispute into a political issue. In early 1151, Stephen finally agreed to recognize Henry Murdac, as the king campaigned for religious approval for the coronation of his son and heir Eustace, but the archbishop was still unable to gain access to York and died on 14 October 1153, to be succeeded by his ejected predecessor William Fitz Herbert.

As he had been given the power by the pope to do, Archbishop Theobald released all of the English bishops from their suspension, with the sole exception of Bishop Henry. The Bishop of Winchester was instead required to set out for Rome to seek the personal forgiveness of the pope. Bishop Henry secured absolution with relative ease, but he used his time in Rome to try and improve his position at home once more. He sought a pallium, which would be a signal of high honour usually bestowed on archbishops. That seemed to be part of a scheme to carve out an archbishopric for himself with control over western England. The move was not, perhaps, entirely selfish, since that was the region still holding firm for the empress and the Angevin cause and increased authority there could be used to Stephen's benefit too. When he could raise no interest in that idea, Bishop Henry tried to have himself appointed Legate again so that he would be superior to Theobald, but the archbishop's current high favour with the pope made such a move unlikely.

When he was refused a request to exempt the see of Winchester from subservience to Canterbury, he made no headway, and his final plea for a personal exemption from Canterbury's jurisdiction fell on deaf ears. Whilst he was still in Rome, news arrived that Stephen was oppressing the church once more in some way, and Henry loudly proclaimed, 'How glad I am that I am not there now, or this persecution would be laid at my door.' The pope smiled and offered the following fable in response:

> The devil and his dam were chatting to each other, as friends do, and whilst she was endeavouring to curb her son's evil-doing by rebuking him and chiding him for his misdeeds, a storm arose in their sight and many ships were sunk. 'See,' said the devil, 'if I had been there you would have blamed me for this mischief.' Said she, 'Even if you were not actually on the spot, you have certainly trailed your tail there beforehand.'

As the meaning sank in, the pope added wryly 'Ask yourself, my brother, if you have not been trailing your tail in the English sea.' Scolded, Bishop Henry asked for permission to leave but bought a large number of Roman statues to take back to Winchester before he departed. To avoid any trouble in Tuscany, Lombardy or Burgundy, he elected to travel back through Spain, visiting St James of Compostella on the way.[14]

Stephen was finding trouble in more quarters than just the south-west. That was nothing new, but problems with the church affected by changing priorities and outlooks in Rome and partly driven by a monk sitting in Clairvaux Abbey were something he had no control over at all. Archbishop Theobald, who seems to have undergone something of a transformation during 1148, was able to use the political turmoil in England to the advantage of the church and force Stephen to come to terms the king had avoided. It is another mark not only of the mountainous numbers but also the wide-ranging variety of problems that Stephen faced, all of which seems to make it all the more impressive that he was still King of England at all, even if parts of his realm had been hacked away from him. He had handled the Matildine War well enough, without actually managing to win it. How he would face the Henrician War remained to be seen.

24

Empress Matilda

> While the kingdom of England was in this wretched and frightful state of disorder and disturbance Henry, the lawful heir to England, received advice from his adherents to get the emblems of a knight's rank from his father, or else from the King of Scots, his intimate and special friend, and then with renewed vigour rise up against the king and gain with resolution and spirit what was rightfully his.[1]

As the campaigning season of 1149 neared, it became apparent that Empress Matilda had taken a back seat, but that she was still involved in coordinating efforts from Normandy. The fight would now be carried by her son, who had his sixteenth birthday on 5 March 1149. Stephen might look to the boy's rather pathetic attempt at invasion a couple of years earlier for encouragement, but Henry was a little older now, better able to lead men and probably came this time with the full backing of both his mother and his father. The king could consider that Henry would feel some obligation to be gentle with his first cousin once removed since Stephen had magnanimously bailed out the previous botched invasion, but Henry FitzEmpress had no intention of relinquishing his claim to the crown that adorned Stephen's head.

Young Henry was advised that he should now arrange to have himself knighted. Stephen was doing the same for Eustace as a prelude to a coronation and Henry could not be left behind. He would need to ensure that he was equally prepared for an inauguration as soon as he could drive Stephen from the throne. Duke Geoffrey might have been an appropriate man to knight his son, but Henry seemed to want something even better, dripping with more prestige. He set his heart on being knighted by his great-uncle, King David of Scotland. No doubt part of the attraction, alongside the status it would afford him, was the excuse to traipse through Stephen's kingdom and ensure that he was seen by all those he planned to rule.

King David, happy to oblige, particularly when it would cause discomfort to Stephen, agreed to the plans and arranged to meet his great-nephew at Carlisle. On 22 May 1149, Henry FitzEmpress arrived in the city and was knighted amid great pomp by King David. The young knight had been accompanied by Roger, Earl of Hereford, the son and heir of Miles of Gloucester, and a small group of Angevin supporters. Henry and David managed to entice Ranulf, Earl of Chester to meet with them and the three men agreed a pact of mutual aid to work together against King Stephen. Not wishing to pass up the opportunity presented by their present gathering, they determined to take an army to York and try to capture the city. Moving south into Lancashire, perhaps to allow Earl Ranulf to raise more men, they then struck east towards York.

Their plans were scuppered before they could come to anything. King Stephen had arrived in York with a large army and was waiting for them. Henry of Huntingdon believed that Stephen had seen the danger in the meeting at Carlisle and feared they would target York, so rushed to defend the city.[2] The *Gesta Stephani* claims that the citizens of York had sent a desperate plea for help to Stephen and he had immediately marched north to protect them.[3] If the latter is true, then it would be significant for the king that one of the farthest corners of his reduced kingdom still looked to him as their first and best hope of assistance. It is telling too that Stephen was still able to raise a large enough force to counter the King of Scotland, the Angevin Henry and Earl Ranulf all banded together, and to move quickly enough to be ahead of them.

As the hostile force approached York, they received word of the king's presence there and were sent into a panic. There was no fighting, and no siege was begun. The coalition was apparently unwilling to confront the king. David took his men back to Carlisle, and Earl Ranulf retired to Chester. Henry was forced to make his way south to his late uncle Robert's old stronghold at Bristol, but his journey was not made easy. Stephen's son Eustace had been based at Oxford with an army of his own and tasked with harassing the lands around Bristol, Devizes, Salisbury and Marlborough that many had vacated to travel north with Henry FitzEmpress for his knighting, and now he was able to make things difficult for his rival as Henry pressed south. Eustace discovered that Henry was staying at Dursley Castle in Gloucestershire on one of the nights and prepared three ambushes to cover the roads out in the early morning. Henry had got wind of the plan and fled in the middle of the night, finally reaching Bristol before moving to Devizes to prepare a new campaign, apparently in defiance of his mother's assurance that none of her allies would use the castle there again. From here, he tried to plan his next move.

Stephen remained in York throughout August and set about demolishing some castles and erecting others to make the defence of his northern borders easier and more efficient. This seems to have met with the approval of the city since many of the castles he destroyed were considered burdensome.[4] The city also encouraged the king to take his army to nearby Beverley and demand the payment of a fine from the town for having admitted Henry Murdac in his quest to take possession of the archbishopric at York.[5] The king then moved south to London in September, where he spent some days deliberating his next move. Making up his mind, he gathered more men and joined Eustace in Wiltshire to take the fight to the intruder Henry. The king gave every appearance of being so far in the ascendant that victory must have felt within his grasp.

As the royal forces entered the county, there must have been some fear that young Henry was in real danger because Earl Ranulf launched a conspicuous assault on Lincoln again. Stephen sped away to repel the earl and was occupied for some time at Lincoln. The two pressed each other hard, and the conflict swung from favouring one to the other and back again. It is likely that Ranulf's only real intention was to draw Stephen away from the south-west to buy Henry time to regroup. Had he captured Lincoln, it would have been an added bonus, but the primary objective seemed to be to occupy the king for as long as possible. Finally, Stephen built a new castle strategically placed to restrict Ranulf's ability to raid the region and decided it was time to return to dealing with Henry.[6] In his absence, Eustace had also been drawn away by fresh trouble from Hugh Bigod in Norfolk. There is an increasing sense of Stephen's once disparate enemies beginning to cohere around Henry's cause. Even the writer of the *Gesta Stephani* refers to the Angevin boy consistently from this point onwards as 'Henry, the lawful heir to England'.[7]

Henry FitzEmpress had not been idle in the room provided by Ranulf and Hugh. Along with his cousin William, Earl of Gloucester, the oldest son of his uncle Robert, and Roger, Earl of Hereford he raised as many men as he was able and plunged into Devon, planning to snuff out what remained of the king's authority there. Stephen was faced once more with a war on three fronts and could only meet two of them. Henry captured Bridport, which had been holding out for the king, but found he was unable to defeat Henry de Tracy, one of Stephen's men who was still able to maintain a powerful force in the county. Henry de Tracy harrassed lands held in Henry FitzEmpress's name but swiftly retreated behind the walls of a stout castle whenever the Angevin army drew near. Eventually, Henry got word that Eustace was heading back towards Devizes and decided that he would have to return there too or risk losing land and castles in the area. Displaying an increasing maturity and military understanding, Henry quickly sent some men ahead to protect Devizes Castle and managed his own withdrawal from Devon slowly and carefully, securing as many castles and stamping out as much resistance as he could without becoming bogged down again.[8]

Eustace arrived at Devizes before Henry and managed to break into the outer defences, burning buildings to make the rest of the castle easier to assault. Soon enough, though, Henry and the rest of his army began to arrive in Devizes, and the conflict intensified, the author of the *Gesta Stephani* describing skirmishing and archery battles all around the town. Finally, Eustace was forced back and realized that he would have to withdraw to avoid a severe defeat.[9] Despite the appearance of gaining a victory, Henry opted to leave England immediately after defending Devizes. It is possible that the young knight had never really intended to conquer England on this visit, unless it fell into his lap, and that the campaign had been more about probing Stephen's authority and reminding those who had backed his mother that her claim, now living in him, had not been abandoned and neither had they. There was an understanding that Henry had returned to Normandy on the advice of those close to him in England. If he had sought to understand Stephen's strength, then it had been amply demonstrated. Perhaps to his disappointment, Henry had found, just as his mother had before him, that the nobles of England had not flocked to support him, but remained loyal to Stephen, or maintained a safe distance and neutrality.

Henry's advisors had apparently suggested that he go back to his father and try one more time to secure more men and assistance. A coalition of King David, Earl Ranulf and Henry had been spooked into abandoning an assault on York by the mere presence of the king, and there must have been some sense that, had Ranulf and Hugh Bigod not drawn the king and Eustace away, Henry might have been in very real trouble at

Devizes. Either way, it was clear that they could still not defeat Stephen as things stood. Geoffrey was not displeased or unimpressed by his son's performance in England and in early 1150, allowed his son to formally assume the mantle of Duke of Normandy. This development adds weight to the idea that the 1149 visit to England had been a kind of training exercise, a challenge from father to son to prove Henry was worthy of taking up power and ready to rule in his own right. It is striking quite how unwilling Henry would later be to act in the same way with his own sons, but for now, it strengthened his arm and served as a warning to Stephen. The fight was not over, and the king no longer faced a woman seeking a throne, but a Duke of Normandy, a grandson of Henry I. Having lost most of the backing of the church, it altered the king's position significantly, but for now, Henry remained across the Channel.

The sense that the barons of England had, by now, had enough of the fighting, if they were ever all that keen on it, was reinforced in this period of renewed stalemate by the creation of conventio, or a covenant, between several of them. Dissatisfied with the ongoing uncertainty and unrest, they sought out ways to try and manage the conflict so that as much peace as possible could be enjoyed. As discussed previously, that was what made landowners and traders their money. Some might have revelled in the odd bit of fighting, but on the whole, a state of perpetual war did not serve the nobility's long-term interests. An example of the kind of arrangments being drawn up is the conventio between Ranulf, Earl of Chester and Robert Beaumont, Earl of Leicester. Ranulf was in open opposition to Stephen, but Robert remained loyal to the king. He had some responsibility for supervising the lands of his twin brother Waleran around the earldom of Worcester too, and it is not impossible that Robert was being courted, perhaps willingly, by the Angevin cause. Publically, at least, Robert was still the king's man and so might have considered Ranulf an enemy.

At some undeterminable date between 1149 and 1153, the earls of Chester and Leicester set out to agree on peace between themselves, setting aside the ongoing dispute over the crown. The document set out to achieve a *finalis pax et concordia* – a final peace and concord – between the magnates.[10] The two earls opened the arrangements by stating that they had no desire for conflict with each other but acknowledged that their respective masters were at war. Should the earls be forced to take the field on opposing sides, they each swore not to go against the other with any more than twenty knights, ensuring that any future fighting would be on a limited and controllable scale. The conventio further stipulated that any goods taken by one lord from the other during any such confrontation were to be returned without ransom after the battle was over.

More serious was the agreement that both earls would not allow their respective liege lord to launch assaults on the lands or castle of the other from their own properties. Such an attempt to restrict the actions of, in Robert's case, the king and in Ranulf's, the Duke of Normandy who intended to be king, was risky. Denying their liege lord access to their lands and castles might cause them serious problems and had previously been Stephen's reason for arresting men and confiscating their property. If either earl was forced to move against the other or felt compelled to act for any reason, he was not to do so without giving fifteen days' notice of his intention to attack. Also, neither was to build any castle close to the borders between their lands.

Robert and Ranulf further agreed that they would come to the aid of the other against all men, excepting only their respective liege lord and one other selected, named person. Robert, Earl of Leicester chose his son-in-law, a fellow servant of the king, Simon de Senlis, Earl of Northampton and Huntingdon. Ranulf's selection was more of a surprise and is hard to explain. He took as his named ally Robert de Ferrers, Earl of Derby. Robert de Ferrers had succeeded his father in 1139 and remained loyal to Stephen. He would be active against Henry FitzEmpress after this date so Ranulf cannot have believed that he was sympathetic to the earl's cause. There must have been some reason Ranulf made that particular choice, but it is hard to discern.

Ranulf made other agreements with Robert de Ferrers and with William Peverel of Nottingham on the king's side, and Robert, Earl of Leicester agreed on conventio with Roger, Earl of Hereford and his own twin brother Waleran as Earl of Worcester from those favouring Henry FitzEmpress. The settlements were tenuous and, if tested too vigorously, may have collapsed in a domino effect, but there is a clear demonstration amongst the senior nobility of both factions that they were fed up of being constantly at odds. If Stephen and Matilda, and now Stephen and Henry, could not find a way to make peace for the whole country, then they were willing to create a patchwork of agreements to blanket as much of England as possible. One of the critical responsibilities of a monarch and one that his vassals expected most keenly was the preservation of peace, law and order. In the absence of an effective resolution at the top, the next layer down strove to fill in the gaps themselves.

When King Louis VII of France returned from the embarrassing failure of the Second Crusade in November 1149, he was unhappy to find Henry FitzEmpress installed as Duke of Normandy by his father without reference to Louis as their liege lord. He was encouraged to outrage by Eustace, who was not only Count of Boulogne but also Louis' brother-in-law. Together, they launched a campaign into Normandy, but by August 1151, Louis had given up. In the summer they had taken Arques and Séez but had been unable to progress further. Bernard of Clairvaux set about convincing Louis to seek peace with Henry, thus causing trouble for Stephen once more, and Louis eventually agreed to a reconciliation. On 31 August 1151 at Paris, a concord was formally sealed, and Henry was invested by Louis as Duke of Normandy.

In the immediate aftermath of this victory, Duke Henry, now eighteen, summoned all of the barons of Normandy to attend him at Lisieux on 14 September 1151 to prepare for a full-scale invasion of England. Before the young Duke could mobilize his army, news reached him that his father had died suddenly and unexpectedly on 7 September at Château-du-Loir on his way back to Angers. William of Newburgh offers a deathbed demand on Geoffrey's part that no other chronicler seems to have picked up. The writer claimed that as he lay dying from a fever, Geoffrey insisted that his body should not be buried until his oldest son Henry had sworn to observe the stipulations he laid down. Geoffrey left Anjou to Henry, but only on the condition that if he ever won England, he would hand the county over to his younger brother Geoffrey. According to William of Newburgh, Henry agreed to take the oath, but he would never relinquish Anjou to his brother, and the story does not appear anywhere else. His father may have felt that Henry would be stretched too far, as he seems to have believed Matilda would be. He could not have known his oldest son very well if he tried to force this measure on him.

With the chance to attack England lost for the year, Henry set about further establishing himself in Normandy and Anjou. By March 1152, he was receiving increasingly desperate pleas from his allies in England to come to their aid. His uncle, Reginald, Earl of Cornwall, in particular sent messages encouraging his nephew to hurry to England before Stephen succeeded in annihiliating them. On 6 April 1152, Duke Henry again summoned his barons to Lisieux to make ready an invasion of England. Again, he failed to set sail. This time, news from an ecclesiastical council that had met on 21 March reached the young duke and sent him in the opposite direction. The council, led by the archbishops of Rouen, Rheims, Sens and Bordeaux had been convened at the request of King Louis to investigate the legitimacy of his own marriage to Eleanor of Aquitaine. The couple had been married for fifteen years and in that time had been blessed with two daughters, but no sons. Eleanor had accompanied Louis on the Second Crusade, but their relationship had not stood the strain of the campaign. There were even sordid rumours that Eleanor had engaged in an affair with her uncle, Raymond, Prince of Antioch. Many onlookers in France seemed to think that Louis would not risk losing the wealthy territories in Aquitaine that Eleanor brought to the French crown, but the need for a male heir, and perhaps some unsavoury scandal, had outweighed any desire to hold on to land. The marriage was declared null and void, and the couple separated.

On 18 May 1152, less than two months after the annulment of her marriage, Eleanor was wed to Duke Henry. He was nineteen, and she was about thirty, but there had been rumours the young duke had courted her in Paris during the previous August when he had been invested by Louis. Eleanor was a fierce, independent woman, but she was also the most fabulous prize on the marriage market in western Europe. It is hard to know what won Henry's heart, but when they married, he claimed Aquitaine on her behalf. Louis seemed to think that the lands should remain in his hands on behalf of their daughters, but he was unable to win the argument. If he feared Angevin expansionism, he had just gifted Duke Henry a new and unexpected jewel to add to his growing collection. For all his fury, Louis could do nothing.

By late June, Henry was back at Barfleur, determined to reach England that year. Fate was once more against him, and he was forced to return south by the news that Louis had renewed his alliance with Eustace and, along with Henry, Count of Champagne and, most worryingly, his own brother Geoffrey, had launched an assault on southern Normandy. The French king quickly secured Neufmarché-sur-Epte, but when Duke Henry arrived, he punched hard into the Norman Vexin, which had been in Louis' possession since 1144. Geoffrey tried to rebel within Anjou, but Henry was able to orchestrate the crushing of his revolt. It is to be wondered whether this was the incident that Henry felt released him from any obligation to hand Anjou over to Geoffrey if such an agreement existed. Certainly, it may help to explain Henry's future aversion to the devolving of power anywhere in his territories.

It was increasingly apparent that Henry was unassailable in Anjou and Normandy. Although it took the remainder of 1152 to settle things, there was little real danger of Henry losing anything, even against the King of France. All of that was positive. Henry was receiving ever greater tuition in the arts of war, politics and rule, but none of it helped those in England clinging to the idea that he would come to help them. Reginald had been desperate in March 1152, but the year ended with no aid. As Henry accumulated and solidified possessions in greater swathes across western France, it remained to be seen whether his friends in England could hold out until he was able to return. The young duke's eye seems never to have been very far from England, and his mind was preoccupied, perhaps his mother pricking his conscience repeatedly, convinced now that her son was ready to deliver the end game to Stephen. It had been postponed by fate, but Henry was increasingly the master of his own destiny, and he was coming to England as soon as it was possible.

25

King Stephen

When Henry, archbishop of York, made his peace with king Stephen of England, he promised to endeavour by every means at his disposal to induce the pope to crown Eustace the king's son; for the coronation would never be possible unless the pope's favour were secured.[1]

It might have been during one of the joint initiatives that Louis had suggested to Eustace the idea that the latter should ensure he was crowned during his father's lifetime. There had been moves afoot in England that might have indicated a desire to achieve this end, but knighthood for Eustace and efforts to bring an end to the rift with the church may not have been connected. Louis was terrified by Angevin expansionism. They held Anjou, Maine, Normandy and now Aquitaine, with an eye on England. They might soon turn their voracious gaze to Louis' own rich crown. The French king, therefore, had an interest in propping up Stephen's regime and ensuring Angevin eyes were kept looking further north for as long as possible. Of course, if Eustace did succeed his father, then Louis' sister would also become his queen consort.

In 1151, King Stephen was forced to face the disturbing re-emergence of an almost forgotten threat. Eystein Haraldsson, King of Norway had decided in his mid-twenties to launch raids reminiscent of the old Viking attacks to his west. He captured Harald Maddadson, Earl of Orkney in the far north of Scotland before marauding along the coast and attacking Aberdeen, Hartlepool and Whitby. Whether the Norwegian king had intended anything more than a few sharp incursions to snatch plunder is unclear, but Stephen confronted the invaders at Whitby and drove them away from his shores. Whitby was severely damaged by the attentions of the raiders, but the king had once more successfully come to the defence of his subjects and had beaten back another threat.

During March 1151, Theobald, Archbishop of Canterbury, and now favoured with the powers of Papal Legate coveted by Bishop Henry, had held his first Legatine Council in London. Stephen, Eustace and most of the nobility loyal to Stephen attended. One notable absentee was the newly reconciled Henry Murdac, Archbishop of York, who was travelling to Rome, perhaps to seek the pope's approval for a coronation for Eustace. Murdac's absence almost certainly suited Theobald, who was still trying to formally establish the superiority of Canterbury over York. The council discussed illegal secular exactions against clerics and churches, but there was no real hostility directed at the king and no hint of the previous rift between Stephen and Archbishop Theobald. The former was surely being careful to nurse his relationship with the church because without its support, his reign might falter and his son's coronation was sure not to take place.

John of Salisbury, writing of Henry Murdac's efforts in Rome to secure permission for Eustace's coronation, understood that the blockage was a result of earlier work by Empress Matilda. Guido di Castello had been Cardinal of San Marco and Papal Legate to France before being elected Pope Celestine II in 1143. He only reigned until his death the following year on 8 March 1144, but John of Salisbury knew that Guido had only attained the papal throne 'with the empress's support'. In return for that aid, as Pope Celestine II he had written to Archbishop Theobald expressly forbidding him from doing anything that would change the position of the English crown 'since the transfer of it had been justly denounced, and the matter was still under dispute'. Celestine's successors, Lucius II and Eugenius III, had repeated the prohibition and although it sounded like a measure that might well affect the empress's claims, it specifically prevented Stephen from crowning his son and obtaining for Eustace the same protection Stephen had enjoyed as a result of papal recognition.[2]

Henry of Huntingdon was clear in his understanding that 'the pope had by his letters prohibited the archbishop from crowning the king's son, because King Stephen appeared to have broken his oath of fealty in mounting the throne.'[3] That may have been Celestine's view, in support of the empress's position, but it probably does not represent a new and ongoing rupture between Stephen and Rome. Celestine's successors doubtless felt bound by their predecessor's explicit commands, but they remained insistent that Stephen was the legitimate and lawful King of England. It is more likely that Lucius and then Eugenius maintained

Celestine's line simply as an expedient so that they were excused from contributing to the prolonging of the civil strife in England. While the kingdom gazed into its own navel, it could add little to any efforts in the Holy Land, and the papacy rarely saw Christians fighting Christians as a just war that it could approve of.

As Duke Henry made ever more threatening preparations in Normandy to invade England, Stephen refused to give up on the idea of securing Eustace's coronation. He summoned Archbishop Theobald and all the bishops to him at London in early 1152 and demanded that they crown Eustace. Politely, but firmly, Theobald refused. Henry of Huntingdon wrote that it was here that Archbishop Theobald produced the letters from the pope ordering him not to crown Eustace because of Stephen's oath-breaking, but it is likely that they were the decade-old instructions from Celestine rather than fresh ones from Eugenius. Theobald was perhaps as acutely aware as Stephen that Duke Henry was imminently expected to arrive in England. If the church took sides now, it could not only prolong the coming conflict but if they chose the wrong side, place them in the path of the victor's wrath. The archbishop might have considered that it was time for the church to step back and keep out of what was coming, not least because it might force Stephen and Henry to find some final resolution between them.

It is striking, though, that Theobald now felt confident enough to point out the letters and the enclosed sentiment that Stephen had usurped his throne unjustly. It was a stronger stance than the church had ever taken before against Stephen, at least on that point. It initially backfired, and Stephen moved to a desperate display of his superiority. All of the bishops were arrested, stripped of their lands and imprisoned. Theobald managed to escape and flee to the continent, his sympathy for the king surely disintegrating again. Those held by Stephen were threatened and cajoled in an effort to force them to change their minds, but they remained resolute until the king was left with no option but to relent and set them free, restoring their lands and offering his apologies.[4] In desperation, Stephen is reported to have caused all of the barons to swear fealty to Eustace, but of all people, King Stephen cannot have believed such a move would afford his son much real protection.[5]

On 3 May 1152, King Stephen was hit by a personal blow. His wife of twenty-seven years, Queen Matilda, died in her mid-forties. She had been taken by a sudden fever at Hedingham Castle in Essex.

Stephen arranged for her to be buried at Faversham Abbey, which they had founded together. Stephen himself was approaching sixty, and the loss of his wife was a sharp reminder of his own mortality and what his death might mean for England and for their son. The failure to secure a coronation for Eustace must have suddenly burned more deeply. The king could also reflect on what he owed his wife of more than a quarter of a century. They had two sons, Eustace and William, and a daughter, Mary, but Stephen also owed his wife the throne he was still fighting to retain. In 1141, when Stephen had been a prisoner of the empress, it was Queen Matilda who had kept his cause alive. She had acted impeccably, and importantly in the way the men around her expected a woman and a queen to behave. She had highlighted the empress's unreasonableness by carefully applying for Eustace to be allowed to retain the County of Boulogne, and she had succeeded in putting armies into the field in her husband's name to force the Rout of Winchester. It was this that had eventually secured her husband's release, and Matilda even travelled to Bristol to give herself up as a hostage as part of the prisoner exchange. It is impossible to see the nature of their personal relationship at such a distance and without evidence, so there is no way to speculate about love. That they worked together in perfect harmony and shared trust in and respect for one another is plain to see. The death of Queen Matilda was a personal blow to a king struggling to keep a grip on his realm.

Stephen now turned his attention to military matters, hoping to make the most of Duke Henry's prolonged absence, which was moving into its third year. If the young duke was likely to appear in England at any moment, then the king had a small window in which to try and erode even further the support that still lingered for the empress's cause in the west. Taking an army, Stephen laid siege to Newbury Castle, winning it in short order from John Fitz Gilbert. It is here that the later legend contained in the *History of William the Marshal* relates that William's father, John Fitz Gilbert, had previously given William to King Stephen as a hostage during a truce as an assurance that he would give up the castle if help failed to come. When John refused to hand over Newbury, Stephen supposedly threatened to have the boy catapulted over the walls, but at least was entitled to have him executed, and warned John that he would do it. John sent back the reply that 'he still had the anvils and hammers to produce even finer ones', a callous and crude retort.

Stephen, unable to continue with the threat, consoled the little boy: 'I'll spare you this torture, you can be sure you won't die here now.' The story may be apocryphal and is certainly anecdotal, but it fits with Stephen's tendency towards leniency and honourable behaviour. He was never a cruel man. Whatever else, England perhaps owed Stephen thanks for sparing William Marshal that day so that he could, justifiably, become a legend in the decades that followed.[6]

The next target on Stephen's list was Wallingford. He set about his third attempt since 1139 to reduce the stubborn outpost. Brian Fitz Count appears to have passed away by this point, though his date of death is not recorded. His absence may have led Stephen to believe that the castle might fall and provide a significant tactical victory before Duke Henry arrived. Switching from his previous tactic of a frontal assault on the fortress, Stephen instead ordered the construction of a counter castle across the river at Crowmarsh. From here, the river was blockaded to prevent supplies from reaching Wallingford, and the siege was begun. The garrison was hard pressed and began to struggle. Roger, Earl of Hereford tried to relieve the castle whenever he could, but Stephen's grip was tightening, and it was clear Wallingford could not hold out much longer.

Earl Roger suddenly sent Stephen an offer. The earl would transfer his allegiance to the king and fight tirelessly at his side if the king would help him recover Worcester Castle from Waleran of Meulan's men, who had imprisoned the castellan William de Beauchamp and taken possession of it. The prospect of gaining the allegiance of the principal supporter of Duke Henry in England on the eve of the invasion was too much for Stephen to resist. Leaving some men to continue the siege of Wallingford, Stephen took the rest of his army to Worcester, where he laid siege to the castle alongside Earl Roger. Unsurprisingly, it was a trick. Whether Stephen was blinded by hope or his own devotion to honour and chivalry is impossible to tell, but Earl Roger immediately sent letters to Duke Henry warning him 'if he had any regard for his own supporters or cared at all to recover his kingdom, to return to England with all speed'.[7] Stephen became aware of Earl Roger's duplicity and left the siege of Worcester, though he ordered some of his men to stay behind so that Roger could not claim the king had been the first to break their pact. As soon as Stephen was gone, Roger negotiated with those inside Worcester, and the castle was surrendered to him.

There was still some encouragement for Stephen, not least in the fact that Henry had not come and he still held the crown. Militarily, Stephen retained a firm grip on much of his country. Those in need turned to him, and he was able to raise large armies as required and travel at speed around the country to face problems. The *Gesta Stephani* comments that Henry was kept busy in Normandy by Louis and Eustace and that King Stephen 'bore himself like a brave man and with success all over England'. Furthermore, at Wallingford, support had been flooding to the king's side, 'with the Londoners fighting valiantly by his side and barons flocking in to help him from all over England'.[8]

The inevitable could not be put off forever. 1153 was to prove the year in which King Stephen and Duke Henry finally met head-on, and before the year was out, The Anarchy would have a resolution.

26

Epoch

Thus, through God's mercy, after a night of misery, peace dawned on the ruined realm of England.[1]

In the second week of January 1153, Henry, Duke of Normandy set sail from Barfleur for England. If his previous efforts had been little more than the dipping of his toe in the waters, he now took the plunge: this was a serious invasion in which he meant to unseat King Stephen and take his kingdom. Continuing problems in Normandy meant that the duke could not empty his lands of knights for the expedition and he was forced to settle for sailing in thirty-six ships with 140 knights and 3,000 men-at-arms.[2] It was not a large army, but Henry must have hoped for a stronger response to his arrival than he had experienced before. He was a different man now, not least because he was a man, no longer a boy. He was Duke of Normandy, Duke of Aquitaine, Count of Anjou and he meant to be King of England before the year was out.

Rather than heading directly to relieve the besieged Wallingford Castle, Henry instead went to Devizes where he was joined by Earl Ranulf, his uncle Reginald, Earl of Cornwall, Roger, Earl of Hereford and Patrick, Earl of Salisbury. Patrick had gained his earldom from Empress Matilda in 1141 and was allied to John Fitz Gilbert of Newbury by his sister's marriage, making him the uncle of William Marshal. Although not particularly active, he had remained loyal to the empress and had in fact been minting his own coins in Salisbury as royal authority lapsed in the region. From Devizes, these men struck at Stephen's own precious outpost at Malmesbury. They began to undermine the walls as the townsmen flocked to defend them and Henry sent others with ladders to scale sections while archers loosed volleys of arrows into the town.

Despite some emerging, perhaps politically motivated, sympathy for Duke Henry's cause, the writer of the *Gesta Stephani* still attributes to his men terrible atrocities. He relates that

> when the defenders, unable to bear their fierce assault any longer, fled to the church, containing a convent of monks living according to monastic rule, the attackers burst into the church with them and, after plundering and murdering monks and priests all over it, did not shrink from laying hands on the very altar.[3]

They went on to pillage more churches, committing wanton murder in all quarters of Malmesbury. The English barons who had joined Henry were horrified and advised him to send the Normans and Angevins home before they cost him support. Henry, equally disgusted by their actions (a nod to the writer's shifting sympathies, perhaps), agreed and ordered most of them to leave. The writer has his speedy sample of God's righteous retribution when a storm smashes the ships apart as they cross the Channel, providing timely punishment for those who would defy God's laws.[4]

Henry had just ordered the castle to be encircled and besieged when King Stephen arrived with an army to relieve Malmesbury. The king had come via Cirencester and camped for the night on the northern bank of the River Avon, planning to attack the next morning. When morning broke, Stephen withdrew rather than press forward, blaming a torrential rainfall that had flooded the river and made it impassible.[5] This might have been true, but Stephen may also have begun to doubt the willingness of some of those with him to fight Henry, particularly if they had already started to suggest a confrontation would be a bad idea. The *Gesta Stephani* claims Stephen had 'noticed that some of the leading barons were slack and very casual in their service and had already sent envoys by stealth and made a compact with the duke.'[6] Robert, Earl of Leicester may have been amongst those under increasing suspicion. Somehow the two sides managed to open negotiations in spite of the blockage between them, and they arrived at the odd conclusion that Malmesbury Castle should be demolished because they were unable to fight over it.

The king sent one of his men, named Jordan, into Malmesbury to explain to the garrison what was to happen, but once inside,

Jordan barred the gates, subdued the garrison and let Henry know that he would hand the castle over to the duke.[7] That is the *Gesta Stephani*'s version of the loss of Malmesbury, though Henry of Huntingdon believed that the castellan had surrendered to Duke Henry when Stephen had been forced to withdraw by the heavy rain that made fighting impossible.[8] It seems likely that some form of truce was agreed at the same time as Malmesbury was lost, or in the aftermath at least. There was a cessation of hostilities for a few months, which may have been the result of the bad weather which, combined with the early time of year, made campaigning difficult for both sides. Lent was also approaching, during which fighting was traditionally suspended.

Although Henry might have appeared in the ascendant, if he had been forced to send a portion of his Norman knights home again and had not received the rousing welcome he had hoped for, then he may have been willing to take some time to gather himself. The longer he was in England unchallenged, the higher his stock would rise. For Stephen's part, the king would appreciate time to organize himself and draw in as many men as possible from all corners of the kingdom for the showdown that was to come. Like Henry, he might also have felt that doing nothing served his ends. Empress Matilda had spent years in England and failed to depose him. If Henry chose to sit in the west, just as she had done, and achieve nothing, then few would be inspired to join the young adventurer. Stephen probably had more to fear from a stirring, relentless assault on him than returning to the kind of stalemate he had been used to for fifteen years now.

Duke Henry spent some time at Bristol before moving to Gloucester, where his mother had also initially positioned herself after her arrival in England. On 18 April 1153, Henry held an Easter court in the city and made much of his formal adoption of the title Duke of Aquitaine during the festivities. If a truce was in place, it ended just after Easter, when Duke Henry marched out of Gloucester and headed east, to take the fight to King Stephen. The Angevin army paraded through Worcestershire, Warwickshire and Northamptonshire in a display of confidence. They won Tutbury Castle just west of Derby, and when Robert, Earl of Leicester joined the assault on Earl Ferrers and his fortress, there could be no further doubt where his loyalties now lay. It was a bitter blow to Stephen, who had been so generous to the Beaumont twins in the past, but it might not have been a great surprise. Waleran had defected before, and Robert had followed, but it must have said a great deal about how some nobles now viewed the conflict. On paper, Stephen was still firmly in control and looked unassailable, but Duke Henry offered something that caused senior men in the kingdom to pause and consider their positions carefully.

Warwick Castle was also taken by Duke Henry and his army. The wife of Roger de Beaumont, Earl of Warwick had offered no resistance and, it was claimed, had welcomed the Angevins in and given them the castle. Earl Roger, who was with Stephen and who the author of the *Gesta Stephani* believed 'was truly not at fault', was so overcome by grief and shame when news of his wife's actions reached him at court that he dropped dead.[9] Duke Henry's sudden success in the Midlands was less due to his own military prowess than the defection of Robert, Earl of Leicester and support of Ranulf, Earl of Chester. Their disinclination to block his progress and preference for offering him encouragement and even help laid the region open to Angevin triumph, but there was no real, hard-won military victory. There is some evidence after this that Henry moved south to Bedford, but although some accounts suggest damage to the castle there, none is clear as to whether a siege was attempted or what the outcome was. Henry may simply have passed through and indulged in a bit of light ravaging if it seemed too well defended, or it may have given in after a brief resistance.

Towards the end of July or the beginning of August, Henry decided to move his focus to Wallingford to relieve the ongoing siege there. It had been almost six months since he had been begged for urgent assistance. When he arrived, the duke assaulted the counter castle Stephen had built at Crowmarsh to blockade the river. That was enough to bring Stephen and Eustace rushing west with an army. The reluctance of both sides to bring the matter to a confrontation led to another stand-off. This time, they arrayed themselves on either side of the River Avon. Stephen made no effort to cross but neither did Duke Henry seek to give chase. Had the bailing out of Henry's previous campaign had a softening effect on both men?

The barons, watching their respective leaders find excuses not to give battle, began to see an opportunity to force them to try and find terms if they would not fight: 'Wherefore the leading men of each army, and those of deeper judgement, were greatly grieved and shrank, on both sides, from a conflict that was not merely between fellow-countrymen, but meant the desolation of the whole kingdom.'[10] Stephen and Henry seem to have had a private meeting at a narrow section of the river, away from prying eyes, in which both perhaps bemoaned the fickle loyalties and unreliability of their nobles.[11] Henry of Huntingdon saw malice in the work of the nobility here:

> Then the traitorous nobles interfered, and proposed among themselves terms of peace. They loved, indeed, nothing better than disunion; but they had no inclination for war, and felt no desire to exalt either the one or the other of the pretenders to the crown, so that by humbling his rival they themselves might become entirely subject to the other. They preferred that, the two being in mutual fear, the royal authority should, with respect to themselves, be kept in abeyance.[12]

It is almost certain that the reverse was true. It was the nobles who had been trying to find ways to coexist peacefully without the enforcement of royal rule and in the prevailing uncertainties. Led by Earl Ranulf and Earl Robert, they had been arranging agreements that would keep order and limit the scale of any confrontation that could not be avoided. The prevalence of these is not known with certainty, and Earl Robert was now firmly in Duke Henry's camp, but they may well have been keen to avoid fighting in order not only to prevent breaches of these carefully balanced contracts of peace but because of the complexity involved. Each would have to work out who he was able to fight and against whom he had to limit his efforts, and what plunder might have to be returned. It could prove very difficult to monitor, and the slightest sign of a rupture could be enough to bring down the whole house of cards.

In contrast, King Stephen and Duke Henry had no interest in peace. There was only one crown available, and for as long as Henry wanted it and Stephen refused to give it up, there were no terms that would be acceptable to both men. For them, the best solution might have been a conclusive battle to settle the matter, from which only one of them would walk away. Neither seemed keen on that idea, not least because it was fraught with risk and their adherents were not up for a fight. Stephen and Henry seemed to have abdicated negotiations for a possible peace to their supporters, preferring not get involved and leaving the door ajar for a disavowal of any unpalatable terms. Crowmarsh Castle was torn down, and both armies withdrew from Wallingford.

Although Stephen and Henry had evaded making peace, they actively avoided each other for a time. Military action was not stopped, but neither gave chase to the other directly. Duke Henry besieged and captured Stamford before the end of August, then moved to sack Nottingham. Stephen focused his efforts on subduing Hugh Bigod in Norfolk again, laying siege to the earl in his castle at Ipswich. They seemed happy to dance around each other and indefinitely postpone the inevitable. One person, though, was not willing to leave questions unanswered. Eustace appears to have been annoyed by his father's attitude towards Henry and the failure to seek resolution in battle. The young man, heir to his father's throne, must have known that any negotiated settlement was likely to adversely impact his own prospects more than any other. Keeping Henry satisfied would involve concessions that Eustace would be burdened with when his father was gone. Abandoning his father's court, Eustace set about laying waste to parts of Cambridgeshire and around Bury St Edmunds, probably in an attempt to incite Duke Henry to meet him in battle.

On 17 September 1153, just a few weeks after this impasse at Wallingford, Eustace died. The *Gesta Stephani* blamed grief at his father's failure to protect his son's inheritance.[13] Henry of Huntingdon could offer no explanation for the young man's sudden demise but noted that he was 'a good soldier, but an ungodly man, who dealt harshly with the rulers of the church, being their determined persecutor.'[14] This was perhaps little more than a monkish explanation for his untimely demise, but it was a death that immediately and radically altered the face of the conflict between Stephen and Henry. Eustace was laid to rest with his mother at Faversham Abbey, and in the aftermath, many, led by Archbishop Theobald, saw a new hope of peace. Henry of Huntingdon believed the time was right for an end to war because 'God, which makes peace, and is the giver of good, withdrew the scourge which tormented England'.[15] If England had been punished for its sins, God had decided the penance had been paid. So great was the desire to bring an end to the prolonged dispute that even Bishop Henry joined the negotiations.

Archbishop Theobald was considered neutral, though he appeared to favour Duke Henry. He 'had frequent consultations with the king, in which he urged him to come to terms with the duke, with whom also he communicated by messengers',[16] acting as a go-between. Henry of

Huntingdon thought Bishop Henry suddenly repented of all his evils in securing his brother the crown, but it is more likely that political pragmatism forced him to realize something had to give and the time had come to find that something. With Eustace gone, there was a window through which a final settlement and lasting peace might be dragged into England. If some had realized that there was an ideal solution, but that Eustace would be a blockage to reaching it, then his sudden death must have seemed like providence, however devastated his father was.

Eustace's was not the only death that hastened the country along the road – that seemed so long and winding – to peace. King David of Scotland had died on 24 May 1153. David's son and heir, Prince Henry, who had been close to Stephen for a time, had passed away the previous year and David was succeeded by his grandson, the twelve-year-old Malcolm IV, leaving Scotland to face a minority government for some years to come. In late August or early September, Simon de Senlis, Earl of Huntingdon and Northampton died. Simon had been David's rival in Huntingdon, and the threat of Empress Matilda's favouring of her Scots uncle had kept Simon firmly on Stephen's side. The death of Roger de Beaumont, Earl of Warwick had robbed Stephen of another faithful supporter, and soon, on 16 December 1153, the mighty and troublesome Ranulf, Earl of Chester would join these other great men in trying to explain their part in The Anarchy to God. William of Ypres, Stephen's reliable mercenary captain, was now blind and in retirement. Although Eustace's death was perhaps the most potent catalyst in advancing the peace process, the removal of so many men with long-entrenched interests, often at odds with each other, made finding a settlement significantly easier. Dead men could not grumble and disrupt the peace and their approval was no longer needed.

On 6 November 1153, King Stephen and Duke Henry were finally persuaded to meet each other at Winchester to try and find an agreement. Another potentially troublesome matter had been settled with very little bother, and a great deal of luck, before the negotiations got underway. Eustace's younger brother, Stephen's second son, William, who was by this point around sixteen years old, let it be known that he had no desire to succeed his father. If he were able to keep the County of Boulogne along with all of the lands in Normandy and England that his father had held before he became king, William would renounce any claim to the throne. Those favouring peace must have leapt at the offer. William would be hugely wealthy with vast tracts of land on both sides of the Channel but would have to endure none of the struggles that had blighted his father's life and cost his older brother his. Added to that, he was married to Isabel de Warenne, one of the most valuable heiresses in England. Duke Henry and the clergy negotiating the peace agreed immediately, perhaps mindful that William should not be given too long to get used to the idea of succeeding to a crown. Robert de Torigni summed up the settlement reached at Winchester:

> In the assembly of bishops, earls and other magnates, the king first recognized the hereditary right which Duke Henry had in the kingdom of England; and the duke graciously conceded that the king should hold the kingdom all his life, if he wished, provided the king himself, the bishops and other magnates should declare on oath, that after the death of the king, the duke should have the kingdom, if he survived him, peacefully and without contradiction. An oath was also taken that those landed possessions which had fallen into the hands of intruders should be restored to the ancient and lawful possessors who had them in the time of the excellent King Henry. Also concerning those castles which had come into being since the death of the king; their number was said to be more than 1,115 and they were to be destroyed.[17]

It was a momentous shift in the conflict that immediately sucked all of the air out of the dispute. Stephen made Henry his heir to the crown, Henry of Huntingdon going as far as to suggest that Stephen formally adopt Duke Henry as his son.[18] It must have seemed to all who heard the news trickling out of Winchester that it was too good to be true. Stephen and Henry spent Christmas together in London, and after Stephen led Duke Henry through the streets, the Treaty of Westminster was promulgated, giving final form to the agreements reached in Winchester.[19]

The nobility paid homage to Duke Henry, saving only their allegiance to Stephen for as long as he lived. Some castles were placed into the hands of specified castellans who were required to swear an oath to hand them over to Henry on Stephen's death. Roger de Bussy was installed at Oxford Castle, Jordan de Bussy at Lincoln, and both were Henry's liege men who were to provide hostages for their promise while Stephen lived.

Compromise was the final key to a peace acceptable to all. The stated intention was to return all landholdings to the owners in the time of Henry I, but it was not specified whether this was to be at his accession or death, leaving room for manoeuvre. In practice, this plan was left deliberately vague so that individual cases could be dealt with sensitively and on their own merits, wherever possible by marriage alliances or treaties.

1154 began with a great deal of promise and harmony. A series of joint courts was held at which both Stephen and Henry sat to adjudicate on matters that arose in the immediate aftermath of the peace agreement. At the third of these councils at Oxford on 13 January 1154, all of the senior nobility were required to pay homage to Henry. The king and his heir began to address the problem of the number of castles and counter castles that had sprung up during the troubles, often in close proximity to each other. William of Newburgh commented that these new fortresses suddenly 'melted away like wax before a flame',[20] but it is hard to be sure how many castles there were and how many were actually torn down. Henry of Huntingdon claimed that the issue was raised at the fourth joint council held at Dunstable, where Henry accused Stephen of dragging his heels and leaving his own men in charge of too many castles. Stephen denied the charge and Henry, 'wishing to preserve a good understanding with his new father', agreed to defer the matter for another time.[21] It is unlikely that Henry believed Stephen or was sure that the king could be trusted, but Henry could not risk being the one to break the accord and shatter the peace since that would jeopardize his support and the long-term victory he could see on the horizon.

More joint sessions were held at Canterbury and Dover through February and March, and all seemed settled and amicable. Shortly after Easter 1154, which fell on 4 April, Henry returned to Normandy. Gervase of Canterbury believed Henry had got wind of a plot by Stephen's son William to have the duke assassinated, forcing Henry to flee in a hurry,[22] but it seems unlikely that William would seek to unbalance an agreement he had done so well out of. Henry may simply have realized that he could add nothing to the situation in England now and that his presence might serve to make things worse if he stepped on Stephen's toes. The duke may have felt that the best thing he could do now was to keep out of the way and trust that Stephen would not be willing to break their treaty.

Not long after Henry left, Stephen took himself on a slow progress all around his kingdom, 'encircling the bounds of England with regal pomp, and showing himself off as if he were a new king'.[23] What he was really thinking during this ponderous journey is impossible to tell. If he had intended to buy time with his agreement to allow Henry to succeed him, then the tour may have been designed not only to show himself but to measure support around the country for a fresh offensive. If he asked, he probably found little will for it. Even if he did not mean to upset the newly settled accord, he might have been keen to make sure everyone knew that he was still king and was going nowhere. Stephen's motives at this point can be suspected, and it remains possible that he planned to renew the fight once Henry was out of England.

A more satisfactory explanation lies in the reality of the king's circumstances. He was nearly sixty and had spent the nineteen years of his reign thus far almost constantly in harness, in the saddle and fighting fires. Before 1135, he had been a feted favourite nephew of the king, rich and with an impressive portfolio in Normandy and England. His wife had brought to him the County of Boulogne along with three children who had survived youth in Eustace, William and Mary. Stephen also had at least three illegitimate children, probably sired before his marriage to Matilda of Boulogne. All were the children of one mistress, Damette. Gervase was Abbot of Westminster and Ralph and Almaric, though lower in profile, survived childhood. He had become a king, but it had not brought him peace or security. It is doubtful that he would look back and see too many happy, carefree days. His wife was gone, and now his oldest son and heir Eustace lay beside her at Faversham Abbey. William would be well provided for but had no heart to fight for the crown that had blighted his father's life.

In the end, Stephen had probably just had enough. He was an old man. If he fought on, what would it be for? A throne his son did not want? The agreement with Henry at least promised Stephen peace for the rest of his days, without the need to be constantly rushing from one scrap to the next. If he had ever considered himself a caretaker, perhaps asked by his uncle on his deathbed to keep the crown safe for his grandson, then he could consider his work done, though he had tried to buck against it in the end. The progress may have been the first time he was able to travel around England at leisure and see the beautiful lands that he had ruled for nineteen years without the weight of armour, without a helmet narrowing his vision and without looking over his shoulder. This might have been the first time he enjoyed the tranquil green hills and forests, from north to south and east to west. Just relaxing.

On 25 October 1154, at Dover on the south coast, King Stephen died. He had lived at war, but passed away cradled by an unfamiliar peace. The lack of activity and challenge may have made Stephen feel suddenly old, his body allowing time to catch up with itself once no longer required to perform super-human feats of travel and warfare. The melancholy of his losses – not a throne, but a wife and a son –may have gripped him once he had nothing else to worry about. It is striking, and might have provided some comfort to a proud, honourable man as he lay dying, that Stephen would leave this earth still a king, despite The Anarchy that had tried to unseat him. No one had actually beaten him, and he would greet God wearing the crown of England. As he had wished, his body was interred next to his wife and son at Faversham Abbey in Kent, just twenty-five miles from Dover where he died. Perhaps, in the end, he saw death coming and went to greet it, dying as he had lived: on his own terms.

Duke Henry did not hurry to return to England when news arrived that Stephen had died. It was a risky move. His mother's lethargy had cost her the throne, but Henry perhaps felt more confident in his inheritance. He might have been willing to wait and see whether anyone would dare to challenge him too, daring his enemies to show themselves now, or remain silent under his rule. It was not until 7 December that Henry sailed from Barfleur. He was crowned at Westminster Abbey on 19 December 1154, and the delay between Stephen's death and Henry's coronation was the longest between monarchs in over 100 years. It is possible that part of Henry's broader plan was to make it clear that from now on, the crown would be entirely hereditary, ending the Anglo-Saxon principle, clung to by the church and the Londoners, that a king could be elected. If the nobles wanted their lands back on the basis of hereditary right, then they would have to recognize the same precedent for the crown. No longer would they be able to disrupt the descent from father to son and throw the kingdom into turmoil by trying to insert some other candidate.

King Henry II was now King of England, Duke of Normandy, Duke of Aquitaine and Count of Anjou. He ruled over an empire that stretched from the Pennines in the north of England to the Pyrenees in the south of France, touching the chilly North Sea at one end and dipping a toe in the warm Atlantic at the other. Whether he could hold such a vast domain together remained to be seen, but his dynasty was destined to have an immense impact on the history of medieval Europe.

The Anarchy was over.

Epilogue

My lord pope sent to me, enjoining me, for the remission of my sins, to interfere to renew peace and concord between you and the king, my son, and to try to reconcile you to him.

Letter from Empress Matilda to Thomas Becket, 1165[1]

In her retirement, Empress Matilda could reflect that she had achieved victory in the end, just as Stephen might have. She settled in Normandy and now found herself able to take on a role more familiar to a medieval noblewoman. She promoted religion and acted as a peacemaker where she could, notably when her son spectacularly fell out with Thomas Becket, his Archbishop of Canterbury and a protégé of Archbishop Theobald. She remained busy, though, especially on her son's behalf.

As early as 27 May 1154, Empress Matilda was acting as Henry's agent in Normandy when he was forced to visit Aquitaine. The chronicler Robert of Torigny was elected Abbot of Mont-Saint-Michel, and the appointment was confirmed by Hugh, Archbishop of Rouen and Empress Matilda. Her reach still extended to England in 1159 when she wrote to the Sheriff of Herefordshire ordering him on her own authority as well as that of her son to prevent any action being taken in court against the monks of Reading Abbey that would affect their land and chattels. Reading had been her father's foundation, and he was buried there, so she retained a particular interest in the abbey. The letter ended with the menacing warning that 'Unless you do this, the justiciar of England is to see it done'.[2]

There were times when the empress was active in Normandy alongside her son too. A dispute between William de Bacton and his cousin Robert de Valognes about the possession of the Honour of Bacton was settled before both Henry and his mother. In 1164, it was to Empress Matilda that King Louis VII wrote as the person responsible for justice in Normandy to complain about the treatment a French merchant was receiving in Rouen. The empress replied that Louis' merchant would be treated fairly, offering that the king could send men to sit in on the proceedings if he wished. Her authority was reinforced by her son, who was not averse to ending letters containing his orders 'Unless you do it, let my lady and mother the empress see that it is done'.[3]

In 1165, Empress Matilda refused an audience to the Archbishop of Cologne and other representatives of the Holy Roman Emperor Frederick Barbarossa on the basis that the Emperor supported the schismatic Pope Victor IV against Alexander III, who was recognized by her son and the King of France. Rotrou, Archbishop of Rouen wrote to Cardinal Henry of Pisa to explain the empress's actions and felt confident enough to assure the cardinal: 'Do not imagine for a moment that she will vacillate in any way.'[4] Although Thomas Becket insisted the empress had made no public objection, some of the bishops of England believed that she had tried to block his selection as Archbishop of Canterbury on the death of Theobald, but that she had been overruled by her son.[5] Her authority may have begun to wane as Henry's confidence increased and he saw less need to lean on his mother's experience. It was one piece of advice Henry might have done well to heed, since his mother had seen the danger of political appointments to high offices in the church during her time in the Empire. Her son, though, was surrounded by his own counsellors and was ruling a vast domain in his own right. He could not turn to his mother forever.

Empress Matilda died at Rouen on 10 September 1167, aged sixty-five. She had been actively engaged in trying to maintain peace between her son and Louis VII until the very end, and Henry was about to launch an invasion of Brittany when he heard of her death and immediately turned back. At her request, the empress was buried at the Abbey of Bec-Hellouin in front of the High Altar. The empress's mortal remains have since undergone almost as much adventure as she did in life. In 1263, the Abbey of Bec-Hellouin was seriously damaged by fire and her tomb was left covered in rubble. Restoration only took place in 1282, when her body was sown into an ox skin, as was common at the time, and her tomb repaired. In 1421, the church was ransacked by the English as part of the Hundred Years' War, and her tomb was smashed to pieces. In was not until 1684 that efforts were made to reinstate the monument. In March of that year, human remains were discovered near the High Altar along with scraps of silk and a partial inscription that identified them as those of Empress Matilda. The body was wrapped in a cloth of green and gold silk and placed into a coffin lined with lead and then wood.

During the Napoleonic Wars, the abbey was completely destroyed by Emperor Napoleon's army. It was excavated in 1846, and the empress's coffin was rediscovered. Norman archaeologists sought permission from King Louis-Philippe to rebury the empress at St Denis, where French monarchs had traditionally been laid to rest, but the request was refused. Instead, they were allowed to reinter Empress Matilda at Rouen Cathedral. Ironically, she has since rested in the place her father had selected for her in 1134 when it looked like she might die. She had appealed against it and won him over, but Henry I seemed to have a way of getting what he wanted in the end, even if it took a long time and a difficult struggle.

The epitaph supplied for Empress Matilda is poetic and witty, but it hardly does her justice. For all of her faults, and they appear to have been many, she achieved more than many of her sex in her period and came within a hair's breadth of being England's first queen regnant. She kept the claim of Henry I's line alive and bequeathed to her son a position from which he was able to become one of the most potent and powerful European rulers in medieval history. It seems an injustice to only remember her for the men in her life and ignore her own achievements and contributions.

Great by birth,
greater by marriage,
greatest in her offspring:
here lies Matilda,
the daughter, wife, and mother of Henry

Conclusion

> They oppressed greatly the wretched men of the land with the making of castles; when the castles were made, they filled them with devils and evil men.[1]

Did they? The lingering perception of the period of King Stephen's reign from 1135 to 1154 is that it was an era of brutality and barbarism that is best forgotten. The voices of the chroniclers that echo through the centuries as they used to ring around their cloisters are adamant that the suffering was so great that only God's outrage and indignation could explain it. The perpetrators must be those secular men of power who live outside the monasteries and beyond the reach of the church, so that each of their deaths must be the punishment delivered by God, measuring out their evil for all to see.

Those writers provide an invaluable insight into the reign of King Stephen that would otherwise be left shrouded in shadow and mystery. There were surely outbursts of violence and destruction of property and crops when action took place at a nearby castle or town, but these cannot have been as widespread or sustained as the writers wish us to believe. The opportunity to provide a moral lesson needed to be wrapped in a good read and nothing reads better than war, blood, torture and the fall of kings. It is striking how many of these commentators lived on the frontiers of the conflict. William of Malmesbury's town was a constant focus throughout. The author of the *Gesta Stephani* was possibly the Bishop of Bath, or at least one of his associates, so was also in the same region. The famous lines from *The Anglo-Saxon Chronicle*, in which Christ and his saints sleep as England is punished, come from a continuation written at Peterborough, the area where Hugh Bigod caused almost constant trouble for one reason or another, drawing conflict to the region. Foreign writers heard news from these monks, and painted an ever bleaker picture.

That is not to say that no one suffered. Anyone in the path of a hungry, careless army or near the site of a siege or skirmish would face the terror of losing all of their food and perhaps seeing their home burnt to clear space for siege machinery. It mattered little how widespread the troubles were if they landed at your threshold. For the vast majority of England, though, it is likely that they saw little of the fighting and felt minimal impact from the rumblings of their betters. Some knights and noblemen indulged in pillaging to make a quick coin, that much is almost certain, but for the majority, the return of order, certainty and prosperity was what they craved. The desire for it can be seen in the increasing unwillingness of any to take the field and the way that they compensated for their master's shortcomings by working together and reaching agreements to plaster over the cracks.

Royal authority, of some kind, was not really lacking in any part of England. Borders shifted a little, but King David ruled the parts of the north he controlled in peace. Empress Matilda in the west kept order where she had authority and Stephen's reach extended across the rest of England, from York to Dover. The government had a different face regionally, but it performed its role whatever mask it wore and whichever banner flew above it. Although the monkish chroniclers were the first to trumpet the peril that waited along every road, Stephen's reign saw an explosion of monastic activity, with new foundations springing up throughout England and monks travelling from established communities to fill the new ones. Bernard of Clairvaux's Cistercians had six houses in England in 1135 and by 1154, that number had rocketed to fifty-four, despite their frequently fraught relationship with Stephen. They cannot have felt too frightened to step outside the walls of their cloisters, even if they claimed they were. The ability of those wishing to travel to Portugal on a crusade to organize themselves, fund the trip and the security they must have felt to leave the country and their families behind strongly suggests there was not perpetual terror.

When Stephen took the throne in 1135, he faced a myriad of problems Henry I had left behind. The prevalence of these might have caused Henry to ask Stephen to step up in Matilda's place on his deathbed. King David threatened the north, the Welsh reacted to a change of ruler by trying to break their bonds, and Normandy only ceased to tear itself apart when it was invaded by the Count of Anjou on an annual basis. When Matilda added to his problems in the west and Hugh Bigod determined to unsettle the east, Stephen was fighting a war on every front that he had. Although he still languishes in the historical gloom of the umbrella of The Anarchy, he perhaps deserves more sympathy and admiration than he has been able to garner in the eight centuries since his death. When he was succeeded by his enemy, the struggle to maintain a reputation immediately became all the more impossible. From that perspective, it is worth considering what Henry FitzEmpress, then King Henry II, made of his predecessor. It was Stephen who had bailed out Henry's abortive campaign when he was fourteen after his own mother and uncle refused to help. In 1153, the unwillingness of Henry to actually fight Stephen is remarkable. Henry was never one to shy away from a confrontation, but he consistently avoided, and facilitated the avoidance of, a final clash. He may have learned from his father's careful patience in Normandy, but it is also possible that he had respect for Stephen, maybe even that he liked his first cousin once removed. Stephen was, all agreed, a likeable man, almost to a fault, lacking the killer instinct of a king.

Empress Matilda is a likewise admirable, if flawed, figure. The easy way to get what she wanted when she arrived in England was to play the part of the dutiful wife and mother, there to protect the rights of her husband and their son. Never one to take an easy path, she insisted that she not only had a right to rule, but that she could do it as well as any man, and she didn't need one with her to do it. Military activity in her own name remained impossible, but in her half-brother Robert, she had someone more than capable of fulfilling that necessary role without wanting to be her equal as a fee for his service. By early 1141, she had manoeuvred her cause onto the brink of the throne, and she had achieved it by herself and in her own name (accepting that Robert played a significant part in that, but meaning without her husband or son as even a talisman). Unfortunately, she would lose the chance that had been crafted in part through her own stubbornness, but it cannot have been entirely her own fault. The men she sought to rule had little desire to pay homage to a woman. They had no reference point for it and wouldn't know where to begin. Matilda might have sought a way to nurture them through the thorny maze, but she saw no reason to. A man would not have had to, so she would not. Otherwise, she dangerously distinguished herself from kings. Had a king, her father or her son, for example, behaved the way she did in 1141 in London it would have been applauded as a signal of strength and a firm stamping of authority, but in a woman, it created shock and perplexed disgust.

It is a myth of the history written by the victors that King Stephen was despised throughout his reign. He was welcomed to the throne, elected as king even, by London and the clergy in 1135. The north was willing to fight off King David in his name even when he could not be there, and throughout his troubles, the farthest reaches of his kingdom consistently turned to Stephen for help when they needed it most. The majority of the significant and lasting losses that he suffered were the result of his absence and imprisonment in 1141. The case for Matilda's legitimacy as Henry I's heir seems inevitable with the dangerous benefit of hindsight, but it had little traction in England in the 1140s. Robert's unassailable fortress at Bristol and a handful of capable men such as Miles of Gloucester and Brian Fitz Count propped up her cause, but the overwhelming majority of the rest of the country's knight and nobles unfailingly turned out for Stephen, at least before 1153. Those living through Stephen's kingship accepted it. The pope explicitly approved Stephen's accession, and the papacy never withdrew that legitimacy.

A large part of the anathema that still surrounds this period has its roots in Victorian histories of the era. The nineteenth century was all about the glory of empire, even if that glory only looked polished at a distance and the real grime of it went unseen. Devolution was the enemy of Victorian imperialism but is embraced today as fair and enlightened, so Stephen is perhaps overdue, and worthy of, reconsideration. Victorians sought out what they approved of: the establishment and development of institutions as models for centralizing authority. These marked the footprints of England and Great Britain's inexorable march to superiority across the globe. Henry I's Exchequer and Henry II's Common Law were interesting to them as building blocks that laid the foundations of the empire they enjoyed and took pride in.[2] Henry VIII can only have been a force for good because he brought control of the church and religious authority within his own shores. For Stephen, who favoured the placement of capable men he could trust in local, regional roles to represent him, there was no bunting or brass band. It was abhorrent, a retrograde stumble on the path to empire that should be swept under the carpet. They managed to miss something even bigger than the Exchequer and the Common Law that they ought to have appreciated.

One of the real legacies of The Anarchy is the establishment and reinforcement of the strength of the institution of monarchy. The crown was not yet an hereditary right that could be automatically passed from father to son, but Stephen demonstrated its power as a symbol of national unity. Despite assertions that Henry I and Henry II were 'better' kings than Stephen, he was never unseated. Compare his steadfastness to that lacking in Richard II, Henry VI and Edward IV, all of whom lost their crowns, Henry VI twice. Stephen's willingness to devolve his authority was not only effective but seemed popular. It was more in line with Anglo-Saxon styles of rule, a concept embraced at the very beginning of Stephen's reign by his election. Henry I had seen the benefits of marrying an Anglo-Saxon princess from the House of Wessex in a country that still felt the yolk of Norman subjugation. What better way to integrate than to return to the old ways of doing things? What his contemporaries may have seen as desirable and popular, later commentators have sneered at. His real achievement was in demonstrating that the institution of kingship could not be broken. Even when a prisoner, Stephen did not become irrelevant because the office he held was vital and no one else filled it. In fact, his release only polished his authority to a new sheen, buffed by God's explicit approval of him. In nineteen years of rule, none was able to unseat him because the removal of a crown was unconscionable, and would remain so for another 250 years.

Henry II was quick to get a handle on his new realm of England. This was not through administrative magic or the immediate resurrection of institutions lying in the dust for nineteen years. Henry was able to reap the rewards of the Exchequer, a functioning justiciary and a well-oiled local administration because it had never gone away. Some of Henry's most complete and profitable early returns came from the south-east, in regions utterly loyal to Stephen and firmly under his control. The north of England was easy to regain from a minor King of Scotland, like taking cake from a child. All of the problems that had faced Stephen on his accession did not hinder Henry II, and it is to be wondered how much that was due to Stephen's careful, assiduous skill as a king.

In summation, The Anarchy is perhaps a colourful handle to give a period during which a former king's daughter claimed the crown that sat on the current king's head, but it does a disservice to King Stephen to label his entire reign as lawless and lacking in government. If it were, then the fault would lie equally with Empress Matilda, King David and Count Geoffrey, each of whom had control over some area of Stephen's domain. In fact, it was probably a far more settled era than it appears and the lingering distaste, a vestige of Victorian prejudices, should be washed away and the innovations of Stephen's kingship, not to mention his success is retaining his throne and dying with the crown on his head, should be afforded new appreciation.

Empress Matilda's achievements and legacy are likewise worthy of admiration. Her impact can perhaps be seen more tangibly in the years, decades and centuries that followed. Walter Map wrote around the turn of the thirteenth century of the advice Empress Matilda had given her son on ruling, and it perhaps sums up her enduring legacy:

> His mother taught him, I have heard, to prolong every case of every man, to hold fast for a long time whatever fell into his hands and thus reap its advantages, and to keep in suspense those women who were in high hope, confirming this opinion by the following heartless parable, to wit: 'An untamed hawk, when raw flesh is often offered to it, and then withdrawn or hidden from it, becometh greedy, and is more ready to obey and to remain' She used to tell him also to be 'free in bed, infrequent in business'; to see that no one's bequest, except of what he had seen or known, should have validity, and other evil advice of this sort.[3]

Notes

Introduction

1. *Collins English Dictionary, Home Edition*, HarperCollins Publishers, 2011, p. 20.
2. *The Anglo-Saxon Chronicle*, p. 246.
3. Ibid, p. 248.
4. *William of Malmesbury*, pp.75-7.

Prologue

1. *Orderic Vitalis*, p. 39.
2. *Orderic Vitalis*, p. 33. pp. 33-7 provide Orderic's detailed account of the *White Ship* disaster.
3. Ibid, p. 34.
4. Ibid, p. 36.
5. Ibid, p. 37.

1. The Death of Henry I

1. *Orderic Vitalis*, pp. 151-2.
2. Ibid, p. 153.
3. *The Anglo-Saxon Chronicle*, p. 245.

2. Empress Matilda

1. *Chroniques des ducs de Normandie par Benoit*, ed. Carin Fahlin, Lund, 1951–67, pp. 604-6.
2. *Opera Omnia, Vol V*, Anselm, ed. F.S. Schmitt, Edinburgh, 1851, pp. 410-2.
3. *Henry of Huntingdon*, pp. 343-4.
4. *The Empress Matilda*, M. Chibnall, Blackwell Publishers, 1991, p. 16, n. 34 citing *Regesta*, ii, n. 919. Original charter can be found in the British Library, Cart. Harl. 43, C11.
5. *Chroniques des ducs de Normandie par Benoit*, ed. C. Fahlin, Lund, 1951–67, pp. 604-6.

6. *The Empress Matilda*, M. Chibnall, Blackwell Publishers, 1991, p. 26, n. 26 cites *Anonymi Chronica Imperatorum Heinrico V dedicata*, ed. F.J. Schmale and I. Schmale-Ott, 1972, p. 262.
7. *The Empress Matilda*, M. Chibnall, Blackwell Publishers, 1991, p. 11. n. 21 cites *Eadmeri Historia Novorum in Anglia*, ed. M. Rule, RS, 1884, p. 127.
8. *William of Malmesbury*, p. 5.
9. *The Anglo-Saxon Chronicle*, p. 238.
10. *William of Malmesbury*, p. 7.
11. Ibid, p. 19.
12. Ibid, p. 9.
13. Ibid, p. 5.
14. Ibid, p. 11.
15. Ibid, p. 19.
16. *Henry of Huntingdon*, p. 258.
17. *Robert of Torigny's Interpolations in the Gesta Normannorum ducum*, ed. Jean Marx, Société de l'histoire de Normandie, Paris, 1914.
18. *Henry of Huntingdon*, p. 259.
19. Ibid, p. 263.
20. *William of Malmesbury*, p. 25.
21. *The Gesta Stephani*, pp. 13-5.

3. King Stephen

1. *The Gesta Stephani*, p. 5.
2. *King Stephen*, R. H. C. Davis, Longmans, Green and Co, 1967, p. 2. n. 4. cites *Die Kreuzzugsbriefe aus der Jahren 1088–1100*, Innsbruck, 1901, pp. 138-40 for Count Stephen's letter.
3. *The Ecclesiastical History of England and Normandy by Orderic Vitalis, Vol III*, T. Forester, London, 1854, pp. 133-4.
4. *The Gesta Stephani*, p. 7.
5. Ibid.
6. Ibid.
7. Ibid.
8. Ibid, p. 11.
9. Ibid.
10. Ibid.
11. *Orderic Vitalis*, p. 155.
12. Ibid.

4. Empress Matilda

1. *Orderic Vitalis*, p. 167.
2. Ibid, pp. 156-7.

3. Ibid, p. 157.
4. Ibid, p. 158.
5. Ibid, pp. 164-9 for the detail of Geoffrey's incursion into Normandy.
6. Ibid, p. 165.
7. Ibid.
8. Ibid, p. 166.
9. Ibid, p. 167.
10. Ibid, p. 169.
11. Ibid.
12. Ibid.

5. King Stephen

1. *Documents Illustrative of English Church History*, H. Gee and W. J. Hardy, London, 1896, pp. 66-8 & *William of Malmesbury*, pp. 35-7.
2. Ibid, p. 67.
3. *Henry of Huntingdon*, p. 264.
4. *Scottish Annals from English Chronicles AD 500 to 1286*, A. O. Anderson, London, 1908, pp. 172-3
5. Ibid, p. 173.
6. *The Gesta Stephani*, p. 27.
7. *William of Malmesbury*, p. 33.
8. *Adami de Domerham de rebus gestis Glastoniensibus*, ed. T. Hearne, 2 vols, Oxford, 1727, ii, p. 310.
9. *William of Malmesbury*, p. 33.

6. Empress Matilda

1. *The Gesta Stephani*, p. 33.
2. Ibid, p. 37.
3. Ibid, p. 39.
4. Ibid, pp. 39-41.
5. Ibid, p. 43.
6. Ibid, p. 45.
7. Ibid.

7. King Stephen

1. *Orderic Vitalis*, p. 174.
2. Ibid, p. 173.
3. Ibid, p. 174.
4. *The Anglo-Saxon Chronicle*, p. 248.
5. *Orderic Vitalis*, p. 176.
6. Ibid, p. 178.

7. Ibid, p. 184.
8. Ibid.
9. *William of Malmesbury*, p. 39.
10. Ibid.
11. Ibid, p. 41.

8. Empress Matilda

1. *Orderic Vitalis*, p. 175.
2. Ibid, p. 196.
3. Ibid.
4. Ibid.
5. Ibid, p. 197.
6. Ibid, p. 206.
7. Ibid, p. 207 for Orderic's account of the attack on Touques and William Trussebot's plan to drive the Angevins out.
8. *William of Malmesbury*, p. 24.
9. *The Gesta Stephani*, pp. 13-5: 'When he was advised, as the story went, to claim the throne on his father's death, deterred by sounder advice he by no means assented, saying it was fairer to yield it to his sister's son, to whom it more justly belonged, than presumptuously to arrogate it to himself.'

9. King Stephen

1. *William of Malmesbury*, p. xlviii citing Annals of Winchester, in Ann. Mon. ii, p. 51.
2. Ibid, p. 41.
3. *The Gesta Stephani*, p. 67.
4. Ibid, p. 69.
5. *The Church Historians of England, Vol IV, Part I*, Rev. J. Stevenson, London, 1856, p. 9.
6. *Henry of Huntingdon*, p. 266.
7. *The Church Historians of England, Vol IV, Part I*, Rev. J. Stevenson, London, 1856, p. 9.
8. Ibid.
9. Ibid.
10. *Henry of Huntingdon*, pp. 267-8.
11. *The Church Historians of England, Vol IV, Part I*, Rev. J. Stevenson, London, 1856, p. 10.
12. *Henry of Huntingdon*, p. 269.
13. Ibid, pp. 269-70.

14. *Henry of Huntingdon*, p. 270 gives the Scottish casualties as 11,000, claiming the English 'gained this victory with very little effusion of blood'. He also mentions Scots being killed where they were found wandering later. *The Church Historians of England, Vol IV, Part I*, Rev. J. Stevenson, London, 1856, pp. 10-1 gives the name Bagmoor for the field 'in scorn of this affair' and states that no pursuit was made and that the Scots became lost 'straggling in ignorance of the locality'.
15. *Henry of Huntingdon*, p. 269.
16. 'de Gant' was used to denote 'of Ghent'. The toponym is similar to that applied in the fourteenth century to John of Gaunt; 'of Gaunt' being an Anglicized form of 'of Ghent'.
17. Earl of Albemarle and Count of Aumale were interchangeable titles relating to the county of Aumale in Normandy. *The Chronicle of Florence of Worcester*, T. Forester, London, 1854, p. 264 gives William le Gross, Earl of Albemarle as one of the leaders of the English army.
18. *The Church Historians of England, Vol IV, Part I*, Rev. J. Stevenson, London, 1856, p. 11.

10. Empress Matilda

1. *William of Malmesbury*, p. 61.
2. *King Stephen*, D. Matthew, Hambledon and London, 2002, pp. 88-9.
3. Ibid, p. 89, citing *Herimann of Tournai, Liber de restauratione monasterii S. Martini Tonacensis*, ed. G. Waltz, MGHSS, xiv, pp. 276-317, at p. 282.
4. *The Gesta Stephani*, p. 87 and *William of Malmesbury*, p. 61.
5. *William of Malmesbury*, p. 61. This is what the quote at the opening of the chapter refers to.
6. *The Gesta Stephani*, p. 87.
7. *William of Malmesbury*, p. 63.
8. *The Gesta Stephani*, p. 97.
9. *William of Malmesbury*, p. 61.
10. *The Gesta Stephani*, p. 101.

11. King Stephen

1. *Orderic Vitalis*, p. 121.
2. The dating of some creations of earldoms is difficult to pinpoint in time. It was long believed that Hugh received his title in 1137, but R. H. C. Davis has been able to convincingly suggest that the creation took place in 1138. They will perhaps remain uncertain and shifting as new evidence comes to light, but the key thing is Stephen's broader programme in 1138–40 rather than the specific dates of individual grants.

3. *Henry of Huntingdon*, p. 271: 'Having got hold of the bishop's treasures, he used them to obtain in marriage for his son Eustace the hand of Constance, Lewis the French king's sister.' There was apparently an understanding that Roger had stockpiled wealth which the king had confiscated.
4. *William of Malmesbury*, p. 47.
5. *The Gesta Stephani*, p. 73.
6. Ibid, p. 77.
7. *William of Malmesbury*, p. 47.
8. *The Gesta Stephani*, p. 77.
9. *William of Malmesbury*, p. 49.
10. Ibid, p. 51.
11. Ibid.
12. Ibid, p. 53.
13. Ibid, p. 55.
14. Ibid, p. 57.
15. Ibid, pp. 57-9.
16. *The Gesta Stephani*, p. 99.
17. Ibid, p. 101.
18. *Henry of Huntingdon*, p. 273.

12. Empress Matilda

1. *William of Malmesbury*, p. 73.
2. This kind of thing seems to pass for entertainment today. I'm sure I've seen this in an episode of *I'm a Celebrity, Get Me Out of Here*.
3. *William of Malmesbury*, pp. 75-7 for the episode with Robert Fitz Hubert.
4. *The Gesta Stephani*, p. 107.
5. *William of Malmesbury*, p. 77.
6. Ibid, p. 71.
7. *The Gesta Stephani*, p. 111 shows two leaves missing between the Robert Fitz Hubert incident and the build-up to the events of 1141.
8. *William of Malmesbury*, p. 77.
9. Ibid, pp. 73-5.
10. Ibid, p. 77.

13. King Stephen

1. *Orderic Vitalis*, p. 214.
2. Ibid, p. 214 for Orderic's telling of this story.
3. *The Gesta Stephani*, p. 113.
4. Ibid, p. 111 and *Henry of Huntingdon*, p. 276. Henry adds the detail of the pix falling from its fastenings.
5. *Henry of Huntingdon*, p. 274.

6. Ibid, p. 277.
7. Ibid.
8. Ibid, pp. 277-8.
9. Ibid, p. 279 and *Orderic Vitalis*, pp. 216-7.
10. *The Gesta Stephani*, p. 113.
11. *Orderic Vitalis*, p. 217.
12. *Henry of Huntingdon*, p. 279.
13. *Orderic Vitalis*, p. 217.
14. Ibid.
15. Ibid.
16. *Chronicles of the Reigns of Stephen, Henry II and Richard I, Vol IV*, ed. R. Howlett, London, 1889, pp. 139-41.
17. *William of Malmesbury*, p. 87.
18. *The Gesta Stephani*, p. 113.
19. *Wiliam of Malmesbury*, p. 87.
20. Henry of Huntingdon, p. 280.
21. *The Gesta Stephani*, p. 115.
22. *Henry of Huntingdon*, p. 280.
23. *The Gesta Stephani*, p. 115.

14. Empress Matilda

1. *The Gesta Stephani*, p. 117.
2. *William of Malmesbury*, p. 87.
3. Ibid.
4. *The Gesta Stephani*, p. 119.
5. Ibid.
6. Ibid, p. 117: 'But still the greater part of the kingdom at once submitted to the countess and her adherents.'
7. Ibid, p. 119.
8. Ibid, p. 121.
9. *Henry of Huntingdon*, p. 280.
10. *William of Malmesbury*, p. 91.
11. Ibid.

15. King Stephen

1. *Henry of Huntingdon*, p. 315. Bishop Henry was not the king's son but his nephew. The letter seems to have been written around 1135, before Stephen's accession, so Henry of Huntingdon is somewhat prophetic in his assessment of Bishop Henry at least in terms of the part he is perceived to have played during his brother's reign.
2. *William of Malmesbury*, p. 91.

3. Ibid, p. 93.
4. Ibid.
5. Ibid.
6. Ibid.
7. *The Gesta Stephani*, p. 7.
8. *William of Malmesbury*, p. 95.
9. Ibid.
10. Ibid.
11. *The Empress Matilda*, M. Chibnall, Blackwell Publishers, 1991, p. 99. The full list is: 'And I call the following to witness that what I say you commanded is true: Theobald, called archbishop of Canterbury, Bernard, bishop of St David's, Robert, bishop of Hereford, Simon, bishop of Worcester, the bishop of Bath (whose name escapes me), Robert, bishop of Exeter, Seffrid, bishop of Chichester, Roger, bishop of Chester, Adelolf, bishop of Carlisle, Everard, bishop of Norwich, Robert, bishop of London, Hilary, dean of Christchurch, David, king of Scotland, Robert, earl of Gloucester, Miles of Gloucester, Ralph Paynel, Earl Ranulf of Chester, William Peverel of Nottingham, William de Roumare, Earl Hugh of Norfolk, Aubrey de Vere, Henry of Essex, Roger of Valognes, Gilbert fitz Gilbert, Geoffrey de Mandeville, Osbert Eightpence and all the Londoners, William of Pont de l'Arche and all the men of Winchester, Robert of Lincoln, Robert Arundel, Baldwin de Redvers, Roger de Nonant, Reginald the son of your uncle, William de Mohun, William de Curcy, Walter de Chandos, Walter de Pinkeney, Elias Giffard, Baderon, Gilbert de Lacy, Robert de Euias, William de Beauchamp, Miles de Beauchamp, John de Bidun, Robert de Aubigny, William Peverel of Dover, William de Sai, William fitz Richard, Roger of Warwick, Geoffrey de Clinton, William fitz Alan. These are the men who heard.'

16. Empress Matilda

1. *William of Malmesbury*, p. 97.
2. *The Gesta Stephani*, p. 121.
3. *William of Malmesbury*, p. 97.
4. *The Gesta Stephani*, p. 121.
5. Ibid, pp. 121-3.
6. Ibid, p. 123.
7. *William of Malmesbury*, p. 99.
8. *The Gesta Stephani*, p. 123.
9. I am aware that understanding this requires a degree of misogyny distasteful to most twenty-first-century ears. I do not approve of the views expressed in this passage, but it is important to appreciate what Queen Matilda's peers

expected and how they would have reacted. The queen offered them what they were used to, what they anticipated and wanted. The empress represented an unknown, the dropping off of a cliff edge that would always inspire more fear than willingness to leap in medieval noblemen.

10. *The Gesta Stephani*, p. 123.
11. *William of Malmesbury*, p. 101.
12. Ibid.

17. King Stephen

1. *The Gesta Stephani*, p. 119.
2. Ibid, p. 125 for the attack of the Londoners on Empress Matilda.
3. Ibid.
4. *William of Malmesbury*, p. 101.
5. Ibid, p. 105.
6. Ibid, p. 103.
7. Ibid, p. 105.
8. *The Chronicle of Florence of Worcester*, trans. T. Forester, London, 1854, p. 284 and *The Anglo-Saxon Chronicl*e, p. 250. Florence of Worcester's account has Bishop Henry proclaiming peace throughout the city and then calling in Queen Matilda's army when the Angevins relaxed.
9. *Stephen and Matilda*, J. Bradbury, The History Press, 2009, p. 123, n. 45 quoting H. W. C. Davis, *'Henry of Blois and Brian fitz Count'*, EHR, xxv, 1910, pp. 297-303, p. 298.
10. *The Chronicle of Florence of Worcester*, trans. T. Forester, London, 1854, p. 284.
11. *The Gesta Stephani*, p. 135.
12. *The Chronicle of Florence of Worcester*, trans. T. Forester, London, 1854, pp. 284-5.
13. *William of Malmesbury*, p. 107.
14. Ibid.
15. Ibid, p. 117.
16. Ibid, pp. 117-9.
17. Ibid, p. 119.

18. Empress Matilda

1. *William of Malmesbury*, p. 127.
2. Ibid, p. 123.
3. Ibid.
4. Ibid, p. 125.
5. Ibid.

6. Ibid, 'The count came without reluctance'.
7. Ibid. I have inferred this from the protestation recorded from Geoffrey that 'he was kept from coming to England because a number of castles were in revolt against him in Normandy'.
8. Ibid, p. 127.
9. Ibid. William of Malmesbury seems insistent that Stephen burned every place he visited. Whilst it is possible that some suburban structures were cleared away to make an area either more defensible or easier to assault, both sides would have been as capable of such action. It seems unlikely, though not impossible, that Stephen actively sought to reduce entire towns to ash everywhere he went. After all, he would hope to rely on income from areas he took back under his authority.
10. *The Gesta Stephani*, p. 139.
11. *William of Malmesbury*, p. 127.
12. Ibid, pp. 127-9. 'But it was not their plan to assail him within the city, which the earl of Gloucester had so strongly fortified with earthworks, that it seemed impregnable unless it were set on fire'. This also seems to suggest that Stephen had not, in fact, already burned the city.
13. Ibid, p. 127.
14. Ibid, p. 129.
15. Ibid, pp. 129-131.
16. Ibid, p. 131.
17. *The Gesta Stephani*, p. 143 and *Henry of Huntingdon*, p. 281 for their respective accounts of this incident, which are relied on below.
18. *William of Malmesbury*, p. 133.
19. *The Gesta Stephani*, p. 145.

19. King Stephen

1. *The Gesta Stephani*, p. 141.
2. Ibid, p. 145.
3. Ibid, p. 147.
4. Ibid.
5. Ibid, p. 149.
6. Ibid, pp. 149-51.
7. Ibid, p. 151.
8. Ibid, p. 161.
9. *Chronicles of the Reigns of Stephen, Henry II and Richard I, Vol I*, ed. R. Howlett, London, 1884, p. 45.
10. *The Gesta Stephani*, p. 161.
11. *Henry of Huntingdon*, p. 282.

12. *The Gesta Stephani*, p. 165.
13. *Henry of Huntingdon*, p. 282.
14. *King Stephen*, R. H. C. Davis, Longmans, Green and Co, 1967, p. 84.
15. *The Anglo-Saxon Chronicle*, pp. 247-8. Part of this quote appears earlier but is repeated both for its relevance to the episode involving Geoffrey de Mandeville at Ramsey Abbey and because it is so poetic, and paints such a desperate picture in its entirety, even if it might have been exaggerated.
16. *The Gesta Stephani*, pp. 153-5.
17. *Chronicles of the Reigns of Stephen, Henry II and Richard I, Vol I*, ed. R. Howlett, London, 1884, p. 146.
18. *Henry of Huntingdon*, p. 282.
19. Ibid, p. 283.
20. Ibid.
21. *The Gesta Stephani*, p. 167.
22. Thank you to Dan Jones for clarifying this. I was uncertain why the Templars would accept the remains of an excommunicated man, and wanted the chance to name-drop.
23. *Liber Eliensis*, ed. E. O. Blake, Royal Historical Society, 1962, p.324.

20. Empress Matilda.

1. *The Gesta Stephani*, p.181
2. Ibid, p. 151; pp.151-3 provide the Gesta's account of the William de Pont de l'Arche affair recounted here.
3. *The Gesta Stephani*, p. 153.
4. Ibid, pp. 159-61.
5. *Chartes de Saint-Julien de Tours (1002-1227)*, ed. L'Abbé L. J. Denis, Société des archives historiques du Maine 12, Le Mans, 1912, no. 87, pp. 113-4.
6. *The Gesta Stephani*, p. 179.
7. Ibid.
8. Ibid.
9. Ibid, p. 181.
10. Ibid.

21. King Stephen

1. *The Gesta Stephani*, p. 199.
2. *King Stephen*, R. H. C. Davis, Longmans, Green and Co, 1967, p. 70, n. 8.
3. *The Reign of King Stephen*, K. J. Stringer, Routledge, 1993, p. 57.
4. *The Gesta Stephani*, p. 185 in particular.
5. Ibid, p. 191.
6. Ibid, p. 195.

7. Ibid, also for the suggestion that Ranulf might have meant the king harm.
8. Ibid, p. 199.
9. Ibid, p. 203.
10. Ibid, p. 209 for the description of Eustace.

22. Empress Matilda

1. *The Gesta Stephani*, p. 211.
2. Ibid, p. 205.
3. Ibid, p. 205 on the belief Henry had come with a large force and much treasure, and pp. 205-7 for the events of the campaign.
4. Ibid, p. 207.
5. Ibid.
6. Ibid, pp. 207-9, quoting Romans 12:20: 'If your enemies are hungry, feed them. If they are thirsty, give them something to drink. In doing this, you will heap burning coals of shame on their heads.'
7. *Charters and Documents Illustrating the History of the Cathedral Church and Diocese of Salisbury in the Twelfth and Thirteenth Centuries*, ed. W. R. Jones and W. D. Macray, London, 1891, pp. 12-3
8. Ibid, pp. 14-5.
9. *The Empress Matilda*, M. Chibnall, Blackwell Publishers, 1991, p. 153, n. 55.
10. *The Letters of St Bernard of Clairvaux*, trans. B. S. James, London, 1953, p. 462.
11. *De Expugnatione Lyxbonensi: The Conquest of Lisbon*, ed. C. W. David, Columbia, 1936, pp. 5-6, 55-7, 101-5.
12. *The Gesta Stephani*, p. 193

23. King Stephen

1. *John of Salisbury*, p. 11.
2. *King Stephen*, R. H. C. Davis, Longmans, Green and Co, 1967, p. 98.
3. *The Letters of St Bernard of Clairvaux*, trans. B. S. James, London, 1953, n. 205.
4. Ibid, n. 204.
5. Ibid, n. 266.
6. *John of Salisbury*, p. 6.
7. Ibid, p. 7.
8. Ibid, pp. 7-8.
9. Ibid, p. 10.
10. Ibid, p. 11.
11. Ibid, p. 42.
12. Ibid, p. 49.

13. Ibid.
14. Ibid, pp. 78-80.

24. Empress Matilda

1. *The Gesta Stephani*, p. 215.
2. *Henry of Huntingdon*, p. 287.
3. *The Gesta Stephani*, p. 217.
4. Ibid, p. 219.
5. *King Stephen*, R. H. C. Davis, Longmans, Green and Co, 1967, p. 108.
6. *The Gesta Stephani*, p. 221. The writer typically paints a picture of pitched battles and ruined countryside, but it seems more likely that it was akin to a game of cat and mouse to waste the king's time.
7. Ibid, p. 223.
8. Ibid.
9. Ibid, pp. 223-5.
10. *The First Century of English Feudalism*, F. M. Stenton, Oxford, 1961, pp. 250-6, 286-8.

25. King Stephen

1. *John of Salisbury*, p. 83.
2. Ibid, 86.
3. *Henry of Huntingdon*, p. 289.
4. Ibid, pp. 288-9.
5. *King Stephen*, D. Matthew, Hambledon and London, 2002, p. 203, n. 9 quoting *Annales Waverleiensis, AM*, ii, p. 234; *Annales Wintoniae, anno 1152*, Ungedruckte anglo-normannische Geschichtsquellen (Strasburg, 1879), pp. 56-83. '*Apud Londoniam Eustachio filio regis Stephani fide et jusjurando universi comites atque barones Angliae se subdiderunt*'.
6. www.medievalists.net/2014/01/how-young-william-marshal-was-saved-from-being-catapulted-into-a-castle/ provides a good account of the story.
7. *The Gesta Stephani*, p. 229.
8. Ibid, p. 227.

26. Epoch

1. *Henry of Huntingdon*, p. 294.
2. *Chronicles of the Reigns of Stephen, Henry II and Richard I, Vol I*, ed. R. Howlett, London, 1884, p. 88 for William of Newburgh *and Chronicles of the Reigns of Stephen, Henry II and Richard I, Vol IV*, ed. R. Howlett, London, 1889, p. 171 for Robert of Torigni.
3. *The Gesta Stephani*, p. 231.

4. Ibid, pp. 231-3.
5. *Henry of Huntingdon*, pp. 291-2.
6. *The Gesta Stephani*, p. 235.
7. Ibid, p. 233.
8. *Henry of Huntingdon*, p. 292.
9. *The Gesta Stephani*, p. 235.
10. Ibid, p. 239.
11. Ibid suggests the private meeting. *Henry of Huntingdon*, p. 293 adds 'the king and the duke had a conference without witnesses, across a rivulet, on the terms of a lasting accommodation between themselves, during which the faithlessness of their nobles was anxiously considered'. How he knew what was discussed without witness is hard to tell.
12. *Henry of Huntingdon*, p. 293.
13. *The Gesta Stephani*, p. 239.
14. *Henry of Huntingdon*, p. 293.
15. Ibid, p. 294.
16. *The Gesta Stephani*, p. 294.
17. *Chronicles of the Reigns of Stephen, Henry II and Richard I, Vol IV*, ed. R. Howlett, London, 1889, p. 177.
18. *Henry of Huntingdon*, p. 294: 'for the king received him as his son by adoption, and acknowledged him heir to the crown!'
19. *Regesta Regum Anglo-Normannorum 1066-1154*, Vol III, ed. H.A. Cronne and R. H. C. Davis, Oxford, 1968, p. 97, n. 272 for the text of the treaty.
20. *Chronicles of the Reigns of Stephen, Henry II and Richard I, Vol I*, ed. R. Howlett, London, 1884, p. 94.
21. *Henry of Huntingdon*, p. 295.
22. *King Stephen*, R. H. C. Davis, Longmans, Green and Co, 1967, p. 126.
23. *Chronicles of the Reigns of Stephen, Henry II and Richard I, Vol I*, ed. R. Howlett, London, 1884, p. 94.

Epilogue

1. *Letters of Royal and Illustrious Ladies of Great Britain, Vol I*, M. A. E. Wood, London, 1846, p. 10
2. *Regesta Regum Anglo-Normannorum 1066 1154, Vol III,* ed. H. A. Cronne and R. H. C. Davis, Oxford, 1968, pp. 261-2, n. 711.
3. *The Empress Matilda*, M. Chibnall, Blackwell Publishers, 1991, p. 161.
4. *Materials for a History of Thomas Becket, Vol V*, ed. J. C. Robertson, London, 1881, pp. 194-5.
5. Ibid, pp. 410, 516-7.

Conclusion

1. *The Anglo-Saxon Chronicle*, p. 246.
2. I don't approve of empire. Please don't think that I do.
3. *De Nugis Curialium*, Walter Map, trans. F. Tupper and M. B. Ogle, London, 1924, pp. 298-9.

Bibliography

Primary Sources

Anderson, A. O., *Scottish Annals from English Chronicles AD 500 to 1286*, London, 1908.

anon, *A Chronicle of London*, London, 1827.

Blake, E. O. ed., *Liber Eliensis*, Royal Historical Society, 1962.

Chibnall, M. ed., *The Historia Pontificalis of John of Salisbury*, Thomas Nelson and Sons, 1956.

Cronne H. A. and R. H. C. Davis eds, *Regesta Regum Anglo-Normannorum 1066-1154, Vol III*, Oxford, 1968.

David, C. W. ed., *De Expugnatione Lyxbonensi: The Conquest of Lisbon*, Columbia, 1936.

Fahlin, Carin ed., *Chroniques des ducs de Normandie par Benoit*, Lund, 1951-67.

Forester, T. ed., *The Chronicle of Henry of Huntingdon*, London, 1853.

_________, *The Chronicle of Florence of Worcester*, London, 1854.

_________, *The Ecclesiastical History of England and Normandy by Orderic Vitalis, Vol IV*, London, 1856.

Gasquet, F. A., *Some Letters of St Bernard Abbot of Clairvaux*, London, 1904.

Gee, H. and W. J. Hardy *Documents Illustrative of English Church History*, London, 1896.

Gomme, E. E. C., *The Anglo-Saxon Chronicle*, London, 1909.

Hearne, T. ed., *Adami de Domerham de rebus gestis Glastoniensibus*, 2 vols, Oxford 1727.

Howlett, ed., *Chronicles of the Reigns of Stephen, Henry II and Richard I, Vol I*, London, 1884.

_________, *Chronicles of the Reigns of Stephen, Henry II and Richard I, Vol II*, London, 1885.

________, *Chronicles of the Reigns of Stephen, Henry II and Richard I, Vol III*, London, 1886.

________, *Chronicles of the Reigns of Stephen, Henry II and Richard I, Vol IV*, London, 1889.

James, B. S., *The Letters of St Bernard of Clairvaux*, trans. London, 1953.

Jones, W. R. and W. D. Macray eds, *Charters and Documents Illustrating the History of the Cathedral Church and Diocese of Salisbury in the Twelfth and Thirteenth Centuries*, London, 1891.

Keeler L., *Geoffrey of Monmouth and the Late Latin Chroniclers*, University of California, 1946.

King, E., ed., *William of Malmesbury's Historia Novella*, Oxford Medieval Texts, 1998.

Marx, Jean ed., *Gesta Normannorum ducum*, Société de l'hstoire de Normandie, Paris, 1914.

Potter, K. R. ed., *Gesta Stephani*, Oxford Medieval Texts, 1976.

Riley, H. T. trans., *Ingulph's Chronicle of the Abbey of Croyland*, London, 1908.

________, *The Annals of Roger of Hoveden, Vol I*, London, 1853.

________, *The Annals of Roger of Hoveden, Vol II*, London, 1853.

Robertson, J. C. ed., *Materials for a History of Thomas Becket, Vol V*, London, 1881.

Schmitt, F. S ed., *Opera Omnia, Vol V*, Anselm, Edinburgh, 1851.

Sharpe, R. R., *London and the Kingdom, Vol I*, London, 1894.

Sheppard, J. B. ed., *The Letter Books of the Monastery of Christ Church, Canterbury, Vol I*, London, 1887.

Stevenson, Rev. J., *The Church Historians of England, Vol I, Part II*, London, 1853.

________, *The Church Historians of England, Vol II, Part I*, London, 1853.

________, *The Church Historians of England, Vol II, Part II*, London, 1854.

________, *The Church Historians of England, Vol III, Part I*, London, 1854.

________, *The Church Historians of England, Vol III, Part II*, London, 1855.

________, *The Church Historians of England, Vol IV, Part I*, London, 1856.

________, *The Church Historians of England, Vol IV, Part II*, London, 1856.

________, *The Church Historians of England, Vol V, Part I*, London, 1858.

Stubbs, W. ed., *Select Charters and Other Illustrations of English Constitutional History*, Oxford, 1905.

Tupper, F. and M. B. Ogle trans., *De Nugis Curialium*, Walter Map, London, 1924.

Weaver, J. R. H. ed., *The Chronicle of John of Worcester*, Oxford, 1908

Wood, M. A. E., *Letters of Royal and Illustrious Ladies of Great Britain, Vol I*, London, 1846.

Secondary Sources

Bradbury, J., *Stephen and Matilda: The Civil War of 1139–53*, The History Press, 2009.

Chibnall, M., *The Empress Matilda*, Blackwell, 1991.

Davis, R. H. C., *King Stephen*, Longmans, Green & Co, 1967.

James, M. R, *Two Ancient English Scholars*, Glasgow, 1931.

Matthew, D., *King Stephen*Hambledon and London, 2002.

Norton, E., *She Wolves: The Notorious Queens of England*, The History Press, 2009.

Norwich, J. J., *The Popes*, Vintage, 2012.

Stenton, F. M., *The First Century of English Feudalism*, Oxford, 1961.

Stringer, K. J., *The Reign of King Stephen*, Routledge, 1993.

Abbreviations

Henry of Huntingdon: *The Chronicle of Henry of Huntingdon*, ed. T. Forester, London, 1853.

The Anglo-Saxon Chronicle: *The Anglo-Saxon Chronicle*, E. E. C. Gomme, London, 1909.

John of Worcester: *The Chronicle of John of Worcester 1118–1140*, J. R. H. Weaver, Oxford, 1908.

Orderic Vitalis: *The Ecclesiastical History of England and Normandy* by Orderic Vitalis, Vol IV, T. Forester, London, 1856.

Gesta Stephani: *Gesta Stephani*, ed. K. R. Potter, Oxford Medieval Texts, 1976.
William of Malmesbury: *William of Malmesbury Historia Novella*, ed. E. King, Oxford Medieval Texts, 1998.
John of Salisbury: *The Historia Pontificalis of John of Salisbury*, ed. M. Chibnall, Nelson's Medieval Texts, 1956.

Index